本教材受教育部中外语言交流合作中心 2020 年国际中文教育重点项目“国际中文教育教材的研发和课程建设”资助

我是医学生

I Am a Medical Student

基础医学汉语 课本 4

Preclinical Medicine Chinese Textbook 4

总 主 编：朱瑞蕾 甄 珍
本册主编：李晓婧
副 主 编：朱瑞蕾 甄 珍
编 者：李晓婧 朱瑞蕾 甄 珍 张举英 张杏春

北京语言大学出版社
BEIJING LANGUAGE AND CULTURE UNIVERSITY PRESS

图书在版编目（CIP）数据

我是医学生. 基础医学汉语. 4. 课本 / 朱瑞蕾, 甄珍总主编；李晓婧分册主编. —北京：北京语言大学出版社, 2023.5

ISBN 978-7-5619-6259-6

Ⅰ. ①我… Ⅱ. ①朱… ②甄… ③李… Ⅲ. ①医学—汉语—对外汉语教学—教材 Ⅳ. ①H195.4

中国国家版本馆CIP数据核字（2023）第057416号

我是医学生：基础医学汉语　课本 4

WO SHI YIXUESHENG : JICHU YIXUE HANYU　KEBEN 4

排版制作：华伦图文制作中心
责任印制：周　燚

出版发行：北京语言大学出版社
社　　址：北京市海淀区学院路 15 号，100083
网　　址：www.blcup.com
电子信箱：service@blcup.com
电　　话：编辑部　8610-82303395
发行部　8610-82303650/3591/3648
北语书店　8610-82303653
网购咨询　8610-82303908
印　　刷：北京市金木堂数码科技有限公司

版　　次：2023 年 5 月第 1 版　　印　　次：2023 年 5 月第 1 次印刷
开　　本：787 毫米 ×1092 毫米　1/16　　印　　张：21.25
字　　数：268 千字
定　　价：88.00 元

PRINTED IN CHINA
凡有印装质量问题，本社负责调换。售后 QQ 号 1367565611，电话 010-82303590

前　言

《我是医学生：基础医学汉语》系列教材是一套在“中文＋医学”理念指导下，依据《新汉语水平考试大纲》《国际中文教育中文水平等级标准》《医学汉语水平考试（MCT）大纲》编写的综合性医学专用汉语教材。教材重在提高学习者在日常生活交际和医院日常交际场景中运用汉语的能力，同时也注重提升学习者的文化素养和医生职业素质。

本套教材主要适用于来华学习基础医学专业的汉语零起点医学生，同时也适用于：（1）来华学习临床医学专业的医学生；（2）来华学习中医学专业的医学生；（3）来华工作的医学专家及短期研修的医学生；（4）有汉语学习需求的海外医学生。

一、编写理念

本套教材将医学专业汉语学习者的日常汉语学习和HSK应考能力提高相结合，将医学专业知识和社会文化知识相结合，以实现汉语、医学和文化相互融合的编写目标。本套教材从零起点开始培养学习者的听、说、读、写技能，帮助学习者逐步掌握HSK一至四级所规定的词汇、语言点和话题任务，熟悉《医学汉语水平考试（MCT）大纲》所规定的医学专业词汇、话题和任务，提高在日常生活交际和医院日常交际场景中运用汉语的能力，同时通过汉语学习了解医生的职业特点，感受“医者仁心”“医德为先”的高尚情操。

二、教材架构

《我是医学生：基础医学汉语》系列教材包括课本4册、配套练习册4册，每册15课。具体安排如下：

第1册侧重汉语日常交际能力的培养，适度增加简单的医学场景交流。其中，正课前的“汉语拼音”和“拼音练习”部分对现代汉语语音知识进行了集中的讲授和练习，后面的1—5课也对其不断进行复现和强化。完成第1册的学习，学习者汉语水平可以达到HSK二级，能够熟悉常用的医学专业词汇，并进行简单的医学场景交流。

第2册将汉语日常交际能力的培养与医学场景中交流能力的提升相结合，所涉及的交际场景更加多样，交流范围更加广阔，所反映的中国社会文化也更加丰富。完成第2册的学习，学习者汉语水平可以达到HSK三级，医学专业词汇进一步增加，并能进行常见的医学场景交流。

第3册和第4册进一步拓展汉语日常交际的广度和深度，日常交际任务更加丰富；所涉医学场景更加侧重医院常见科室的寻医问诊，医患交流场景更加具体、真实，多是通过专科医生了解常见疾病的症状和治疗方案。完成第3册和第4册的学习，学习者汉语水平可以达到甚至超过HSK四级，能够掌握常用的医学专业词汇，了解常见疾病的基本知识，感受医生的职业特点和高尚情操。

三、教材特点

1. 汉语、医学和文化相互融合

《我是医学生：基础医学汉语》系列教材的编写目标包括汉语、医学和文化三个方面。汉语目标是核心目标，主要包括汉语知识目标和汉语技能目标，是实现医学目标和文化目标的基础。本套教材是医学专用汉语教材，医学目标包括医学词汇目标、医学场景交流目标和医学文化目标，主要通过营造医学场景的方式实现。文化目标包括知识文化目标和交际文化目标，本套教材致力于加深学习者对中国社会文化的了解，提高学习者的跨文化交际能力，促进学习者对多元文化的理解。文化目标的实现依赖于语言教学内容中具体文化目标的完成。汉语目标和文化目标属于中文目标，医学目标属于专业目标，三者完美融合于本套教材中。

2. 听、说、读、写并重

本套教材是综合性医学专用汉语教材，在语言技能培养方面，听、说、读、写并重。每篇课文后的“综合练习”部分针对重点词汇、语法、汉字、句型和课文内容进行反复练习，巩固学习者的语言知识；每课后的“语言任务”部分针对口头表达和书面表达能力设计输出型语言任务，重在培养学习者的语言产出能力。配套练习册除进一步巩固汉语重点知识、强化重点能力培养外，还通过丰富的练习题型，训练学习者解决各种语言问题的应用能力，提高HSK应考能力。

3. 通用和专用大纲兼顾

通用汉语词汇、语言点和话题任务重点参照《新汉语水平考试大纲》，同时参照《国际中文教育中文水平等级标准》，医学专业词汇、话题和任务重点参照《医学汉语水平考试（MCT）大纲》。本套教材覆盖《新汉语水平考试大纲》一至四级全部词汇、语言点和话题任务，同时覆盖《医学汉语水平考试（MCT）大纲》一至三级全部话题和任务，以及大部分词汇。

4. 依据试用反馈不断调整完善

本套教材在山东大学临床医学专业（外国留学生）已进行了三轮试用，每次试用后我们都会进行教学效果和学生需求的实证研究与分析，根据教师教学反馈和学生学习反馈进行调整和修改。教材试用结果表明，本套教材可以有效满足医学相关专业学生日常交流、临床实习、通过HSK四级考试和了解中国社会文化的需要。

除此之外，本套教材还在江西中医药大学试用了一个学期，在美国阿拉巴马大学（University of Alabama）试用了两个学期，都取得了显著的教学效果，我们根据试用反馈进行了进一步的调整和修改。

四、编写体例

根据语言学习规律和医学能力培养规律，本套教材各册的编写体例略有差异，具体如下：

1. 第1册编写体例

◎课本

《课本1》开篇便针对现代汉语语音基础知识进行了集中的讲授和练习，并在后面的1—5课中不断复现和强化。1—15课每课均由学习目标、热身活动、课文与生词、语言点讲解与操练、综合练习、语言任务六部分组成。

学习目标：根据课文内容设置语言功能和语言点目标，帮助学习者了解本课的学习重点。鉴于学习者为零起点的外国留学生，本部分以英文形式呈现。

热身活动：设置两个问题，引入本课主题，激发学习者对学习内容的兴趣，激活学习者已有的背景知识和相关词汇。问题围绕日常交际话题设计。

课文与生词：每课包含两篇课文，课文（一）和课文（二）均为对话体，以医学生的日常交际话题为主，后期逐渐增加医学场景的交际话题。两篇课文之间注重内容的关联和生词、语法的复现。生词紧扣《新汉语水平考试大纲》和《医学汉语水平考试（MCT）大纲》。

语言点讲解与操练：语言点讲解简洁清晰，例句典型而丰富，同时突出语法格式的归纳、易错点的提醒及近义词的辨析。每个语言点后均配有针对性练习。

综合练习：课文（一）和课文（二）后均有紧扣课文内容和知识能力培养的综合练习，前5课主要以"听录音，选出你听到的音节""根据汉字写拼音""朗读语句""完成对话"和"汉字书写"为主，后10课主要以"根据汉字写拼音""朗读语句""替换练习""选词填空""根据课文内容回答问题""根据课文内容填空"和"汉字书写"为主。

语言任务：以现实情景为场景，引导学生完成综合性语言任务，主要包括"阅读理解"和"口头表达"。语言任务以日常交际情景为主，以医学情景为辅。

◎练习册

第1—5课所学习的词汇、语言点和课文相对简单，我们将之融入第6—15

课的练习中。

第6—15课每课包括听力、阅读和书写三个部分。听力部分的练习包括“看图片，听词语，判断对（√）错（×）”“看图片，听句子，判断对（√）错（×）”和“听对话，选择正确答案”，阅读部分的练习包括“看图片，并将图片序号填在相关句子后”“选词填空”和“选出下列词语在句子中的位置”，书写部分的练习包括“读句子，根据拼音写汉字”和“组词成句”。

2. 第2册编写体例

◎课本

《课本2》每课均由学习目标、热身活动、课文与生词、语言点讲解与操练、综合练习、语言任务、补充词汇七部分组成。

学习目标：根据课文内容设置语言功能、语言点、医学知识和社会文化目标，帮助学习者了解本课的学习重点。同样，鉴于学习者汉语水平较低，本部分以英文形式呈现。

热身活动：设置两个问题，引入本课主题，激发学习者对学习内容的兴趣，激活学习者已有的背景知识和相关词汇。问题主要围绕日常交际话题和医学话题设计。

课文与生词：每课包含两篇课文，课文（一）和课文（二）均为对话体，以医学生的日常交际话题为主，后期逐渐增加医学场景的交际话题。两篇课文之间注重内容的关联和生词、语法的复现。生词紧扣《新汉语水平考试大纲》和《医学汉语水平考试（MCT）大纲》。

语言点讲解与操练：语言点讲解简洁清晰，例句典型而丰富，突出语法格式的归纳、易错点的提醒及近义词的辨析。每个语言点后均配有针对性练习。

综合练习：课文（一）和课文（二）后均有紧扣课文内容和知识能力培养的综合练习，题型主要包括“根据拼音写汉字”“辨字组词”“替换练习”“选词填空”“用所给词语完成对话”“根据课文内容回答问题”和“根据课文内容填空”。

语言任务：以现实情景为场景，引导学生完成综合性语言任务，主要包括“阅读理解”“口头表达”和“书面表达”。语言任务以日常交际情景为主，以医学情景为辅。

补充词汇：补充与本课内容密切相关的医学专业词汇，每课补充4—6个词，每个词均配有拼音、英文翻译和图片。

◎练习册

《练习册2》每课包括听力、阅读和书写三个部分。听力部分的练习包括“听句子，判断对（√）错（×）”“听对话，选择正确答案”和“听句子，写下你听到的话”，阅读部分的练习包括“选词填空”“选出下列词语在句子中的位置”和“阅读语句，选择正确答案”，书写部分的练习包括“读句子，根据拼音写汉字”和“组词成句”。

3. 第3、4册编写体例

◎课本

《课本3》和《课本4》每课均由学习目标、热身活动、课文与生词、语言点讲解与操练、综合练习、语言任务六部分组成。

学习目标：根据课文内容设置语言功能、语言点、医学知识和社会文化目标，帮助学习者了解本课的学习重点。随着学习者汉语水平的提高，本部分的呈现形式过渡为中文。

热身活动：设置两个问题，引入本课主题，激发学习者对学习内容的兴趣，激活学习者已有的背景知识和相关词汇。问题主要围绕日常交际话题和医学话题设计。

课文与生词：每课包含三篇课文，课文（一）为医学场景对话，课文（二）为日常交流对话，课文（三）为叙述体，其中《课本3》以日常交际话题的叙述为主，《课本4》以医学话题的叙述为主。三篇课文之间注重内容的关联和生词、语法的复现。生词紧扣《新汉语水平考试大纲》和《医学汉语水平考试（MCT）大纲》。

语言点讲解与操练：语言点讲解简洁清晰，例句典型而丰富，突出语法格式的归纳、易错点的提醒及近义词的辨析。每个语言点后均配有针对性练习。

综合练习：课文（一）、课文（二）和课文（三）后均有紧扣课文内容和知识能力培养的综合练习，题型主要包括“根据拼音写汉字”“辨字组词”“选词填空”“选出下列词语在句子中的位置”“用所给词语完成对话”“根据课文内容回答问题”和“根据课文内容填空”。

语言任务：以现实情景为场景，引导学生完成综合性语言任务，主要包括“阅读理解”“口头表达”和“书面表达”。语言任务以医学情景为主。

◎练习册

《练习册3》和《练习册4》每课包括听力、阅读和书写三个部分。听力部分的练习包括“听句子，判断对错”和“听对话，选择正确答案”，阅读部分的练习包括“选择正确的上下文填空”“选词填空”“排列顺序”和“阅读语段，选择正确答案”，书写部分的练习包括“组词成句”“读句子，根据拼音写汉字”和“看图片，用词造句”。

五、教学建议

本套教材建议每课用6—8课时完成。若一周8课时，一学期16周，每学期可完成1册。若选择“主讲＋复练”的教学模式，主讲教师负责教授每课的课文、生词和语言点，并带领学生完成课文后相应的综合练习；复练教师负责生词与语言点的扩展性和交际性练习，并带领学生完成每课的语言任务和练习册上的练习。

六、编写团队

本套教材由长期从事一线医学汉语教学工作的教师编写，总主编为朱瑞蕾、甄珍。

《课本1》和《练习册1》由张杏春、甄珍、张举英、李晓婧、朱瑞蕾编写，张杏春负责统稿。

《课本2》和《练习册2》由张举英、张杏春、李晓婧、朱瑞蕾、甄珍、张海萍、李婷玉编写，张举英负责统稿。

《课本3》和《练习册3》由甄珍、朱瑞蕾、李晓婧、张举英、张杏春编写，甄珍负责统稿。

《课本4》和《练习册4》由李晓婧、朱瑞蕾、甄珍、张举英、张杏春编写，李晓婧负责统稿。

七、鸣谢

本套教材由张杏春、朱瑞蕾、戴丽华、周汶霏、校潇、张云、蔡燕等任课教师在山东大学进行了三个学期的课堂试用，由张海萍、李婷玉在江西中医药大学进行了一个学期的课堂试用，由马玲在美国阿拉巴马大学进行了两个学期的课堂试用，她们都对教材提出了很多切实的修改意见，在此特别致谢！

在教材编写过程中，山东大学李安老师在词频统计方面提供了强大的技术支持，山东大学陈蒙老师在医学词汇选取方面与《医学汉语水平考试（MCT）大纲》进行了严格的对标（参见书后《全四册覆盖MCT大纲词汇表》[①]），李静茹、徐紫钰、温璐妃、刘晓洁、齐梓君、张铭心、曾哲宇等同学在语料整理方面提供了周到的帮助，济南市第二人民医院王旭医师、济南市妇幼保健院侯艳梅医师在医学专业知识和方法方面提供了有力的支持，在此一并感谢。

除此之外，我们还要感谢北京语言大学出版社责任编辑李非飞老师对本套教材提出的宝贵修改意见。

编写团队

2022年4月

① 本成果受教育部中外语言交流合作中心2021年国际中文教育研究青年项目“基于需求分析和文本分析的来华预科生医学汉语教材建设研究”（21YH72D）资助。

Foreword

Under the guidance of the concept of "Chinese + medicine", *I Am a Medical Student: Preclinical Medicine Chinese* is a series of integrated medical Chinese textbooks compiled based on *Chinese Proficiency Test Syllabus*, *Chinese Proficiency Grading Standards for International Chinese Language Education* and *Medical Chinese Test (MCT) Syllabus*. The teaching materials focus on improving the learners' ability to use Chinese for communication in daily life and in the hospital, and also focus on improving the learners' cultural literacy and professional quality as doctors.

This series of textbooks is suitable for international preclinical medical students who are the very beginners of Chinese language. It is also suitable for: (1) medical students who come to China to study clinical medicine; (2) medical students who come to China to study traditional Chinese medicine; (3) medical experts working in China and medical students taking short-term training courses; (4) international medical students with the need of learning Chinese.

1. Writing Principles

This series of textbooks combines medical Chinese students' learning of daily Chinese with their improvement of HSK test-taking ability, and combines their medical knowledge with social and cultural knowledge, so as to achieve the integration of Chinese, medicine and culture. This series of textbooks promotes beginners' listening, speaking, reading and writing skills from scratch, helps them gradually master the vocabulary, language points, topics, and tasks stipulated in HSK Levels 1 to 4, and acquaints themselves with the medical vocabulary, topics and tasks stipulated in the *Medical Chinese Test (MCT) Syllabus*. It improves students' ability to use Chinese for communication in daily life and in the hospital, helping them understand the professional characteristics of doctors using Chinese language, and feel the nobility of a doctor's benevolence and medical morality.

2. Textbook Structure

This series of integrated medical Chinese textbooks includes 4 volumes, each consisting of a textbook and the corresponding workbook. Each volume has 15 lessons. The specific arrangements are as follows:

Volume 1 focuses on the cultivation of daily communicative competence in Chinese, moderately increases communication in simple medical scenarios. The "Chinese Pinyin" and "Pinyin exercises" parts before the lessons teach and practice modern Chinese phonetics, which are repeated and strengthened in the following Lessons 1-5. After studying Volume 1, beginners' Chinese proficiency can reach HSK Level 2. They will be familiar with common medical Chinese vocabulary, and communicate in simple medical scenarios.

Volume 2 combines the development of communication skills in daily life with the improvement of communication skills in medical scenarios. The communication scenarios involved are more diverse, the scope of communication is broader, and the Chinese society and culture reflected are also richer. After studying Volume 2, learners' Chinese proficiency can reach HSK Level 3. Learners will further improve their vocabulary in medical Chinese, and they can communicate in common medical scenarios.

Volumes 3 and 4 further expand the breadth and depth of daily communication in Chinese, and the daily communication tasks are richer; the medical scenarios involved more focused on seeing patients in common departments in hospitals, and the doctor-patient communication scenarios more specific and real, most of which are about learning symptoms and specialists' treatment protocols for common diseases. After studying Volumes 3 and 4, learner's Chinese proficiency can reach or even exceed HSK Level 4. They can master common medical Chinese vocabulary, learn the basics of common diseases, and feel the professional characteristics and noble sentiments of doctors.

3. Characteristics of the Textbooks

(1) Integrating Chinese, medicine and culture

The compilation targets of this series of textbooks include three aspects: Chinese, medicine and culture. Learning Chinese is the core target, mainly including learning Chinese knowledge and skills, which is the basis of learning medicine and culture. These are specialized medical Chinese textbooks. The medical targets mainly include learning medical vocabulary, communication in medical scenes, and medical culture, which are mainly achieved by creating medical scenes. Cultural targets include learning knowledge about culture and communication. These textbooks are committed to enhancing students' understanding of Chinese society and culture, improving their cross-cultural communication skills, and promoting their understanding of multiculturalism. The realization of cultural targets depends on the completion of specific cultural targets in language teaching. Learning Chinese language and culture realizes the language target, and learning medicine realizes the professional target. These three are integrated in these textbooks.

(2) Putting equal emphasis on listening, speaking, reading and writing

This is a series of integrated medical specialized Chinese textbook. In terms of the development of language skills, equal emphasis is put on listening, speaking, reading and writing. The "Comprehensive Exercises" part of the textbooks focuses on repetition drills on major vocabulary, grammar points, Chinese characters, sentence patterns and texts to consolidate learners' mastery of language; at the same time, the "Language Tasks" part after each lesson also designs language output tasks to practice language orally and in written forms, focusing on cultivating learners' language production ability. In addition to further consolidating learners' essential knowledge of Chinese and enhancing their development of primary abilities, the accompanying workbooks of the textbooks also train learners' ability to solve various language problems and improve their ability to take the HSK test through a variety of exercises.

(3) Giving consideration to both general and specific syllabuses

For general Chinese vocabulary, language points, topics and tasks, this series of textbooks is based on *Chinese Proficiency Test Syllabus* and *Chinese Proficiency Grading Standards for International Chinese Language Education*. For medical Chinese vocabulary, topics and tasks, this series of textbooks refers to *Medical Chinese Test (MCT) Syllabus*. This series of textbooks covers all the vocabulary, language points, topics, and tasks at Level 1 to Level 4 in *Chinese Proficiency Test Syllabus* and all the topics, tasks and most of the vocabulary at Level 1 to Level 3 in *Medical Chinese Test (MCT) Syllabus*.

(4) Making continuous adjustment and improvement based on the feedback from the trial

This series of textbooks has been used for three rounds in clinical medicine major (for international students) of Shandong University. After each trial, empirical research and analysis on the teaching effect and students' needs were conducted, and adjustments and revisions were made according to the teaching and learning feedback. The trail use of this series of textbooks showed that it can effectively meet medical students' need for daily communication, clinical practice, passing HSK Level 4 and understanding Chinese society and culture.

In addition, this series of textbooks has been tried out for one semester at Jiangxi University of Chinese Medicine and two semesters at the University of Alabama in the United States, both of which have achieved remarkable teaching effects, and we have made further adjustments and revisions based on the trial feedback.

4. Compilation Layout

Following the law of language learning and medical competence development, this series of textbooks is slightly different in the compilation layout of each volume. The specific compilation layouts are as follows:

(1) The compilation layout of Volume 1

◎ Textbook

Textbook 1 teaches and practices the basics of modern Chinese phonetics and recurs and strengthens in Lessons 1 to 5. Each of Lessons 1 to 15 consists of six parts: learning objectives, warm-up, texts and new words, language points explanation and practice, comprehensive exercises, and language tasks.

Learning objectives: Design the language functions and language points based on the text to help learners understand the learning focus of each lesson. Since the learners are beginner-level foreigners, this part is presented in English.

Warm-up: Ask two questions to introduce the theme of the lesson, stimulate learners' interest in the content, and activate the background knowledge and related vocabulary they already acquired. The questions are on topics in daily communication.

Texts and new words: Each lesson includes two texts. Both Text 1 and Text 2 are conversational, focusing on the topics in medical students' daily communication and gradually discussing those in medical scenes. The correlation between the two texts and the recurrence of new words and grammar are emphasized. The new words are based on *Chinese Proficiency Test Syllabus* and *Medical Chinese Test (MCT) Syllabus*.

Language points explanation and practice: Language points are explained concisely and clearly using typical and abundant example sentences. Meanwhile, it highlights the summary of grammar points, the reminders of error-prone points, and the differentiation of synonyms. Each language point comes with targeted exercises.

Comprehensive exercises: After Text 1 and Text 2, there are comprehensive exercises based on the texts and the development of knowledge and ability. The first 5 lessons ask students to "listen to the recording and pick out the syllables you hear", "write Pinyin according to Chinese characters", "read aloud", "complete dialogues", and "write Chinese characters". And the following 10 lessons ask students to "write Pinyin according to Chinese characters", "read aloud", "substitution drills", "use the following words to fill in the blanks", "answer the following questions according to the text", "fill in the blanks according to the text", and "write Chinese characters".

Language tasks: This part takes real-life situations as scenarios and guides students to complete comprehensive language tasks, such as "reading comprehension" and "oral expression". Most language tasks are based on daily communication situations, supplemented by those based on medical situations.

◎ Workbook

The vocabulary, language points and texts in Lessons 1 to 5 are relatively easy, and thus are incorporated into the exercises in Lessons 6 to 15.

Each of Lessons 6 to 15 consists of three parts: listening, reading and writing. The listening exercises include to "look at the pictures, listen to the words and judge right (√) or wrong (×)", "look at the pictures, listen to the sentences and judge right (√) or wrong (×)", and "listen to the dialogues and choose the correct answers". The reading exercises include to “look at the pictures and fill in the picture numbers after the relevant sentences”, “use the following words to fill in the blanks”, and “choose the correct position of the following words in the sentences”. The writing exercises include to “read the following sentences and write Chinese characters according to Pinyin” and “group the following words into sentences”.

(2) The compilation layout of Volume 2

◎ Textbook

Each lesson consists of seven parts: learning objectives, warm-up, texts and new words, language points explanation and practice, comprehensive exercises, language tasks, and supplementary vocabulary.

Learning objectives: Design the language functions, language points, medical knowledge, and social culture based on the text to help learners understand the learning focus of each lesson. Since the learners are at the novice level, this part is also presented in English.

Warm-up: Ask two questions to introduce the theme of the lesson, stimulate learners’ interest in the content, and activate the background knowledge and related vocabulary they already acquired. The questions are on topics in daily communication and medicine.

Texts and new words: Each lesson includes two texts. Both Text 1 and Text 2 are conversational, focusing on the topics in medical students’ daily communication and gradually discussing those in medical scenes. The correlation between the two texts and the recurrence of new words and grammar are emphasized. The new words are based on *Chinese Proficiency Test Syllabus* and *Medical Chinese Test (MCT) Syllabus*.

Language points explanation and practice: Language points are explained concisely and clearly using typical and abundant example sentences. Meanwhile, it highlights the summary of grammar points, the reminders of error-prone points, and the differentiation of synonyms. Each language point comes with targeted exercises.

Comprehensive exercises: After Text 1 and Text 2, there are comprehensive exercises based on the texts and the development of knowledge and ability. The types of questions mainly include to "write Chinese characters according to Pinyin", "discriminate between Chinese characters and make words", "substitution drills", "use the following words to fill in the blanks", "complete the dialogues with given words", "answer the following questions according to the text", and "fill in the blanks according to the text".

Language tasks: This part takes real-like situations as scenarios and guides students to complete comprehensive language tasks, such as "reading comprehension", "oral expression" and "written expression". Most language tasks are based on daily communication situations, supplemented by those based on medical situations.

Supplementary vocabulary: It supplements medical vocabulary closely related to this lesson. Each lesson is supplemented with 4-6 words with Pinyin, English translations and pictures.

◎ Workbook

Each lesson consists of three parts: listening, reading and writing. The listening exercises include to "listen to sentences and judge right (√) or wrong (×)", "listen to dialogues and choose the correct answers", and "listen to sentences and write down what you heard". The reading exercises include to "use the following words to fill in the blanks", "choose the correct positions of the following words in the sentences", and "read the following sentences and choose the correct answers". The writing exercises include to "read the following sentences and write Chinese characters according to Pinyin" and "group the following words into sentences".

(3) The compilation layout of Volumes 3 and 4

◎ Textbooks

Each lesson consists of six parts: learning objectives, warm-up, texts and new words, language points explanation and practice, comprehensive exercises, and language tasks.

Learning objectives: Design the language functions, language points, medical knowledge, and social culture based on the text to help learners understand the learning focus of each lesson. With the improvement of learners' Chinese proficiency, this part uses Chinese.

Warm-up: Ask two questions to introduce the theme of the lesson, stimulate learners' interest in the content, and activate the background knowledge and related vocabulary they already acquired. The questions are on topics in daily communication and medicine.

Texts and new words: Each lesson includes three texts. Text 1 is a dialogue in medical scenarios, Text 2 is a dialogue in daily life, and Text 3 is a narration. In Volume 3, Text 3 discusses topics in daily life, and in Volume 4, it discusses medical topics. The correlation among the three texts and the recurrence of new words and grammar are emphasized. The new words are based on *Chinese Proficiency Test Syllabus* and *Medical Chinese Test (MCT) Syllabus*.

Language points explanation and practice: The language points are explained concisely and clearly using typical and abundant example sentences. Meanwhile, it highlights the summary of grammar points, the reminders of error-prone points, and the differentiation of synonyms. Each language point comes with targeted exercises.

Comprehensive exercises: After Text 1, Text 2 and Text 3, there are comprehensive exercises based on the texts and the development of knowledge and ability. The types of questions mainly include to "write Chinese characters according to Pinyin", "discriminate between Chinese characters and make words", "use the following words to fill in the blanks", "choose the correct positions of the following words in the sentences" "complete the dialogues with given words", "answer the following questions according to the text", and "fill in the blanks according to the text".

Language tasks: This part takes real-life situations as scenarios and guides students to complete comprehensive language tasks, such as "reading comprehension", "oral expression" and "written expression". Most language tasks are based on medical situations.

◎ Workbook

Each lesson consists of three parts: listening, reading and writing. The listening exercises include to "listen to sentences and judge right or wrong", and "listen to dialogues and choose the correct answers". The reading exercises include to "choose the correct context to fill in the blanks", "use the following words to fill in the blanks", "sort sentences", and "read the following paragraphs and choose the correct answers". The writing exercises include to "group the following words into sentences", "read the following sentences and write Chinese characters according to Pinyin", and "look at pictures and make sentences with given words".

5. Teaching Suggestions

We suggest that each lesson takes 6-8 class hours. If each week has 8 class hours, and each semester completes one volume if it has 16 weeks. If you choose the teaching mode of "main lecture + repetition drills", the "main lecture" teacher is responsible for teaching the texts, new words and language points, and guiding students to complete comprehensive exercises after the corresponding texts; the "repetition drills" teacher is responsible for teaching extended new words and language points, and helping students to complete the language tasks and the exercises in the workbook for each lesson.

6. Authoring Group

This series of textbooks are written by teachers with hands-on experience in medical Chinese. The compilers-in-chief are Zhu Ruilei and Zhen Zhen.

Textbook 1 and *Workbook 1* are written by Zhang Xingchun, Zhen Zhen, Zhang Juying, Li Xiaojing, and Zhu Ruilei. Zhang Xingchun is the finalizer.

Textbook 2 and *Workbook 2* are written by Zhang Juying, Zhang Xingchun, Li Xiaojing, Zhu Ruilei, Zhen Zhen, Zhang Haiping, and Li Tingyu. Zhang Juying is the finalizer.

Textbook 3 and *Workbook 3* are written by Zhen Zhen, Zhu Ruilei, Li Xiaojing, Zhang Juying, and Zhang Xingchun. Zhen Zhen is the finalizer.

Textbook 4 and *Workbook 4* are written by Li Xiaojing, Zhu Ruilei, Zhen Zhen, Zhang Juying and Zhang Xingchun. Li Xiaojing is the finalizer.

7. Accomplishments

This series of textbooks was tried out in Shandong University for three semesters by Zhang Xingchun, Zhu Ruilei, Dai Lihua, Zhou Wenfei, Xiao Xiao, Zhang Yun, Cai Yan, and other teachers. Zhang Haiping and Li Tingyu used it in Jiangxi University of Chinese Medicine for one semester before it is published. Ma Ling conducted a two-semester classroom trial at the University of Alabama. All of them have put forward many practical suggestions for the revision of the textbooks, and I would like to extend my special thanks.

When compiling these textbooks, Li An of Shandong University, provided strong technical support on word frequency statistics, and Chen Meng of Shandong University, conducted strict benchmarking with *Medical Chinese Test (MCT) Syllabus* in the selection of medical vocabulary, and Li Jingru, Xu Ziyu, Wen Lufei, Liu Xiaojie, Qi Zijun, Zhang Mingxin, Zeng Zheyu, and other students provided meticulous help in the organization of language data. Wang Xu, a doctor of Jinan Second People's Hospital, and Hou Yanmei, a doctor of Jinan Maternal and Child Health Hospital, provided their strong support in medical expertise and methods, and I would like to thank them all.

In addition, I would also like to thank Li Feifei, the editor in charge, of Beijing Language and Culture University Press, for her valuable comments on the revision of this series of textbooks.

The Authoring Group

April 2022

目　录

Contents

第一课 Lesson 1

有没有家用除颤器？

学习目标 Learning Objectives

1. 语言功能：能听懂医生或别人提出的建议，能向他人咨询保健知识。
2. 语言点：反问句（2）“难道……吗”、助词“什么的”、副词“恐怕”、连词“因此”、动词“经过”。
3. 医学知识：了解自动体外除颤器（AED）。
4. 社会文化：了解与垃圾分类有关的知识。

热身活动 Warm-up

1. 你了解除颤器（chúchànqì, defibrillator）吗？它有哪些作用？

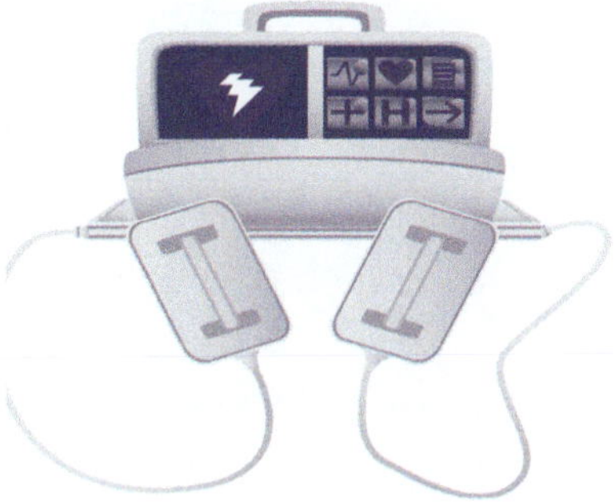

2. 导致猝死（cùsǐ, to die suddenly）的原因主要有哪些？

课文（一）
Text（I）

（心内科病房，护士通知病人去办理出院手续。）

护士：您现在可以去办理出院手续了。

病人：我一想到出院就害怕。

护士：难道您不想回家吗？

病人：当然想。可是我害怕出院以后，心脏再出问题。

护士：如果感觉不舒服，您一定要及时打 120。

病人：我担心打 120 来不及。医院里有急救设备，其他地方都没有。

护士：其实，最近很多大型购物中心、机场、火车站、地铁站等公共场所都安装了除颤器。家用除颤器也可以买到，您不用这么担心。

病人：是吗？有家用除颤器？我想买一台。

护士：您先别着急买。建议您去问问大夫，看看是否需要。

生词 New words

1. 通知	tōngzhī	*v.*	to inform, to notify
2. 手续	shǒuxù	*n.*	procedure
3. 害怕	hàipà	*v.*	to be afraid
4. 难道	nándào	*adv.*	*used in a rhetorical question for emphasis*
5. 急救	jíjiù	*v.*	to give first aid treatment
6. 设备	shèbèi	*n.*	equipment
7. 大型	dàxíng	*adj.*	large
8. 火车站	huǒchēzhàn	*n.*	railway station
9. 地铁站	dìtiězhàn	*n.*	subway station
10. 公共场所	gōnggòng chǎngsuǒ		public place
场所	chǎngsuǒ	*n.*	place
11. 安装	ānzhuāng	*v.*	to install
12. 除颤器	chúchànqì	*n.*	defibrillator
13. 家用	jiāyòng	*adj.*	household
14. 台	tái	*m.*	*a measure word for machines and instruments*

语言点 Language Points

反问句（2）：难道……吗

副词“难道”用在反问句中，可以加强反问的语气，句尾常常有“吗”。例如：

1. 病人：我一想到出院就害怕。

   护士：难道您不想回家吗？

2. 已经八点半了，你怎么还不去学校？难道今天没有课吗？

3. 一进门就是医院的服务台，难道你没看见吗？

※ 练习：请根据给出的场景，用副词“难道”提问

1. 场景：星期一上午九点，你看到同屋还在宿舍睡觉。

____?

2. 场景：你送给妹妹一条裙子，但是她不太高兴。

____?

3. 场景：病人今天要出院了，可是他不太高兴。你是护士。

____?

4. 场景：你的朋友是心内科医生，你向他咨询怎么治疗高血压，可是他说不知道。

____?

综合练习 Comprehensive Exercises

一、根据拼音写汉字

1. shǒuxù __________ 3. tái __________ 5. jíjiù __________

2. hàipà __________ 4. nándào __________ 6. chǎngsuǒ __________

二、辨字组词

1. 火__________ 3. 台__________

水__________ 胎__________

2. 续__________ 4. 怕__________

读__________ 快__________

三、选词填空

安装	害怕	手续	安排	提前

1. 这只是个小手术，你不用（　　）。
2. 你如果要去体检，最好（　　）打电话预约。
3. 今年夏天特别热，我打算在书房（　　）一台空调。
4. 医院专门（　　）李大夫给这位病人做检查。
5. 你恢复得很好，明天就可以办理出院（　　）了。

四、选出下列词语在句子中的位置

1. 你 A 不想 B 去外地 C 旅游 D 吗？（难道）
2. A 如果家人 B 有心脏病，你最好懂 C 一些 D 知识。（急救）
3. A 父母 B 我 C 在国外 D 过得不好。（担心）
4. 如果 A 身体不舒服 B，一定要 C 去医院 D。（及时）
5. 父母 A 允许 B 你做 C 整形手术 D？（是否）

五、用所给词语完成对话

1. 护士：你今天下午就可以出院了。

   病人：______________________________。（一……就……）

2. 月亮：马上就可以回国了，______________________________？（难道）

   朋友：我很高兴，可是我也不想离开这里的朋友们。

3. 医生：______________________________。（其实）

   病人：不用做手术了，太好了，谢谢您！

4. 妈妈：糟糕，我忘了带手机！

   爸爸：______________________________。（来不及）

5. 医生：________________________。（及时）

病人：好的，谢谢大夫。

六、根据课文内容回答问题

1. 护士告诉病人什么事儿？
2. 病人为什么害怕出院？
3. 病人出院后如果觉得不舒服，护士建议他怎么做？
4. 现在除了医院，还有哪些地方也安装了除颤器？
5. 关于是否需要购买家用除颤器，护士给了病人什么建议？

七、根据课文内容填空

护士________病人可以去办理________手续了，可是病人听后并不高兴，他一想到出院就________，因为他担心心脏再出________。护士说，出院以后，如果觉得不舒服，一定要________打120。病人却担心打120________，他觉得医院里有________设备，其他地方都没有。护士告诉病人，最近很多________购物中心、机场、火车站、________等公共________都________了除颤器，家用除颤器也可以买到，让他不用这么________。护士还建议他先别________买家用除颤器，去问问大夫，看看________需要。

课文（二）
Text（II）

（王东和艺文在家聊天儿。）

王东：你发现咱们小区的新变化了吗？

艺文：什么变化？

王东：垃圾桶的数量变了。以前咱们楼下有两个垃圾桶，现在变成四个了，颜色还都不一样。

艺文：这说明要实行垃圾分类了。

王东：你对垃圾分类了解吗？

艺文：知道一点儿。报纸、矿泉水瓶什么的是可回收垃圾，电池是有害垃圾。

王东：你确实是只知道一点儿。说实话，我也不太懂。咱们快点儿了解一下这方面的知识，否则恐怕连垃圾都不会扔了。

生词 New words

1. 变化	biànhuà	*n./v.*	change; to change
变	biàn	*v.*	to change
2. 垃圾桶	lājītǒng	*n.*	trash can
3. 数量	shùliàng	*n.*	quantity
4. 说明	shuōmíng	*v.*	to explain, to demonstrate
5. 实行	shíxíng	*v.*	to implement
6. 分类	fēnlèi	*v.*	to classify
7. 报纸	bàozhǐ	*n.*	newspaper
8. 矿泉水	kuàngquánshuǐ	*n.*	mineral water
9. 什么的	shénmede	*part.*	and the like
10. 回收	huíshōu	*v.*	to recycle
11. 电池	diànchí	*n.*	battery
12. 有害	yǒu hài		harmful
13. 确实	quèshí	*adv.*	indeed
14. 实话	shíhuà	*n.*	truth
15. 恐怕	kǒngpà	*adv.*	maybe, *indicating an estimation*

语言点 Language Points

一、助词"什么的"

助词"什么的"用在一个或者几个并列的成分之后，表示"……之类"的意思。例如：

1. 报纸、矿泉水瓶什么的是可回收垃圾。
2. 我买了水果、蔬菜、牛奶什么的。
3. 我不喜欢跑步、爬山什么的，只喜欢游泳。

※ 练习：请用助词“什么的”完成对话

1. A：你去超市买什么了？

B：________________________________。

2. A：医院有哪些科室？

B：________________________________。

3. A：什么是有害垃圾？

B：________________________________。

4. A：你上网的时候一般做什么？

B：________________________________。

二、副词“恐怕”

副词“恐怕”表示担心或估计。例如：

1. 咱们快点儿了解一下这方面的知识，否则恐怕连垃圾都不会扔了。

2. 快起床吧，都七点四十了，恐怕要迟到了。

3. 我们五个人只点三个菜，恐怕不够吧。

※ 练习：请用副词“恐怕”完成对话

1. A：九点的飞机，咱们八点出发，来得及吧？

B：________________________________。

2. A：________________________________。

B：那我们带上雨伞吧。

3. A：________________________________。

B：那我去药店给你买点儿药吧。

4. A：妈妈说明天下雪，咱们还能去爬山吗？

B：________________________________。

综合练习 Comprehensive Exercises

一、根据拼音写汉字

1. biànhuà ________　　3. shuōmíng ________　　5. quèshí ________

2. shùliàng ________　　4. yǒu hài ________　　6. shíhuà ________

二、辨字组词

1. 量________　　3. 报________

重________　　抱________

2. 实________　　4. 化________

卖________　　花________

三、选词填空

确实　恐怕　否则　什么的　变化

1. 我到处找手机也没找到，（　　）是丢了。
2. 这次考试必须得通过，（　　）就毕不了业了。
3. 回国的时候我要买一些茶叶、零食（　　）当礼物，送给家人和朋友。
4. 几年不回来，国内的发展（　　）太大了，我快不适应了。
5. 你别问我了，我（　　）不知道哥哥得了什么病。

四、选出下列词语在句子中的位置

1. A 我 B HSK 四级 C 考试 D 不太了解。（对）
2. A 你现在 B 怎么 C 手机 D 都不会用了？（连）
3. A 我想 B 了解一些 C 医学 D 的知识。（方面）
4. 你 A 别着急，B 我们 C 先去问问医生 D 需要住院。（是否）

5. A 一定要 B 好好儿吃药，C 你的病会 D 越来越严重的。（否则）

五、用所给词语完成对话

1. 大为：已经七点五十了，快起床！

   同学：糟糕，起晚了，______________________。（恐怕）

2. 美丽：我现在能用汉语跟中国人聊天儿了。

   月亮：______________________。（说明）

3. 老师：你来中国已经一年了，感觉怎么样？

   大为：______________________。（发现）

4. 金龙：老师，HSK 四级考试难不难？

   老师：挺难的，你要好好儿准备，______________________。（否则）

5. 医生：吃了两天药，身体恢复得怎么样了？

   病人：______________________。（确实）

六、根据课文内容回答问题

1. 王东住的小区里有什么新变化？
2. 这个新变化说明了什么？
3. 关于垃圾分类，艺文了解什么？
4. 王东为什么觉得要快点儿了解一下垃圾分类的知识？

七、根据课文内容填空

王东发现小区里有了一些新________——垃圾桶的________变了。以前楼下有________垃圾桶，现在变成________了，颜色还都不一样。这说明要实行________了。艺文对垃圾分类了解一点儿，报纸、矿泉水瓶________是可________垃圾，电池是________垃圾。说实话，王东也不太懂，他想快点儿了解一下这________的知识，否则________连垃圾都不会扔了。

课文（三）
Text（III）

自动体外除颤器（AED）可以帮助人们对心脏病病人进行及时抢救。研究发现，中国每年因为心脏病猝死的人数超过50万。因此，机场、火车站、商场、学校、高速公路服务区等公共场所都需要安装自动体外除颤器。自动体外除颤器的使用方法并不复杂，经过简单的培训，人们都能学会。

生词 New words

1. 自动	zìdòng	*adj.*	automatic
2. 体外	tǐwài	*n.*	in vitro
3. 心脏病	xīnzàngbìng	*n.*	heart disease
4. 抢救	qiǎngjiù	*v.*	to rescue
5. 研究	yánjiū	*v./n.*	to research; research
6. 猝死	cùsǐ	*v.*	to die suddenly
7. 超过	chāoguò	*v.*	to exceed
8. 万	wàn	*num.*	ten thousand
9. 因此	yīncǐ	*conj.*	therefore
10. 高速公路	gāosù gōnglù		expressway
11. 服务区	fúwùqū	*n.*	service zone
12. 方法	fāngfǎ	*n.*	method
13. 经过	jīngguò	*v.*	to go through
14. 培训	péixùn	*v.*	to train

语言点 Language Points

一、连词"因此"

连词"因此"常用在表示结果或结论的小句中。例如：

1. 研究发现，中国每年因为心脏病猝死的人数超过 50 万。因此，机场、火车站、商场、学校、高速公路服务区等公共场所都需要安装自动体外除颤器。
2. 垃圾分类可以减少环境污染，因此越来越多的城市开始实行垃圾分类政策。
3. 电池是有害垃圾，因此我们要把它放到专门的垃圾桶中。

※ 练习：请用连词"因此"完成句子

1. 长时间看电脑和手机对眼睛不好，因此____________________。

2. 坐高铁旅行又快又方便，因此________________。

3. 老年人的体检项目和年轻人不太一样，因此________________。

4. 现在整形技术已经很成熟了，因此________________。

二、动词“经过”

动词“经过”表示通过某动作或事件，后面可以带名词或动词性成分做宾语。例如：

1. 自动体外除颤器的使用方法并不复杂，经过简单的培训，人们都能学会。
2. 宿舍经过打扫，干净多了。
3. 经过七年的专业学习，他终于成为一名医生。

※ 练习：请用动词“经过”完成对话

1. A：怎么才能来中国学习医学？
   B：________________。
2. A：医生，请问我现在就可以做整形手术吗？
   B：________________。
3. A：普通人能学会使用自动体外除颤器吗？
   B：________________。
4. A：我的汉语怎么才能说得像中国人一样好？
   B：________________。

综合练习 Comprehensive Exercises

一、根据拼音写汉字

1. yánjiū ________	3. péixùn ________	5. fāngfǎ ________
2. chāoguò ________	4. yīncǐ ________	6. jīngguò ________

二、辨字组词

1. 培________　　3. 此________

　 倍________　　　 些________

2. 万________　　4. 超________

　 方________　　　 路________

三、选词填空

经过　超过　抢救　研究　培训

1. 这次期中考试，咱们班（　　）一半的同学都考得很好。
2. （　　）半年的努力，他终于通过了 HSK 四级考试。
3. 爷爷突然晕过去了，我们马上把他送到了医院（　　）。
4. 这项（　　）说明，实行垃圾分类有利于减轻环境污染。
5. 每年暑假，学校都会对年轻老师进行教学（　　）。

四、选出下列词语在句子中的位置

1. A 假期出行的人 B 尤其多，C 要特别 D 注意交通安全。（因此）
2. A 我们 B 学校 C 的老师都是 D 培训的。（经过）
3. A 班里 B 一半 C 的学生 D 得了感冒。（超过）
4. 我 A 不太 B 喜欢 C 吃甜 D 的食物。（并）
5. A 在医院、学校、商场 B 公共场所 C 都不能抽烟 D。（等）

五、用所给词语完成对话

1. 金龙：这个学期你的专业课学得怎么样？

　 王晨：____________________________。（经过）

2. 月亮：这次考试你考得怎么样？

朋友：不太好，不过______________________________。（超过）

3. 病人：大夫，我身体恢复得怎么样？

医生：恢复得很好，______________________________。（因此）

4. 儿子：妈妈，你了解我吗？

妈妈：______________________________。（对）

5. 大为：你住在学校宿舍吗？

同学：______________________________。（并）

六、根据课文内容回答问题

1. 自动体外除颤器对心脏病病人有什么帮助？
2. 研究发现，中国每年因为心脏病猝死的人数有多少？
3. 为什么一些重要的公共场所需要安装自动体外除颤器？
4. 自动体外除颤器的使用方法复杂吗？
5. 怎样才能学会使用自动体外除颤器？

七、根据课文内容填空

自动体外除颤器（AED）可以帮助人们对心脏病病人进行________。研究发现，中国每年因为心脏病猝死的人数________50万。因此，机场、________、商场、学校、高速公路________等________都需要________自动体外除颤器。自动体外除颤器的使用方法________复杂，经过简单的________，人们都能________。

语言任务 Language Tasks

一、阅读理解

近年来，不少报道称“年轻人猝死大多因心律失常”，这导致部分人对“心律失常”产生恐惧感。其实，心律失常有很多类型，恶性心律失常才是引起猝死的原因。

心律失常跟人们的生活习惯和饮食习惯有很大的关系。因此，预防心律失常需要平时保持充足的睡眠，不抽烟，不喝酒，注意劳逸结合，规律饮食，保持情绪稳定。突然出现胸闷、眩晕、心悸等症状，有可能是心律失常发生的前奏。出现这些情况，一定要重视，并及时就医。

来源：广州日报《心律失常不等于心脏病》

补充词汇

1. 近年	jìnnián	*n.*	recent years
2. 报道	bàodào	*n.*	report
3. 称	chēng	*v.*	to claim
4. 心律失常	xīnlǜ shīcháng		arrhythmia
5. 产生	chǎnshēng	*v.*	to engender
6. 恐惧感	kǒngjùgǎn	*n.*	a sense of fear
7. 类型	lèixíng	*n.*	type
8. 恶性	èxìng	*adj.*	malignant
9. 保持	bǎochí	*v.*	to keep, to maintain
10. 充足	chōngzú	*adj.*	adequate, sufficient
11. 睡眠	shuìmián	*n.*	sleep
12. 劳逸结合	láoyì jiéhé		to strike a proper balance between work and rest
13. 规律	guīlǜ	*n.*	law, regular pattern
14. 稳定	wěndìng	*adj.*	stable, calm
15. 胸闷	xiōngmèn	*adj.*	chest tightness
16. 眩晕	xuànyùn	*v.*	to get dizziness

17. 心悸	xīnjì	*v.*	to palpitate
18. 发生	fāshēng	*v.*	to happen
19. 前奏	qiánzòu	*n.*	prelude
20. 就医	jiùyī	*v.*	to go to a doctor

回答问题

1. 引起猝死的主要是哪种心律失常？
2. 心律失常跟什么有关系？
3. 如何预防心律失常？

二、口头表达

任务名称：向医生咨询是否需要购买家用除颤器。

任务背景：病人去医生办公室向医生咨询一下是否需要买台家用除颤器。

任务要求：1. 两个学生一组，一个扮演病人，一个扮演医生。

2. 医生询问病人有什么问题，并告诉病人自动体外除颤器需经过培训后才能使用。

3. 病人向医生咨询是否需要购买家用除颤器。

参考语言：一……就……　害怕　急救设备　担心　出问题　越来越……　需要　经过　培训　方法　注意　因此　及时　120

三、书面表达

任务名称：介绍一下垃圾分类的好处。

任务要求：马上要实行垃圾分类了，但很多人并不了解这方面的知识。请你在查阅资料的基础上，向大家介绍一下垃圾分类的好处，要求 200 字以上。

参考语言：对……了解　变化　垃圾桶　实行　说明　回收　有害　确实　方面　环境　污染　减轻

第二课 Lesson 2 老年性耳背比较普遍

学习目标 Learning Objectives

1. 语言功能：能对两种事物或同一事物的两个方面进行详细比较。
2. 语言点：副词“大约”、固定结构“既……又/也……”、助词“之”、固定结构“跟/和……相比”、动词“使”、连词“而”（2）。
3. 医学知识：了解老年性耳背的常见症状和治疗方法。
4. 社会文化：了解科技对生活的改变。

热身活动 Warm-up

1. 你周围有耳背的老人吗？他们有哪些表现？

2. 科技的发展给人们的生活带来了哪些改变？请举例说明。

课文（一）
Text（I）

（病人在耳鼻喉科门诊看病。）

病人家属：大夫，我爸的耳背越来越严重了。

医生：多长时间了？

病人家属：大约半年了。

医生：你们是怎么发现的？

病人家属：刚开始的时候，我们发现他听不到别人敲门，也听不到周围的人跟他打招呼。昨天晚上打雷的声音那么响，他竟然一点儿都没听见。

医生：他多大年纪了？

病人家属：七十三了。大夫，他需要配助听器吗？

医生：老年性耳背比较普遍，你们不用太担心。先做个听力测试，然后根据测试结果治疗。

生词 New words

1. 耳鼻喉科	ěr-bí-hóukē	*n.*	Department of ENT (ear-nose-throat)
2. 耳背	ěrbèi	*adj.*	hard of hearing
3. 大约	dàyuē	*adv.*	approximately
4. 敲门	qiāo mén	*VO*	to knock at a door
5. 周围	zhōuwéi	*n.*	around
6. 打招呼	dǎ zhāohu	*VO*	to greet (sb.)
7. 打雷	dǎléi	*v.*	to thunder
雷	léi	*n.*	thunder
8. 声音	shēngyīn	*n.*	sound
9. 响	xiǎng	*adj.*	loud
10. 年纪	niánjì	*n.*	age (*used to refer to the elderly*)
11. 配	pèi	*v.*	to match
12. 助听器	zhùtīngqì	*n.*	hearing-aid
13. 老年性	lǎoniánxìng	*n.*	senile
老年	lǎonián	*n.*	old age
14. 普遍	pǔbiàn	*adj.*	common
15. 测试	cèshì	*v.*	to test
16. 治疗	zhìliáo	*v.*	to treat
治	zhì	*v.*	to treat

语言点 Language Points

副词“大约”

副词“大约”表示不是很准确的估计，通常用在数量词或动词前做状语。例如：

1. 我爸耳背大约半年了。
2. 老王大约有七十岁了。
3. 买一台自动体外除颤器大约需要多少钱？

※ 练习：请用副词“大约”完成对话

1. A：你早上去公司要多长时间？

   B：______________________________。

2. A：你这次去超市购物花了多少钱？

   B：______________________________。

3. A：你什么时候回国？

   B：______________________________。

4. A：医学院一共有多少留学生？

   B：______________________________。

综合练习 Comprehensive Exercises

一、根据拼音写汉字

1. dàyuē ________ 3. zhìliáo ________ 5. niánjì ________

2. zhōuwéi ________ 4. shēngyīn ________ 6. pǔbiàn ________

二、辨字组词

1. 响________ 3. 约________

   向________ 药________

2. 围________ 4. 纪________

   国________ 记________

三、选词填空

大约　普遍　年纪　响　周围

1. 老爷爷，您今年多大（　　）了？
2. 他去年就结婚了，他（　　）的人竟然都不知道。
3. 我头疼（　　）有三个月了，现在越来越严重。
4. 你房间的音乐实在是太（　　）了，能不能调小点儿？
5. 七十岁以上的老年人（　　）都有耳背的问题，你们不用太担心。

四、选出下列词语在句子中的位置

1. 刚 A 学习汉语的时候 B，我 C 一点儿也 D 听不懂。（开始）
2. A 这些学生每次见了 B 我，都会 C 我 D 打招呼。（跟）
3. 老年人 A 耳背 B 普遍，医生 C 说 D 不用太担心。（比较）
4. 他 A 已经 B 结婚三年了，我们 C 竟然 D 都不知道。（一点儿）
5. A 他做完手术 B 半年了，可是 C 到现在还 D 没好。（大约）

五、用所给词语完成对话

1. 病人：大夫，我的高血压严重不严重？要不要住院？
   医生：不用担心，______________。（普遍）
2. 月亮：你是什么时候发现空调出问题的？
   同屋：______________。（大约）
3. 病人：大夫，这些药苦吗？
   医生：放心吧，______________。（一点儿也不……）
4. 妈妈：这是妈妈的同事王阿姨，______________。（打招呼）
   儿子：王阿姨，您好！

5. 大为：他的汉语说得这么好，____________________________！（竟然）

金龙：我一开始也以为他是中国人呢。

六、根据课文内容回答问题

1. 病人怎么了？
2. 病人出现这种情况多长时间了？
3. 病人家属是怎么发现病人耳背的？
4. 病人今年多大年纪了？
5. 医生认为病人需要配助听器吗？

七、根据课文内容填空

病人耳背________半年了。刚开始的时候，他的家人发现他听不到别人________，也听不到周围的人跟他________。昨天晚上________的声音那么________，他________一点儿都没听见。医生告诉病人家属________耳背比较________，不用太________。先做个听力________，然后________测试结果治疗。

课文（二）
Text（II）

（刘一鸣到张佳乐家做客。）

刘一鸣：我送给你的扫地机好用吗？

张佳乐：太好用了！既能扫地又能擦地，既省时间又省力气，现在打扫卫生变得轻松多了。

刘一鸣：工作的时候，它的声音大不大？

张佳乐：声音不大，一点儿都不吵，这也是它的优点之一。

刘一鸣：有缺点吗？

张佳乐：有一个小缺点：有的地方，它打扫不了。不过跟它的优点相比，这个缺点不算什么。

刘一鸣：看来你非常喜欢这台扫地机。售货员说这台卖得很好，值得买。

张佳乐：但是很贵吧？

刘一鸣：跟它的作用相比，价格不算什么。

生词 New words

1. 扫地机	sǎodìjī	*n.*	sweeper
2. 好用	hǎoyòng	*adj.*	easy to use
3. 既	jì	*adv.*	both ... and ..., as well as
既……又……	jì…yòu…		both ... and ...
4. 擦	cā	*v.*	to wipe, to scrub
5. 省	shěng	*v.*	to save
6. 卫生	wèishēng	*n./adj.*	hygiene; sanitary
7. 轻松	qīngsōng	*adj.*	easy
8. 优点	yōudiǎn	*n.*	advantage
9. 之	zhī	*part.*	of
10. 缺点	quēdiǎn	*n.*	disadvantage
11. 算	suàn	*v.*	to count as
12. 卖	mài	*v.*	to sell
13. 值得	zhídé	*v.*	to be worth
14. 作用	zuòyòng	*n.*	function

语言点 Language Points

一、固定结构"既……又/也……"

固定结构"既……又/也……"连接表并列关系的分句，表示人或事物同时具有两方面的性质或特点。例如：

1. 扫地机太好用了！既能扫地又能擦地，既省时间又省力气。
2. 我打算租公司旁边小区的房子，这样既可以节省上班路上的时间，又可以少花钱。
3. 我既不喜欢打扫房间，也不喜欢做饭。

※ 练习：请用固定结构“既……又/也……”和所给词语完成句子

1. 我很喜欢爬山，______________________________。

（看美丽的风景　锻炼身体）

2. 我不常在外边吃饭，______________________________。

（贵　不太健康）

3. 马大为每周都去踢足球，______________________________。

（运动　和朋友玩儿）

4. 美丽喜欢唱中国歌，______________________________。

（放松　学习汉语）

二、助词“之”

助词“之”相当于结构助词“的”，一般用在比较书面的句子中。“之一”表示同类事物中的一个，前面常常是名词性成分。例如：

1. 声音不大，一点儿都不吵，这也是它的优点之一。

2. 游泳是最好的运动之一。

3. 使用自动体外除颤器是抢救心脏病病人的重要方法之一。

※ 练习：请用“之一”完成句子

1. 西安很有名，______________________________。

2. 老年性耳背很普遍，______________________________。

3. 我在中国有很多好朋友，马大为______________________________。

4. 高铁又快又舒服，______________________________。

三、固定结构“跟/和……相比”

固定结构“跟/和……相比”，表示比较，引出比较对象。例如：

1. 跟它的优点相比，这个缺点不算什么。

2. 跟跑步、踢足球相比，散步更适合老年人。

3. 和飞机相比，我觉得坐高铁更方便。

※ 练习：请用固定结构“跟/和……相比”完成对话

1. A：买房子和租房子，哪一种比较适合年轻人？

   B：________________________________。

2. A：你喜欢在网上看电影，还是去电影院看电影？

   B：________________________________。

3. A：你喜欢去商店买衣服，还是在网上买衣服？

   B：________________________________。

4. A：我觉得汉语课太难了，你觉得呢？

   B：________________________________。

综合练习 Comprehensive Exercises

一、根据拼音写汉字

1. jì ________　3. qīngsōng ________　5. mài ________

2. suàn ________　4. cā ________　6. yōudiǎn ________

二、辨字组词

1. 既________　3. 卖________

   即________　　买________

2. 值________　4. 作________

   直________　　做________

三、选词填空

既　之一　值得　算　相比

1. 花一千多块钱买条裙子，我觉得不（　　）。

2. 你太客气了，我只是帮了一个小忙，不（　　）什么。

3. 上海是世界上最大的城市（　　），我很想去看一看。

4. 跟线下课（　　），线上课交流不太方便。

5. 想成为一名好医生，（　　）要有高水平的医术，又要有热情。

四、选出下列词语在句子中的位置

1. A 这台除颤器的价格 B 跟它的作用 C，不算 D 什么。（相比）
2. A 老年性耳背 B 比较 C 普遍，不 D 什么大问题。（算）
3. A 王晨的哥哥 B 会做中餐 C，又 D 会做西餐。（既）
4. 《玩具总动员》A 是孩子们 B 最喜欢 C 看的电影 D。（之一）
5. 刚开始工作 A 的时候 B，一天三四台手术 C，我完全适应不 D。（了 liǎo）

五、用所给词语完成对话

1. 美丽：你觉得大夫辛苦还是护士辛苦？

   金龙：________________________________。（跟……相比）

2. 儿子：妈妈，你出差为什么总是坐高铁？

   妈妈：________________________________。（既……又……）

3. 病人家属：大夫，我爸爸这种老年性耳背应该怎么治疗？

   大夫：________________________________。（之一）

4. 病人家属：王护士，谢谢您对我母亲的照顾和关心。

   王护士：不用客气，________________________________。（算）

5. 大为：这个电影我看了三遍了。

   朋友：________________________________。（看来）

六、根据课文内容回答问题

1. 扫地机是谁买的？
2. 这台扫地机有哪些优点？
3. 这台扫地机有什么缺点？
4. 这台扫地机为什么值得买？
5. 刘一鸣觉得扫地机的作用和价格哪个更重要？

七、根据课文内容填空

张佳乐觉得刘一鸣送给她的扫地机太________了！既能________又能________，既省________又省________，现在打扫卫生变得________多了。而且，它工作的时候声音________，一点儿都不________。但这台扫地机有一个小缺点，就是有的地方它________。不过，跟它的________相比，这个缺点________。张佳乐很喜欢这台扫地机，售货员也说这台扫地机________得很好，________买。刘一鸣觉得虽然扫地机有点儿贵，但是跟它的________相比，价格________。

课文（三）
Text（III）

科学技术的发展使我们的生活越来越方便。

比如：以前，我们主要通过书、报纸、广播和电视获得信息，进入21世纪以后，互联网逐渐成了人们获得信息的主要方式；以前，我们购物要去商店，寄东西要去邮局，学习要去教室，发文件要用传真，现在这些事情都可以通过互联网完成；以前，很多人觉得坐火车既慢又不舒服，而现在高铁速度提高到了每小时300多千米，各方面的条件也越来越好。

科技就是这样改变着我们的生活。

生词 New words

1. 科学	kēxué	*n.*	science
2. 发展	fāzhǎn	*v.*	to develop
3. 使	shǐ	*v.*	to make, to cause
4. 广播	guǎngbō	*n./v.*	broadcast; to broadcast
5. 获得	huòdé	*v.*	to obtain
6. 进入	jìnrù	*v.*	to enter
7. 世纪	shìjì	*n.*	century
8. 互联网	hùliánwǎng	*n.*	(the) Internet
9. 逐渐	zhújiàn	*adv.*	gradually
10. 方式	fāngshì	*n.*	way, mode
11. 商店	shāngdiàn	*n.*	shop, store
12. 寄	jì	*v.*	to mail, to send
13. 邮局	yóujú	*n.*	post office
14. 文件	wénjiàn	*n.*	document, file
15. 传真	chuánzhēn	*n.*	fax
16. 完成	wánchéng	*v.*	to finish
17. 慢	màn	*adj.*	slow
18. 提高	tígāo	*v.*	to increase
19. 千米	qiānmǐ	*m.*	kilometer
20. 科技	kējì	*n.*	science and technology

语言点 Language Points

一、动词"使"

动词"使"用在兼语句中，表示让、叫，通常出现在"A + 使 + B + 动词性/形容词性短语"结构中。例如：

1. 科学技术的发展使我们的生活越来越方便。

2. 自动体外除颤器的出现使因心脏病猝死的人大大减少。

3. 扫地机使我们节省出大量的时间，让打扫卫生变得轻松不少。

※ 练习：请用动词“使”改写句子

1. 互联网的出现让我们的生活更加方便了。

____

2. 听了医生说的话，病人开始改变原来的生活习惯。

____

3. 高铁越来越快，人们旅行也越来越方便了。

____

4. 使用助听器之后，很多病人的耳背症状减轻了。

____

二、连词“而”（2）

连词“而”前后可以连接语意相反的成分，表示转折。例如：

1. 以前，很多人觉得坐火车既慢又不舒服，而现在高铁速度提高到了每小时 300 多千米，各方面的条件也越来越好。
2. 打扫卫生要花很多时间，而扫地机的出现使人们节省了大量时间和力气。
3. 十月的哈尔滨已经下雪了，而在三亚人们还可以去海边玩儿水。

※ 练习：请用连词“而”造句

1. 马大为喜欢运动　金龙更喜欢在宿舍上网

____

2. 自己打扫很累　用扫地机很方便

____

3. 自动体外除颤器很有用　有的公共场合还没有安装

____

4. 上网买东西很方便　我更喜欢去商店买

______________________________。

综合练习 Comprehensive Exercises

一、根据拼音写汉字

1. kēxué ________　　3. huòdé ________　　5. fāngshì ________

2. fāzhǎn ________　　4. shìjì ________　　6. wánchéng ______

二、辨字组词

1. 科________　　3. 式________

　和________　　　试________

2. 使________　　4. 寄________

　便________　　　奇________

三、选词填空

使　而　逐渐　获得　通过

1. 科学的发展（　　）我们的生活越来越方便。
2. 现在大多数人都是（　　）互联网了解世界。
3. 过了春节，天气（　　）暖和起来了。
4. 通过这几年的学习，我（　　）了很多医学知识。
5. 三床的病人刚来的时候只能躺着，（　　）现在都能走了。

四、选出下列词语在句子中的位置

1. A自动体外除颤器B的出现C越来越多的心脏病病人D有了抢救的机会。

（使）

2. A 现在高铁速度 B 到 C 了每小时 300 千米 D 以上。（提高）

3. 以前很多夫妻 A 怀不上孩子也 B 没有办法，C 现在他们可以考虑 D 使用多种生殖辅助技术。（而）

4. 科学技术 A 正在 B 从各个方面 C 改变 D 人们的生活。（着）

5. A 我们今天的 B 工作是总结 C 最近遇到的困难和问题 D。（主要）

五、用所给词语完成对话

1. 顾客：这台扫地机怎么样？

 售货员：______________________________。（使）

2. 儿子：妈妈，为什么有的树很高，______________________________？（而）

 妈妈：因为它们的种类不同。

3. 医生：你的腿今天感觉怎么样？

 病人：______________________________。（通过）

4. 老师：______________________________？（完成）

 学生：昨天一放学就写完了。

5. 大为：你以前从不吃肉，现在怎么开始吃了？

 朋友：______________________________。（改变）

六、根据课文内容回答问题

1. 以前，我们主要通过哪些方式获得信息？现在呢？
2. 以前，人们怎么购物、寄东西、发文件？现在有什么变化？
3. 以前的火车跟现在的高铁相比，有哪些缺点？
4. 现在的高铁有哪些优点？
5. 你觉得科技还在哪些方面改变着我们的生活？

七、根据课文内容填空

科学技术的________使我们的生活越来越________。

比如：以前，我们主要________书、报纸、________和电视获得信息，进入21________以后，互联网________成了人们获得信息的主要________；以前，我们购物要去________，寄东西要去________，学习要去________，发文件要用________，现在这些事情都可以通过互联网________；以前，很多人觉得坐火车________又不舒服，而现在高铁速度________到了每小时300多千米，________的条件也越来越好。

科技就是这样________着我们的生活。

语言任务 Language Tasks

一、阅读理解

引起听力减退的原因有很多，但对青少年来说，噪声造成的噪声性听力损伤是最主要的损伤方式。专家指出，噪声暴露是青少年听力减退的主要原因，耳机的使用与其关系密切。据科学家分析，如果一个人每天使用耳机累计超过6小时，连续超过2小时，长期下去，听力就会严重受损。如果耳机声音大于100分贝，就可能对人造成不可恢复性听力损伤；当达到110分贝时，就足以使内耳的毛细胞死亡，对人造成永久性听力损伤。

来源：科普中国《经常戴耳机会容易损伤听力吗？》

补充词汇

1. 减退	jiǎntuì	*v.*	to decrease, to go down
2. 青少年	qīng-shàonián	*n.*	teen-agers
3. 噪声	zàoshēng	*n.*	noise
4. 造成	zàochéng	*v.*	to cause

5. 损伤	sǔnshāng	*v.*	to harm
6. 耳机	ěrjī	*n.*	earphone
7. 密切	mìqiè	*adj.*	close
8. 科学家	kēxuéjiā	*n.*	scientist
9. 分析	fēnxī	*v.*	to analyse
10. 累计	lěijì	*v.*	to add up
11. 连续	liánxù	*v.*	to continue
12. 长期	chángqī	*n.*	long-term
13. 受损	shòusǔn	*v.*	to be damaged
14. 大于	dàyú	*v.*	to be greater than
15. 分贝	fēnbèi	*m.*	decibel
16. 达到	dádào	*v.*	to reach
17. 足以	zúyǐ	*v.*	to be enough to
18. 内耳	nèi'ěr	*n.*	inner ear
19. 毛细胞	máoxìbāo	*n.*	hair cell
20. 永久性	yǒngjiǔxìng	*n.*	permanency

回答问题

1. 对青少年来说，噪声性听力损伤是什么造成的？
2. 青少年听力减退的主要原因是什么？
3. 长期使用耳机对耳朵有哪些危害？

二、口头表达

任务名称：向医生咨询是否需要购买助听器。

任务背景：病人耳背，和家属一起向医生咨询是否需要购买助听器。

任务要求：1. 三个学生一组，一个扮演病人，一个扮演病人家属，还有一个扮演医生。

2. 医生询问病人家属病人有什么症状，给病人进行听力测试后建议其购买助听器。

参考语言：耳背　大约　年纪　周围　打招呼　声音　助听器　配　普遍　测试　治疗

三、书面表达

任务名称：科技改变了我们的生活。

任务要求：请你选取和你生活相关的三个方面进行比较，体现科技对你生活的影响，要求 200 字以上。

参考语言：发展　使　获得　进入　世纪　完成　互联网　方式　改变　各方面

第三课 Lesson 3

我最近失眠很严重

学习目标 Learning Objectives

1. 语言功能：能够给别人提出合理建议，能够对别人进行劝说。
2. 语言点：固定结构“从……起”、连词“另外”、副词“偶尔”。
3. 医学知识：了解失眠的原因及治疗失眠的常用办法。
4. 社会文化：了解中国人午睡的生活习惯。

热身活动 Warm-up

1. 你的睡眠质量怎么样？你有午睡的习惯吗？

2. 哪些因素会影响睡眠？

课文（一）
Text（I）

（病人在神经内科门诊看病。）

病人：大夫，我最近失眠很严重。

医生：持续多长时间了？

病人：一个多月了。以前我的睡眠质量很好，每天晚上十一点准时睡觉；可从上个月起，我突然开始失眠，精力变差，脾气也变坏了。

医生：最近在生活、工作方面是否压力太大了？

病人：对，公司遇到了一些法律问题，我压力很大。这跟失眠有关系吗？

医生：很多人失眠都跟压力有关系。你可以试试睡觉前喝杯热牛奶、洗个热水澡，或者看看杂志。

病人：如果还是不行，怎么办？

医生：如果还是不行，那我再给你开点儿安眠药。

生词 New words

1. 失眠	shīmián	*v.*	to suffer from insomnia
2. 持续	chíxù	*v.*	to continue
3. 睡眠	shuìmián	*n.*	sleep
4. 准时	zhǔnshí	*adj.*	punctual, on time
5. 精力	jīnglì	*n.*	energy, vigor
6. 脾气	píqi	*n.*	temper
7. 坏	huài	*adj.*	bad
8. 公司	gōngsī	*n.*	company
9. 遇到	yùdào	*VC*	to run into
10. 法律	fǎlǜ	*n.*	law
11. 关系	guānxì	*n.*	relationship, relevance
12. 洗澡	xǐzǎo	*v.*	to take a shower
13. 杂志	zázhì	*n.*	magazine
14. 安眠药	ānmiányào	*n.*	sleeping pill

语言点 Language Points

固定结构“从……起”

固定结构“从……起”中间可以是表时间的短语，表示从某个时间开始，一般用在句首。例如：

1. 从上个月起，我突然开始失眠，精力变差，脾气也变坏了。
2. 从刚上大学起，我就每天早起跑步。
3. 从现在起，你不能再抽烟、喝酒了。

※ 练习：请用固定结构“从……起”完成对话

1. A：你是从什么时候开始学汉语的？

   B：________________。

2. A：你是从什么时候开始学习做饭的？

B：________________________________。

3. A：你失眠多长时间了？

B：________________________________。

4. A：孩子咳嗽多长时间了？

B：________________________________。

综合练习 Comprehensive Exercises

一、根据拼音写汉字

1. gōngsī __________
2. yùdào __________
3. fǎlǜ __________
4. xǐzǎo __________
5. zázhì __________
6. píqi __________

二、辨字组词

1. 精__________
   请__________
2. 准__________
   谁__________
3. 坏__________
   环__________
4. 续__________
   卖__________

三、选词填空

持续　准时　按时　及时　遇到

1. 爸爸每天晚上七点（　　）打开电视看新闻节目。
2. 病人最近失眠很严重，这种情况已经（　　）一个多月了。
3. 在学习过程中，（　　）不懂的问题，你一定要及时问老师。

4. 每天的作业你们都要（　　）完成，否则会影响你们的成绩。

5. 马大为踢球时摔伤了，他的朋友们（　　）把他送到了医院。

四、选出下列词语在句子中的位置

1. 从 A 上个月 B，他每天晚上 C 都在医院加班 D。（起）

2. 睡觉前 A 喝杯热牛奶 B 洗个热水澡 C 对睡眠 D 很有帮助。（或者）

3. 失眠 A 一般跟压力有 B，压力 C 越大的时候越容易 D 失眠。（关系）

4. 他 A 身体一直 B 非常好，上个星期 C 病了，D 现在还在医院。（突然）

5. 大夫，我觉得 A 我的睡眠情况 B 和以前一样，C 并没有什么 D 变化。（还是）

五、用所给词语完成对话

1. 医生：你失眠多久了？

   病人：______________________________。（从……起）

2. 月亮：你最近怎么总是不开心？

   同屋：______________________________。（遇到）

3. 病人：大夫，我最近总是睡不着，这到底是怎么了？

   医生：____________________，你最近是不是压力太大了？（跟……有关系）

4. 病人：大夫，我最近经常头疼、头晕。

   医生：______________________________？（持续）

5. 李大夫：王主任，明天的会议八点半就开始。

   王主任：放心吧，______________________________。（准时）

六、根据课文内容回答问题

1. 病人以前的睡眠质量怎么样？
2. 除了失眠，病人还有哪些变化？
3. 病人最近遇到了什么问题？
4. 失眠大多跟什么有关系？
5. 除了吃药，医生还建议病人怎么做？

七、根据课文内容填空

病人最近失眠严重，已经________一个多月了。以前他的睡眠________很好，每天晚上十一点________睡觉；可是从________起，他突然________失眠，精力________，脾气也________了。他的公司最近________一些法律问题，他________很大。医生说很多人失眠都________压力有关系，建议他可以试试睡觉前喝杯________、洗个________，或者看看________。如果________不行，医生再给他开点儿________。

课文（二）
Text（II）

（王晨和马大为在聊天儿。）

王晨：今天下午没有课，咱们去看京剧吧。

马大为：太好了，我还没看过京剧呢。演出几点开始？

王晨：三点。

马大为：咱们吃完午饭就出发吧。

王晨：京剧院离学校不远，咱们两点出发也来得及。午饭后，我想睡一会儿。

马大为：你有午睡的习惯？

王晨：对，我从小就养成了午睡的习惯。

马大为：午睡有什么好处？

王晨：午睡可以帮助我们恢复精力和体力，另外还可以降低血压、保护心脏、提高免疫力。

马大为：我以前一直觉得午睡就是浪费时间，原来午睡有这么多好处。

王晨：你也试试吧。

马大为：我还是更喜欢睡懒觉。

生词 New words

1. 京剧	jīngjù	*n.*	Beijing opera
2. 演出	yǎnchū	*n./v.*	performance; to perform
3. 出发	chūfā	*v.*	to set off
4. 午睡	wǔshuì	*n./v.*	afternoon nap; to have a nap after lunch
5. 养成	yǎngchéng	*v.*	to form, to develop
6. 好处	hǎochù	*n.*	benefit, advantage
7. 体力	tǐlì	*n.*	physical strength
8. 另外	lìngwài	*conj.*	in addition
9. 降低	jiàngdī	*v.*	to lower
10. 保护	bǎohù	*v.*	to protect
11. 免疫力	miǎnyìlì	*n.*	immunity
12. 睡懒觉	shuì lǎnjiào	*VO*	to sleep late
懒	lǎn	*adj.*	lazy

语言点 Language Points

连词"另外"

连词"另外"表示除此以外，后面可以加小句。例如：

1. 午睡可以帮助我们恢复精力和体力，另外还可以降低血压、保护心脏、提高免疫力。
2. 在中国留学可以学习汉语，另外也可以了解中国社会和文化。

除做连词外，"另外"还可以做指示代词，指前面所说的范围以外的人或事，后面常加名词或数量短语。例如：

3. 左边的同学先上车，另外的同学坐下一辆车。
4. 这台自动体外除颤器要安装在机场一楼，另外一台安装在二楼。

"另外"还可以做副词，表示在前文所说的范围以外。例如：

5. 手机坏了别担心，你另外买一个新的吧。

6. 这台电脑送给你吧，我另外还有一台。

※ 练习：请用“另外”完成对话

1. A：这两个手机都是你的吗？

   B：这一个是我的，________________。

2. A：你周末要做什么？

   B：我要去超市买东西，________________。

3. A：冬天去哈尔滨旅行好玩儿吗？

   B：当然好玩儿啊！可以看雪，________________。

4. A：你都买了什么东西？

   B：我买了一些水果，________________。

综合练习 Comprehensive Exercises

一、根据拼音写汉字

1. chūfā ________　　3. yǎngchéng ________　　5. jiàngdī ________

2. yǎnchū ________　　4. wūshuì ________　　6. bǎohù ________

二、辨字组词

1. 体________　　3. 疲________

   休________　　　没________

2. 另________　　4. 处________

   别________　　　外________

三、选词填空

降低　原来　养成　好处　另外

1. 他从十岁起，就（　　）了早睡早起的好习惯。
2. 吃了这些药以后，头不晕了，血压也（　　）了。
3. 游泳对身体有很多（　　），你要坚持每周游一次泳。
4. 医学生很忙，除了在学校上课、做实验，（　　）还要去医院学习。
5. 开始锻炼身体后，我每天不但腿不疼了，精力也好了。（　　），锻炼有这么多好处。

四、选出下列词语在句子中的位置

1. A 睡午觉 B 身体 C 有很多 D 好处。（对）
2. 现在 A 已经十一点了 B，我们什么时候 C 去机场 D？（出发）
3. 睡午觉不光能 A 血压，还能 B 保护心脏，C 提高免疫力 D。（降低）
4. A 这个学期，B 他的成绩 C 得很快，你发现了没有 D？（提高）
5. 我们要 A 良好 B 的 C 生活习惯和 D 学习习惯。（养成）

五、用所给词语完成对话

1. 医生：你哪儿不舒服？

   病人：我从昨天早上开始一直头疼，________________。（另外）
2. 哥哥：午饭以后有空儿吗？想不想去看电影？

   弟弟：________________，然后再去看电影，可以吗？（午睡）
3. 病人：大夫，我从上周起就不抽烟了，可是一直觉得全身不舒服。

   医生：________________，需要很长时间才能适应。（养成）

4. 艺文：你该起床了，否则上班就迟到了。

王东：现在才六点半，______________________。（来得及）

5. 儿子：妈妈，______________________，可以吗？（睡懒觉）

妈妈：明天是周六，你不用上学，当然可以。

六、根据课文内容回答问题

1. 马大为以前看过京剧吗？
2. 演出几点开始？
3. 马大为打算什么时候出发？
4. 午饭后，王晨要做什么？
5. 午睡有哪些好处？

七、根据课文内容填空

王晨今天下午没有课，想和马大为一起去看________。马大为还没________京剧呢，他很高兴。演出三点开始，马大为想吃完午饭就________。王晨说京剧院________学校不远，两点出发也________；而且午饭后他想________一会儿，因为他从小就________了午睡的习惯。午睡有很多________，可以帮助我们________精力和体力，________还可以________血压、________心脏、________免疫力。马大为以前一直觉得午睡就是________时间，原来午睡有这么多________。

课文（三）
Text（III）

根据世界卫生组织的调查，全世界大概有四分之一的人出现过睡眠问题，失眠已经成为很多人的烦恼。偶尔一两次失眠是正常的，可是如果经常失眠，就会严重影响身体与精神健康。

为了引起人们对睡眠问题的关注，世界睡眠医学学会设立了“世界睡眠日”。设立“世界睡眠日”的目的是提醒人们重视睡眠。重视睡眠就是重视健康、重视生命。

生词 New words

1. 调查	diàochá	*v./n.*	to investigate; investigation
2. 出现	chūxiàn	*v.*	to appear
3. 成为	chéngwéi	*v.*	to become
4. 偶尔	ǒu'ěr	*adv.*	occasionally
5. 与	yǔ	*conj.*	and
6. 精神	jīngshén	*n.*	spirit, mind
7. 关注	guānzhù	*v.*	to pay attention to, to follow with interest
8. 设立	shèlì	*v.*	to establish
9. 目的	mùdì	*n.*	purpose
10. 生命	shēngmìng	*n.*	life

专名 Proper nouns

1. 世界卫生组织	Shìjiè Wèishēng Zǔzhī	World Health Organization
2. 世界睡眠医学学会	Shìjiè Shuìmián Yīxué Xuéhuì	World Association of Sleep Medicine
3. 世界睡眠日	Shìjiè Shuìmiánrì	World Sleep Day

语言点 Language Points

副词"偶尔"

副词"偶尔"表示间或、有时候。例如：

1. 偶尔一两次失眠是正常的，可是如果经常失眠，就会严重影响身体与精神健康。
2. 美丽平时不太喜欢运动，偶尔会去爬爬山。
3. 我一般都在家做饭吃，偶尔会去饭店吃。

※ 练习：请用副词“偶尔”完成对话

1. A：你一般早上几点起床？

B：______________________________。

2. A：你常常来这家超市买东西吗？

B：______________________________。

3. A：奶奶常常觉得心脏不舒服吗？

B：______________________________。

4. A：这里的冬天经常下雪吗？

B：______________________________。

综合练习 Comprehensive Exercises

一、根据拼音写汉字

1. ǒu'ěr __________　3. mùdì __________　5. shēngmìng __________

2. chūxiàn __________　4. shèlì __________　6. diàochá __________

二、辨字组词

1. 与__________　3. 目__________

写__________　日__________

2. 设__________　4. 尔__________

没__________　你__________

三、选词填空

调查　与　成为　偶尔　精神

1. 失眠会严重影响人们的身体和（　　）健康。

2. 掉头发现在已经（　　）很多年轻人的烦恼。

3. 科学（　　）技术的发展逐渐改变着我们的生活。

4. 一个月（　　）失眠一两次是正常的，不用太担心。

5. 根据学校的（　　），每年大约有百分之一的学生不能正常毕业。

四、选出下列词语在句子中的位置

1. A 每次 B 出门，奶奶 C 总会 D 我要注意安全。（提醒）

2. 你知道 A 在公共场所安装 B 除颤器的 C 是什么 D 吗？（目的）

3. A 父母 B 辛苦工作大多是 C 让家人 D 生活得更好。（为了）

4. 生病 A 以后，B 他的精力 C 体力都 D 比以前下降了不少。（与）

5. 抽烟 A 对身体有害，为了 B 更多人的 C 重视，D 我们做了很多工作。（引起）

五、用所给词语完成对话

1. 病人：我最近经常失眠，不知道是什么原因。

   医生：______________________，你最近生活有什么变化吗？（引起）

2. 哥哥：你们班有多少男生？

   弟弟：我们班男生很多，大约占全班人数的______________________。（之）

3. 病人：大夫，我最近头疼得厉害。

   医生：是一直疼，______________________？（偶尔）

4. 美丽：你父母比较重视你哪些方面的发展？

   月亮：______________________。（与）

5. 大为：你有哪些兴趣爱好？

   金龙：我喜欢踢足球，______________________。（另外）

六、根据课文内容回答问题

1. 根据世界卫生组织的调查，全世界有多少人出现过睡眠问题？
2. 偶尔失眠需要看医生吗？
3. 经常失眠会带来哪些问题？
4. 设立“世界睡眠日”的目的是什么？
5. 我们为什么要重视睡眠问题？

七、根据课文内容填空

根据世界卫生组织的________，全世界大概有________的人出现过睡眠问题，失眠已经成为很多人的________。________一两次失眠是正常的，可是如果经常失眠，就会严重影响________与________健康。

为了引起人们对________问题的________，世界睡眠医学学会________了“世界睡眠日”。设立“世界睡眠日”的________是提醒人们________睡眠。重视睡眠就是重视________、重视________。

语言任务 Language Tasks

一、阅读理解

失眠主要包括急性失眠和慢性失眠。出现失眠情况在一个月之内的，叫作急性失眠。如果一个月内没有完全调整过来，时间往后拖延，就会进入慢性失眠阶段。

失眠的原因非常复杂，总结起来可以分为内外两个方面。内因主要是患者机体自身的条件，比如特别容易焦虑和紧张。而且，年龄的增长也是内因之一。随着年龄的增长，人们的睡眠质量会逐渐下降。另外，失眠还跟患者自身的生活习惯有关系。这些都是内在的原因。外因就是社会的压力，还有居住环境、温度、噪声等，这些都会导致失眠。

来源：科普中国《经常失眠是什么原因？》

补充词汇

1. 包括	bāokuò	*v.*	to include
2. 慢性	mànxìng	*adj.*	chronic
3. 之内	zhīnèi	*n.*	in, within
4. 叫作	jiàozuò	*v.*	to be called
5. 拖延	tuōyán	*v.*	to delay
6. 阶段	jiēduàn	*n.*	stage
7. 内外	nèiwài	*n.*	inside and outside
8. 内因	nèiyīn	*n.*	internal cause
9. 机体	jītǐ	*n.*	organism
10. 自身	zìshēn	*n.*	oneself
11. 之一	zhīyī	*n.*	one of
12. 下降	xiàjiàng	*v.*	to decline
13. 内在	nèizài	*adj.*	intrinsic
14. 外因	wàiyīn	*n.*	external cause
15. 社会	shèhuì	*n.*	society
16. 居住	jūzhù	*v.*	to reside

回答问题

1. 失眠分为哪两类？
2. 急性失眠和慢性失眠有什么关系？
3. 导致失眠的原因有哪些？

二、口头表达

任务名称：向医生咨询失眠问题。

任务背景：病人有失眠的烦恼，来医院咨询医生。

任务要求：1. 两个学生一组，一个扮演病人，一个扮演医生。

2. 医生询问病人有什么症状，并给病人提出改善睡眠的建议。

参考语言：持续　偶尔　失眠　影响　精神　脾气　压力　跟……有关　为了　洗热水澡　重视　好处　帮助　遇到　精力

三、书面表达

任务名称：午睡的好处。

任务要求：请根据自己的了解介绍一下午睡的好处，要求 200 字以上。

参考语言：养成　习惯　体力　另外　帮助　降低　提高　保护　好处　精力　使

第四课 Lesson 4 这些都是更年期的症状

学习目标 Learning Objectives

1. 语言功能：能够向别人寻求或提供帮助，能够对问题进行深入分析。
2. 语言点：固定结构“在……上”、副词“也许”、连词“同时”。
3. 医学知识：初步了解更年期的主要症状和青春期的主要表现。
4. 社会文化：探讨如何促进父母与子女之间进行有效沟通。

热身活动 Warm-up

1. 你了解更年期吗？更年期女性一般有哪些症状？

2. 青春期时，你有哪些表现？

课文（一）
Text（I）

（病人在妇科门诊看病。）

病人：大夫，最近一段时间，我的月经周期不稳定。

医生：你今年多大？

病人：四十七。

医生：除了月经不正常，身体上还有其他变化吗？

病人：晚上总是出汗，经常生气，越来越没有耐心，还特别容易伤心、焦虑，可是体检结果都正常。

医生：这些都是更年期的症状，所有女性都会经历，不用太紧张。

病人：需要吃药吗？

医生：现在不需要，建议你放松心情，坚持锻炼身体，比如散散步、游游泳什么的。

生词 New words

1. 妇科	fùkē	*n.*	gynaecology
2. 段	duàn	*m.*	*used to indicate time or distance*
3. 月经	yuèjīng	*n.*	menstruation
4. 周期	zhōuqī	*n.*	period, cycle period
5. 稳定	wěndìng	*adj.*	stable
6. 生气	shēngqì	*v.*	to get angry
7. 耐心	nàixīn	*n./adj.*	patience; patient
8. 伤心	shāngxīn	*v.*	to be sad
9. 焦虑	jiāolǜ	*adj.*	worried
10. 更年期	gēngniánqī	*n.*	menopause
11. 症状	zhèngzhuàng	*n.*	symptom
12. 所有	suǒyǒu	*adj.*	all
13. 经历	jīnglì	*v./n.*	to experience; experience

语言点 Language Points

固定结构“在……上”

固定结构“在……上”表示范围或者条件。“上”的前边一般是名词或动词性成分，“在”可以省略。例如：

1. 除了月经不正常，身体上还有其他变化吗？
2. 我家孩子学习很努力，在学习上我从来不用担心。
3. 在去哪儿旅游这件事情上，我和姐姐的想法不一样。

※ 练习：请用固定结构“在……上”和所给词语完成对话

1. A：哥哥最近看起来很忙，他怎么了？

   B：________________。（工作）

2. A：爷爷今天去医院了？

B：________________________________。（身体）

3. A：爸爸，您觉得我应该选择哪个专业呢？

B：________________________________。（专业）

4. A：你现在适应中国的生活了吗？

B：________________________________。（生活）

综合练习 Comprehensive Exercises

一、根据拼音写汉字

1. wěndìng ________
3. nàixīn ________
5. jiāolǜ ________
2. shēngqì ________
4. shāngxīn ________
6. suǒyǒu ________

二、辨字组词

1. 段________
   设________
3. 气________
   汽________
2. 稳________
   和________
4. 所________
   听________

三、选词填空

段　所有　坚持　经历　上

1. 最近一（　　）时间，这个病人都住在九号病房，没有换过。
2. 我们班（　　）的同学都去参观学校对面的医院了。
3. 学习的苦与累，是每个学生都要（　　）的。

4. 我的中国朋友在学习（　　）给了我很多帮助。

5. 运动对身体有很多好处，你（　　）一段时间，一定会有效果。

四、选出下列词语在句子中的位置

1. 下雪后 A 走路 B 一定要小心，因为 C 路滑，很 D 摔倒。（容易）

2. A 我们医院的 B 医生对病人 C 都很有 D 耐心，也很有爱心。（所有）

3. 考试前 A 每个学生 B 都会感到 C，这很 D 正常。（紧张）

4. 最近 A 这段时间，B 他 C 失眠，还经常 D 发脾气。（总是）

5. A 这个学期 B 我们 C 汉语课以外，还有 D 五门专业课。（除了）

五、用所给词语完成对话

1. 病人家属：大夫您好，最近一段时间我父亲经常头晕。

   医生：____________________，还是偶尔这样？（总是）

2. 金龙：你适应这里的生活了吗？

   马大为：____________________。（在……上）

3. 病人：医生您好，这是我的病历。

   医生：____________________？怎么没有最近的？（所有）

4. 丈夫：你去过黄河公园吗？

   妻子：____________________，现在好久没去了。（经常）

5. 病人家属：你觉得这种药效果怎么样？

   病人：现在才吃了三天，____________________。（坚持）

六、根据课文内容回答问题

1. 这位病人为什么来医院？

2. 除了月经不正常，她身体上还有哪些变化？

3. 对女性来说，这些更年期症状普遍吗？

4. 医生给了病人哪些建议？

七、根据课文内容填空

一位四十七岁的女性病人来妇科门诊看病。她最近月经周期不________，晚上总是________，经常________，越来越没有________，还特别容易________、________，可是________结果都正常。医生说这些都是________的症状，________女性都会________，让她不用太________。现在也不需要________，医生建议她________心情，坚持________，比如散散步、游游泳________。

课文（二）
Text（II）

（美丽和月亮在聊天儿。）

美丽：我特别担心妈妈和弟弟。

月亮：他们怎么了？

美丽：我弟弟今年十二岁，上六年级，经常被妈妈批评。

月亮：为什么批评他？

美丽：妈妈觉得他学习态度不好，喜欢玩儿游戏，还不做家务，很懒。

月亮：那你弟弟接受妈妈的批评吗？

美丽：不接受，而且做错了事情也不道歉，经常跟妈妈发生矛盾。

月亮：他们一直这样吗？

美丽：以前不这样。可是现在弟弟是青春期，妈妈是更年期，两个人都缺少耐心，都不冷静。我在中国留学，爸爸在外地做生意，都不在家。

月亮：中国有部电视剧，叫《家有儿女》，建议你们看看，也许有帮助。

生词 New words

1. 年级	niánjí	*n.*	grade
2. 批评	pīpíng	*v.*	to criticize
3. 态度	tàidù	*n.*	attitude
4. 家务	jiāwù	*n.*	housework
5. 接受	jiēshòu	*v.*	to accept
6. 道歉	dàoqiàn	*v.*	to apologize
7. 发生	fāshēng	*v.*	to happen
8. 矛盾	máodùn	*n.*	contradiction
9. 青春期	qīngchūnqī	*n.*	puberty
10. 缺少	quēshǎo	*v.*	to lack
11. 冷静	lěngjìng	*adj.*	calm
12. 做生意	zuò shēngyi	*VO*	to do business
生意	shēngyi	*n.*	business
13. 部	bù	*m.*	*a measure word for books, movies, etc.*
14. 电视剧	diànshìjù	*n.*	TV series
15. 也许	yěxǔ	*adv.*	maybe

语言点 Language Points

副词“也许”

副词“也许”表示猜测或不太肯定，后面常加动词性成分或小句。例如：

1. 中国有部电视剧，叫《家有儿女》，建议你们看看，也许有帮助。

2. 我回国以后也许会跟家人去旅游。

3. 金龙还没到，也许他今天不来了。

“也许”可以单独回答问题，后面常常带“吧”。例如：

4. A：金龙会不会今天不来了？

B：也许吧。

※ 练习：请用副词“也许”完成对话

1. A：今天太热了！不知道明天天气怎么样。

B：______________________________。

2. A：下星期我们放假，你打算做什么？

B：______________________________。

3. A：我的口语太差了，怎么办呀？

B：______________________________。

4. A：马大为今天没来上课，他是不是感冒了？

B：______________________________。

综合练习 Comprehensive Exercises

一、根据拼音写汉字

1. niánjí ________
2. pīpíng ________
3. tàidù ________
4. jiēshòu ________
5. dàoqiàn ________
6. quēshǎo ________

二、辨字组词

1. 级________
   纪________
2. 剧________
   到________
3. 受________
   爱________
4. 部________
   都________

三、选词填空

也许	接受	发生	缺少	部

1. 他从来不（　　）别人的建议，喜欢自己做决定。

2. 这段时间（　　）了这么多事情，你为什么不告诉我？

3. 你失眠这么久了，（　　）应该去医院找个医生看看。

4. 我看了很多（　　）中国电视剧，它们对我的汉语学习很有帮助。

5. 这里的药不全，还（　　）几种，你得去药店买。

四、选出下列词语在句子中的位置

1. 我 A 上小学的时候 B 经常 C 老师 D 批评。　（被）

2. A 你 B 去找张大夫看看吧，他 C 能帮助你 D。　（也许）

3. A 你说的这些我 B 都能 C，但是请你注意 D 说话的态度。　（接受）

4. 最近 A 一段时间，他们 B 夫妻俩经常因为孩子的 C 事儿发生 D。　（矛盾）

5. A 刚毕业的学生，B 肯定 C 经验，D 要多学多练。　（缺少）

五、用所给词语完成对话

1. 医生：你的腿怎么了？

   病人：______________________________。（被）

2. 金龙：毕业以后你还要继续学习吗？

   大为：______________________________。（也许）

3. 妈妈：听说你把同学的足球踢坏了，你给他道歉了吗？

   儿子：道歉了，______________________________。（接受）

4. 丈夫：你怎么又不高兴了？我刚才说错了吗？

   妻子：你没说错，______________________________。（态度）

5. 儿子：我不小心把哥哥的电脑弄坏了，哥哥很生气。

   爸爸：________________________，我相信他会原谅你的。（道歉）

六、根据课文内容回答问题

1. 美丽的弟弟多大了？上几年级？
2. 美丽为什么很担心妈妈和弟弟？
3. 美丽的妈妈为什么经常批评她的弟弟？
4. 弟弟为什么不接受妈妈的批评？
5. 月亮给了美丽什么建议？

七、根据课文内容填空

美丽的弟弟今年十二岁，上________，经常被妈妈________。因为妈妈觉得他学习________不好，喜欢玩儿________，还不做________。弟弟不接受妈妈的________，而且做错了事情也不________，经常跟妈妈发生________。他们以前不这样，可是现在弟弟是________，妈妈是________，两个人都缺少________，都不________。美丽在中国________，爸爸在外地________，都不在家。月亮建议美丽一家看看《家有儿女》这部________，________有帮助。

课文（三）
Text（III）

更年期是所有女性都要经历的一个时期。通过自己的调整，大部分女性都可以顺利度过更年期。专家建议，更年期女性生活要规律，按时起床和睡觉。如果实在睡不着，可以在医生的指导下吃点儿安眠药。更年期女性更要注意营养均衡，蔬菜、水果和蛋白质都不能少；同时，积极乐观的态度也可以帮助女性顺利度过这个特殊时期。

生词 New words

1. 时期	shíqī	*n.*	period, stage
2. 度过	dùguò	*v.*	to spend
3. 专家	zhuānjiā	*n.*	expert
4. 规律	guīlǜ	*n.*	law, regularity
5. 指导	zhǐdǎo	*v.*	to guide
6. 均衡	jūnhéng	*adj.*	balanced
7. 蛋白质	dànbáizhì	*n.*	protein
8. 同时	tóngshí	*conj.*	at the same time
9. 积极	jījí	*adj.*	active
10. 乐观	lèguān	*adj.*	optimistic
11. 特殊	tèshū	*adj.*	special

语言点 Language Points

连词"同时"

连词"同时"表示并列关系，含有进一层的意味；常用在后一小句中，与"也、还、又"等搭配使用。例如：

1. 更年期女性更要注意营养均衡，蔬菜、水果和蛋白质都不能少；同时，积极乐观的态度也可以帮助女性顺利度过这个特殊时期。
2. 如果遇到心脏病病人猝死，而且旁边有自动体外除颤器的话，请马上使用自动体外除颤器进行急救，同时立即打120。
3. 每周坚持踢足球，不但可以锻炼身体，同时还可以交更多的朋友。

"同时"还可以做时间名词，表示动作行为在同一时间发生。例如：

4. 今天早上，马大为和金龙是同时到的教室。
5. 我喜欢看中国电影，因为看电影的同时还可以学习汉语。
6. 我和好朋友同时来中国留学，我们都学习医学。

※ 练习：请用“同时”和所给词语完成句子

1. 我家离公司很远，早上______________________________。（坐车　听英语）

2. 弟弟习惯______________________________。（写作业　听音乐）

3. 这台扫地机不错，扫得很干净，______________________________。（不太贵）

4. 我周末喜欢去爬山，这不仅可以锻炼身体，____________________。（欣赏风景）

综合练习 Comprehensive Exercises

一、根据拼音写汉字

1. shíqī ________　3. tóngshí ________　5. jījí ________

2. dùguò ________　4. tèshū ________　6. zhǐdǎo ________

二、辨字组词

1. 积________　和________

2. 极________　级________

3. 规________　观________

4. 专________　去________

三、选词填空

度过　同时　特殊　通过　大部分

1. 一般来说，学习好的人都有自己（　　）的学习方法。

2. 这是我们医院的院长，（　　）还是我们大学的校长。

3. 更年期女性在医生指导下都可以顺利（　　）这个特殊时期。

4. 这个假期（　　）时间我都在学习汉语，想提高一下自己的汉语水平。

5. 孩子，祝贺你！这都是你（　　）自己的努力取得的成绩。

四、选出下列词语在句子中的位置

1. 我晚上实在 A 睡不 B 的时候就会 C 起来做一些 D 家务。（着）
2. A 我 B 不明白 C 为什么很多学生 D 连专业课都不上。（实在）
3. 在老师 A 和同学的帮助 B，他顺利 C 通过了 D 期中考试。（下）
4. 经过 A 几年的 B 锻炼，爸爸的身体 C 比以前 D 好了。（更）
5. 你快 A 跟我们 B 说说这几年 C 的留学生活你是怎么 D 的。（度过）

五、用所给词语完成对话

1. 金龙：你期末考试怎么考得那么好呀？

   大为：______________________________，我确实提高了很多。（……下）
2. 医生：我刚才说的这些你都听明白了吗？

   病人：______________________________。（大部分）
3. 丈夫：我下个月有一周的假期。

   妻子：真的吗？______________________________？（度过）
4. 病人：大夫，孩子感冒得厉害，只吃药能行吗？

   医生：______________________________。（通过）
5. 病人：大夫，出院以后，我需要注意哪些问题？

   医生：一定要按时吃药，______________________________。（同时）

六、根据课文内容回答问题

1. 谁会经历更年期？
2. 大部分女性是如何顺利度过更年期的？
3. 专家给更年期女性提出了什么建议？

4. 更年期女性需要注意哪些问题？

七、根据课文内容填空

更年期是所有________都要经历的一个________。通过自己的________，大部分女性都可以顺利________更年期。专家建议，更年期女性生活要________，按时________和________。如果________睡不着，可以在医生的________下吃点儿安眠药。更年期女性更要注意营养________，同时，积极乐观的________也可以帮助女性顺利度过这个________时期。

语言任务 Language Tasks

一、阅读理解

更年期综合征多见于46—50岁的女性，近年来有发病年龄提前、发病率上升的趋势。更年期是女性生理上的一个特殊时期，是身心健康出现状况的敏感期，而睡眠障碍在此期间非常突出。更年期女性在睡眠上最常见的症状就是伴随着盗汗的潮热，大约80%的更年期女性都会出现这种症状并由此引发失眠。潮热在晚间使体温快速上升，造成入睡困难。归根结底，这些睡眠障碍都是更年期雌激素、孕酮生成减少导致的。

来源：医学教育网

补充词汇

1. 综合征	zōnghézhēng	*n.*	syndrome
2. 发病	fābìng	*v.*	(of a disease) to come on
3. 上升	shàngshēng	*v.*	to rise, to go up
4. 趋势	qūshì	*n.*	tendency
5. 身心	shēnxīn	*n.*	body and mind
6. 状况	zhuàngkuàng	*n.*	condition

7. 敏感期	mǐngǎnqī	*n.*	sensitive period
8. 障碍	zhàng'ài	*n.*	obstacle
9. 突出	tūchū	*adj.*	outstanding, prominent
10. 伴随	bànsuí	*v.*	to accompany
11. 盗汗	dàohàn	*v.*	to perspire during sleep
12. 潮热	cháorè	*adj.*	hot flash
13. 引发	yǐnfā	*v.*	to trigger
14. 体温	tǐwēn	*n.*	body temperature
15. 快速	kuàisù	*adj.*	fast, high-speed
16. 入睡	rùshuì	*v.*	to fall asleep
17. 归根结底	guīgēn-jiédǐ		in the final analysis
18. 雌激素	cíjīsù	*n.*	estrogen
19. 孕酮	yùntóng	*n.*	progesterone
20. 生成	shēngchéng	*v.*	to produce, to form

回答问题

1. 什么是更年期综合征?
2. 更年期女性有什么突出症状?
3. 更年期睡眠障碍是什么原因导致的?

二、口头表达

任务名称：如何跟更年期妈妈友好相处。

任务背景：妈妈进入更年期后，脾气和习惯改变很大，还常常失眠。姐妹/兄弟俩讨论让妈妈开心的方法。

任务要求：1. 三个学生一组，一个扮演姐姐/哥哥，一个扮演妹妹/弟弟，还有一个扮演妈妈。

2. 三人讨论如何减轻妈妈/自己的焦虑。

参考语言：段　稳定　生气　伤心　焦虑　耐心　经历　坚持　态度　冷静　时期　度过　规律　积极　乐观　均衡　特殊

三、书面表达

任务名称：我的青春期。

任务要求：请介绍一下自己青春期时的主要表现，并尝试分析其原因，要求 200 字以上。

参考语言：段　时期　特殊　冷静　态度　接受　批评　态度　指导　改变　积极　互相

第五课 Lesson 5 我父亲的记忆力越来越差

学习目标 Learning Objectives

1. 语言功能：能够劝慰别人，能够恰当表达自己的感情或情绪。
2. 语言点：副词“稍微”、副词“互相”、代词“彼此”、固定结构“无论……都/也……”。
3. 医学知识：初步了解阿尔茨海默病。
4. 社会文化：初步了解当代中国人的养老方式。

热身活动 Warm-up

1. 你了解阿尔茨海默病吗？这种病有什么表现？

2. 如果患有阿尔茨海默病的亲人走丢了，你会怎么做？

课文（一）
Text（Ⅰ）

（医生在神经内科门诊坐诊。）

病人的女儿：大夫，我父亲的记忆力越来越差，他常常忘记把东西放在哪里，几乎每天都在找眼镜、钥匙和手机。

医生：还有别的变化吗？

病人的女儿：他以前喜欢交朋友，现在却不愿意跟朋友联系了；以前爱讲笑话儿，现在不讲了，语言能力也变差了。并且，稍微有点儿不舒服，他就怀疑自己得了重病，我们怎么解释他也不相信。

医生：您今年多大年纪了？

病人：五十七了。

病人的女儿：又弄错了，不是五十七，是七十五。他现在常常弄错数字。

医生：能自己吃饭、穿衣服吗？

病人的女儿：可以。大夫，我父亲到底怎么了？

医生：可能是阿尔茨海默病。

生词 New words

1. 记忆力	jìyìlì	*n.*	faculty of memory
记忆	jìyì	*v./n.*	to remember; memory
2. 忘记	wàngjì	*v.*	to forget
3. 眼镜	yǎnjìng	*n.*	glasses
4. 钥匙	yàoshi	*n.*	key
5. 联系	liánxì	*v.*	to contact
6. 讲	jiǎng	*v.*	to tell
7. 笑话儿	xiàohuar	*n.*	joke
8. 语言	yǔyán	*n.*	language
9. 能力	nénglì	*n.*	ability
10. 稍微	shāowēi	*adv.*	slightly
11. 怀疑	huáiyí	*v.*	to doubt
12. 解释	jiěshì	*v.*	to explain
13. 相信	xiāngxìn	*v.*	to believe
14. 数字	shùzì	*n.*	figure, numeral
15. 阿尔茨海默病	ā'ěrcíhǎimòbìng	*n.*	Alzheimer's disease

语言点 Language Points

副词"稍微"

副词"稍微"表示数量不多或程度不深，后面常带动词性或形容词性成分。带动词性成分时，动词常常重叠，或动词后带"一点儿、一下、一些、一会儿"等补语。例如：

1. 快出发了，我要稍微准备准备。
2. 饭马上就做好了，你稍微等一下。
3. 太累了！咱们稍微休息一会儿吧。

带形容词性成分时，形容词后也常带"一点儿、一些"等补语。例如：

4. 金龙的汉语比我的稍微好一点儿。

5. 今天比昨天稍微冷一些。

带形容词性成分时，形容词前常用“有点儿”表示不如意。例如：

6. 稍微有点儿不舒服，他就怀疑自己得了重病。

7. 跑步的时候，稍微有点儿累，我就不想再跑了。

8. 这个超市卖的东西稍微有点儿贵。

※ 练习：请用副词“稍微”完成对话

1. A：这家饭馆怎么样？

   B：________________________________。

2. A：你这学期课多吗？

   B：________________________________。

3. A：我们已经走了一个小时了。

   B：________________________________。

4. A：你病了吗？要不要去医院？

   B：________________________________。

综合练习 Comprehensive Exercises

一、根据拼音写汉字

1. wàngjì ________　　3. yàoshi ________　　5. huáiyí ________

2. yǎnjìng ________　　4. shāowēi ________　　6. xiāngxìn ________

二、辨字组词

1. 讲________　　3. 镜________

   进________　　竟________

2. 信________　　　　4. 怀________

言________　　　　坏________

三、选词填空

稍微　弄　联系　忘记　几乎

1. 我刚才不小心把手弄伤了，现在（　　）动一下就流血。
2. 他很早就来到了教室，（　　）了今天是周末。
3. 你又（　　）错了，我是姐姐，她才是妹妹。
4. 她上周（　　）一半的时间都在实验室做实验。
5. 你只要觉得不舒服就赶紧打电话（　　）我。

四、选出下列词语在句子中的位置

1. A 不要 B 水杯放在 C 电脑旁边 D。（把）
2. A 他一直 B 没告诉我这段时间他 C 去哪儿了 D。（到底）
3. 做完 A 手术以后 B，刘大夫 C 休息了一会儿 D。（稍微）
4. 马上就要 A 办理出院手续了，B 他 C 不想 D 出院了。（却）
5. 我们 A 都 B 那件事儿 C 是哥哥说出来 D 的。（怀疑）

五、用所给词语完成对话

1. 医生：我看看你的检查单。

病人：________________________________？（到底）

2. 金龙：________________________________？（稍微）

朋友：我不着急，现在才两点半。

3. 孩子：________________________________。（把）

爸爸：宝贝，谢谢你，我刚想起来忘了拿手机。

4. 医生：你的月经周期稳定吗？

病人：以前很稳定，很规律，________________________。（却）

5. 金龙：________________________________？（联系）

大为：上个周末，我给父母打了电话。

六、根据课文内容回答问题

1. 病人最近有什么表现？
2. 病人今年是五十七岁还是七十五岁？
3. 病人为什么弄错了自己的年龄？
4. 病人自己能做哪些事情？
5. 医生估计病人得了什么病？

六、根据课文内容填空

有位病人________越来越差，常常________把东西放在哪里，几乎每天都在找眼镜、________和手机。他以前喜欢________，现在却不________跟朋友联系了；以前爱讲________，现在不讲了，________能力也变差了。并且，________有点儿不舒服，他就________自己得了重病，家人怎么________他也不相信，还常常________数字，好在病人现在能自己________、________。根据他的症状，医生判断他可能得了________。

课文（二）
Text（II）

（李真的爷爷走失了，李真在安慰奶奶。）

李真：奶奶，您别担心。警察和很多网友都在帮我们，咱们一定能找到爷爷。

奶奶：我真没想到他竟然在家附近迷了路！早上他只吃了一碗面条儿、一个鸡蛋，现在都晚上了，恐怕早就饿了。

李真：爷爷脚疼，肯定走不远，应该很快就能找到。

奶奶：这几年，你爷爷总是让人担心。

李真：奶奶，以前您和爷爷能互相照顾，现在你们年纪大了，以后跟我们一起住吧。

奶奶：你们都很忙，我们不想给你们添麻烦。

李真：这不是麻烦，是我们的责任。我们是一家人，应该关心彼此。

生词 New words

1. 走失	zǒushī	*v.*	to get lost
2. 安慰	ānwèi	*v.*	to console
3. 网友	wǎngyǒu	*n.*	net friend
4. 迷路	mílù	*v.*	to lose one's way
5. 面条儿	miàntiáor	*n.*	noodles
6. 鸡蛋	jīdàn	*n.*	egg
7. 饿	è	*adj.*	hungry
8. 脚	jiǎo	*n.*	foot
9. 互相	hùxiāng	*adv.*	mutually
10. 添	tiān	*v.*	to add, to get or give more
11. 责任	zérèn	*n.*	responsibility
12. 彼此	bǐcǐ	*pron.*	each other

语言点 Language Points

一、副词"互相"

副词"互相"表示A对B、B对A施加相同的动作行为或具有相同的关系，后面一般带双音节或多音节的动词性成分，不能带单音节动词。例如：

1. 以前您和爷爷能互相照顾，现在你们年纪大了，以后跟我们一起住吧。
2. 我和她互相喜欢已经很久了。
3. 过春节的时候，亲戚朋友之间会互相送礼物。

※ 练习：请用副词"互相"改写句子

1. 我很关心妹妹，妹妹也很关心我。

____

2. 我向朋友学习，朋友也向我学习。

____

3. 我很了解他，他也很了解我。

____

4. 我对她不满意，她对我也不满意。

____

二、代词"彼此"

代词"彼此"表示这个和那个，双方；一般在句中做主语或宾语，也可以加上"的"或"间的"之后做定语。例如：

1. 我们是一家人，应该关心彼此。
2. 我们认识很多年了，非常了解彼此。
3. 我们是老朋友，彼此的生日都记得很清楚。

※ 练习：请用代词"彼此"完成对话

1. A：你了解你的丈夫吗？

   B：______________________________。

2. A：你和男朋友的关系怎么样？

   B：______________________________。

3. A：你和母亲________________________？

   B：当然了！她理解我，我也理解她。

4. A：________________________，对吧？

   B：对，我很关心我的同屋，他也很关心我。

综合练习 Comprehensive Exercises

一、根据拼音写汉字

1. ānwèi ________	3. zérèn ________	5. jīdàn ________
2. mílù ________	4. miàntiáor ________	6. hùxiāng ________

二、辨字组词

1. 迷________　　3. 脚________

　米________　　　却________

2. 饿________　　4. 此________

　我________　　　些________

三、选词填空

突然　竟然　互相　彼此　恐怕

1. 我们是姐妹，当然要关心（　　）。
2. 下午我们正踢着球，（　　）下雨了。
3. 今天早上我一起床就头疼得厉害，（　　）只能请假休息了。
4. 他才四岁，（　　）会写这么多汉字。
5. 他是我最好的朋友，我们俩（　　）学习，共同进步。

四、选出下列词语在句子中的位置

1. A 孩子 B 生病，父母 C 都很 D 着急。（肯定）
2. 作为一名 A 医生，治病救人 B 是 C 我的 D。（责任）
3. A 现在 B 晚上十一点了，你 C 怎么还不回家 D？（都）
4. 我过生日 A 那天，妈妈给我 B 做了 C 一大 D 面条儿。（碗）
5. 你到 A 爷爷奶奶家以后 B，要多 C 帮忙，少 D 麻烦。（添）

五、用所给词语完成对话

1. 大为：这次搬家真是太谢谢你了！

　同学：我们是同学，________________________。（互相）

2. 病人：医生，我这个月还得来复查吗？

医生：____________________________。（恐怕）

3. 金龙：听说你们班赢了篮球比赛。

朋友：____________________________。（没想到）

4. 李真：你了解金龙吗？

王晨：____________________________。（彼此）

5. 病人：大夫，我才吃了两天的药，____________________________。（竟然）

医生：你恢复得确实很快。

六、根据课文内容回答问题

1. 李真的爷爷怎么了？
2. 谁在帮忙找爷爷？
3. 爷爷走丢多长时间了？
4. 李真的爷爷是在哪儿走丢的？
5. 李真为什么想让爷爷奶奶跟他们一起住？

七、根据课文内容填空

李真的爷爷在家附近迷路了，警察和很多________都在帮忙找。爷爷早上只吃了一碗________、一个________，现在都晚上了，________早就饿了。李真觉得爷爷脚疼，肯定________，应该很快就能找到。以前奶奶和爷爷能________照顾，现在他们________大了，李真希望爷爷奶奶能跟他们________。奶奶觉得孩子们都很忙，不想给他们________，可是李真觉得一家人就应该关心________。

课文（三）
Text（III）

今天上午，爷爷在家附近走丢了。我们全家都非常着急，到处找他。晚上，一位警察在附近的街道上找到了他，当时他正在一家加油站的入口站着。警察对爷爷非常有耐心，也很友好，还把他送回了家。我们全家都特别感谢那位警察。

以前，我们觉得爷爷在熟悉的地方不会迷路，现在看来这种想法是错误的。爸爸打算给爷爷买一部电话手表，以后无论他在哪里，我们都能准确找到他的位置。我和父母已经商量好了，无论多忙，我们都要照顾好爷爷。

生词 New words

1. 街道	jiēdào	*n.*	street
2. 加油站	jiāyóuzhàn	*n.*	gas station
3. 入口	rùkǒu	*n.*	entrance
4. 站	zhàn	*v.*	to stand
5. 友好	yǒuhǎo	*adj.*	friendly
6. 感谢	gǎnxiè	*v.*	to thank
7. 熟悉	shúxi	*v.*	to be familiar with
8. 错误	cuòwù	*adj./n.*	wrong; error
9. 手表	shǒubiǎo	*n.*	(wrist) watch
10. 无论	wúlùn	*conj.*	no matter (what, where, how, etc.)
11. 准确	zhǔnquè	*adj.*	accurate
12. 位置	wèizhì	*n.*	location

语言点 Language Points

固定结构“无论……都/也……”

固定结构“无论……都/也……”连接表条件关系的分句，表示在任何条件下，结果或结论都不会发生变化。“无论”后边经常有疑问代词“什么、哪里、多么、谁、几、多少、怎么”等或并列短语。例如：

1. 无论他在哪里，我们都能准确找到他的位置。
2. 无论天气好不好，妈妈每天早上都坚持跑步。
3. 无论老人还是孩子，都喜欢过春节。

※ 练习：请用固定结构“无论……都/也……”完成对话

1. A：听说明天很冷，咱们就别去踢球了吧。

   B：________________________________。

2. A：已经十二点了，太晚了，别写了，明天再写吧。

B：________________________________。

3. A：这双鞋要一千块？太贵了！别买了吧。

B：________________________________。

4. A：听说美丽明天不去爬山了，那咱们还去吗？

B：________________________________。

综合练习 Comprehensive Exercises

一、根据拼音写汉字

1. rùkǒu ________
2. yǒuhǎo ________
3. gǎnxiè ________
4. cuòwù ________
5. shǒubiǎo ________
6. wúlùn ________

二、辨字组词

1. 确________
   角________
2. 表________
   衣________
3. 置________
   直________
4. 无________
   天________

三、选词填空

无论　感谢　熟悉　准确　到处

1. 我们应该（　　）那些帮助过我们的人。
2. 你怎么对这家医院这么（　　）？以前来过吗？
3. 张大夫很快就找到了息肉的（　　）位置。

4. 今天是周末，商场里（　　）都是人。

5.（　　）你的病严重不严重，你都得先做检查。

四、选出下列词语在句子中的位置

1. 医院里人很多 A，一个座位 B 也没有，C 我们只能站 D。（着）

2. 父母 A 不放心我 B 一个人去留学，C 跟我 D 一起出国生活。（打算）

3. 我 A 的小狗 B 是昨天下午 C 在小区附近走 D 的。（丢）

4. A 桌子上的菜 B 是辣的，都 C 不适合 D 小孩子吃。（全）

5. 我 A 以前没来过 B 这 C 医院，你 D 来过吗？（家）

五、用所给词语完成对话

1. 金龙：老师，这次考试咱们班考得怎么样？
   老师：______________________。（全）

2. 病人：大夫，出院后我要注意些什么？
   医生：______________________，一定要按时到医院复查。（无论）

3. 医生：你的身体恢复得很不错，平时还是要多休息。
   病人：______________________。（感谢）

4. 丈夫：你还记得我们刚认识的时候我是什么样子吗？
   妻子：______________________。（当时）

5. 大为：你为什么不喜欢去食堂吃饭？
   朋友：______________________。（到处）

六、根据课文内容回答问题

1. 爷爷是什么时候走丢的？

2. 爷爷是什么时候被找到的？

3. 警察是在哪里找到爷爷的？

4. 警察对爷爷的态度怎么样？

5. 爸爸为什么打算给爷爷买部电话手表？

七、根据课文内容填空

今天上午，爷爷在家附近________了。我们________都非常着急，________找他。晚上，一位警察在附近的________上找到了他，当时他正在一家加油站的入口________着。警察对爷爷非常有________，也很________，还把她送回了家。我们全家都特别________那位警察。

以前，我们觉得爷爷在________的地方不会迷路，现在看来这种想法是________的。爸爸打算给爷爷买一部________，以后________他在哪里，我们都能________找到他的位置。我和父母已经商量好了，________多忙，我们都要________好爷爷。

语言任务 Language Tasks

一、阅读理解

提高记忆力主要在于养成良好的生活方式。平时要按时睡觉、起床，不熬夜，保证充足的睡眠时间，劳逸结合，避免过度劳累。如果睡不着，可以在睡前喝一杯热牛奶或用热水泡脚。同时，要适当进行一些户外运动，比如课间可以出去做操、打球或者跑步。适当的娱乐，比如听音乐、看电影、跳舞，对记忆力改善也有所帮助。“找不同”“拼图”等游戏也可以让大脑充分得到锻炼，帮助有效提高记忆力。

来源：搜狐网《“记忆”被掏空，怎样提高学习记忆力？》

补充词汇

1. 在于	zàiyú	*v.*	to lie in
2. 良好	liánghǎo	*adj.*	good, fine
3. 避免	bìmiǎn	*v.*	to avoid
4. 过度	guòdù	*adj.*	excessive
5. 劳累	láolèi	*adj.*	tired, exhausted
6. 热水	rèshuǐ	*n.*	hot-water
7. 泡脚	pào jiǎo	*VO*	to soak one's feet
8. 户外	hùwài	*n.*	outdoors
9. 课间	kèjiān	*n.*	break
10. 做操	zuò cāo	*VO*	to do exercises
11. 拼图	pīntú	*v.*	to do the puzzle
12. 大脑	dànǎo	*n.*	brain
13. 得到	dédào	*v.*	to get, to obtain
14. 有效	yǒuxiào	*v.*	to be effective

回答问题

1. 提高记忆力主要在于什么？
2. 上文指出哪些游戏可以锻炼大脑？
3. 上文从哪几个方面介绍了提高记忆力的方法？

二、口头表达

任务名称：陪奶奶去看病。

任务背景：奶奶得了阿尔茨海默病，你准备陪她去医院看病。

任务要求：1. 三个学生一组，一个扮演奶奶，一个扮演孙子 / 孙女，还有一个扮演医生。

2. 医生询问病人家属病人的症状及其持续时间，和病人进行简单交流，判断病人患病的程度。

参考语言：记忆力　忘记　练习　语言　稍微　弄错　数字　交流　迷路

三、书面表达

任务名称：寻人启事。

任务要求：奶奶患有阿尔茨海默病，今天下午在公园走丢了，请写一则寻人启事，详细描述奶奶的外貌、衣着等特征，让更多的热心人帮助你找到奶奶。

参考语言：迷路　忘记　街道　家　感谢　警察　无论……都/也……　准确　位置

第六课 Lesson 6

腹腔镜手术费大概需要多少钱？

学习目标 Learning Objectives

1. 语言功能：能够谈论毕业后的打算。
2. 语言点：副词"正好"、固定结构"尽管……可是/但是……"、介词"由"(1)、比较句(4)、固定结构"由于……(因此)……"、固定结构"只有……才……"。
3. 医学知识：初步了解腹腔镜手术和医疗保险。
4. 社会文化：初步了解中国的医疗保险制度。

热身活动 Warm-up

1. 你了解腹腔镜手术吗？病人在什么情况下可以做腹腔镜手术？

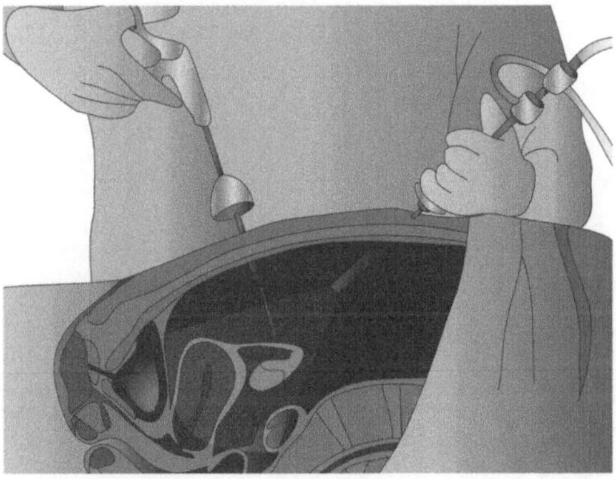

2. 说一说你毕业以后的打算。

课文（一）
Text（Ⅰ）

（病人家属向护士咨询。）

病人家属：护士，我父亲明天要做胃部腹腔镜手术，手术费大概需要多少钱？

护士：差不多需要两万元。他有医疗保险吗？

病人家属：有，正好他的医保卡里还剩两万多，应该够了吧？

护士：手术后的治疗费也不少，建议您再多准备点儿钱。

病人家属：好的。护士，我父亲做完手术后接着就能出院吗？

护士：尽管腹腔镜手术对身体伤害小，可是恢复还需要一段时间。什么时候出院，这要由大夫决定。

生词 New words

1. 腹腔镜	fùqiāngjìng	*n.*	laparoscope
2. 手术费	shǒushùfèi	*n.*	cost of surgery
3. 元	yuán	*m.*	*yuan*, unit of money
4. 医疗保险	yīliáo bǎoxiǎn		medical insurance
医疗	yīliáo	*v.*	(to provide) medical treatment
保险	bǎoxiǎn	*n.*	insurance
5. 正好	zhènghǎo	*adv.*	just enough
6. 医保卡	yībǎokǎ	*n.*	medical card
7. 剩	shèng	*v.*	to be left
8. 治疗费	zhìliáofèi	*n.*	of medical treatment cost
9. 接着	jiēzhe	*adv.*	then
10. 尽管	jǐnguǎn	*conj.*	although
11. 伤害	shānghài	*v.*	to hurt
12. 由	yóu	*prep.*	by (sb.)

语言点 Language Points

一、副词“正好”

副词“正好”表示时间、数量、情况、机会等方面的巧合，后面可以加数量短语、动词性短语或形容词，也可以用在主语前面。例如：

1. 正好他的医保卡里还剩两万多。

2. 我今天早上到教室的时候正好八点。

3. 我高中毕业的时候正好有一个去国外留学的机会。

4. 这件衣服只剩小号了，你穿正好合适。

“正好”还可以做形容词，表示时间、空间、数量等方面的客观情况与实际需要完全相符。此时，它可以做谓语、补语或者独立成句。例如：

5. 明天七点出发正好。

6. 老师的语速不快不慢，正好。

7. A：这双鞋你穿怎么样？

B：正好。

※ 练习：请用“正好”完成对话

1. A：这个包要五百块钱，你带的钱够吗？

B：________________________________。

2. A：今天上班你迟到了吗？

B：________________________________。

3. A：你们怎么一起来了？

B：________________________________。

4. A：这条裙子妈妈穿合适吗？

B：________________________________。

二、固定结构“尽管……可是/但是……”

固定结构“尽管……可是/但是……”连接表转折关系的分句。例如：

1. 尽管腹腔镜手术对身体伤害小，可是恢复还需要一段时间。

2. 尽管更年期会引发一些问题，但是大多数女性都可以顺利度过。

3. 尽管扫地机不便宜，但是我还是想买一台。

※ 练习：请用固定结构“尽管……可是/但是……”完成对话

1. A：你不是很喜欢踢足球吗？最近为什么不去了？

B：________________________________。

2. A：爷爷多大年纪了？每天还去公园锻炼吗？

B：________________________________。

3. A：你为什么不在网上买东西呢？多方便啊！

B：________________________________。

4. A：这双鞋太贵了！

B：________________________________。

三、介词“由”（1）

介词“由”用来引出负责做某事的人。例如：

1. 什么时候出院，这要由大夫决定。

2. 什么时候考试，不由学生决定，要由老师决定。

3. 旅行要带的东西由我来准备。

※ 练习：请用介词“由”改写句子

1. 孩子自己决定买哪件衣服。

____

2. 今天晚上哥哥做饭。

____

3. 病人自己决定要不要住院。

____

4. 父母不能决定孩子学习什么专业。

____

综合练习 Comprehensive Exercises

一、根据拼音写汉字

1. bǎoxiǎn ________　3. shèng ________　5. jǐnguǎn ________

2. zhènghǎo ________　4. jiēzhe ________　6. yóu ________

二、辨字组词

1. 元________　3. 疗________

完________　病________

2. 尽________　　　　4. 剩________

迟________　　　　乘________

三、选词填空

保险　正好　剩　尽管　由

1. 失眠是（　　）哪些原因引起的？
2. 没有医疗（　　）的话，自己需要支付的费用就比较多。
3. （　　）父母反对我做整形手术，可是我还是坚持要做。
4. 我钱包里（　　）有零钱，够你坐公共汽车的。
5. 你做的菜太多了，每次都（　　）不少，以后少做点儿吧。

四、选出下列词语在句子中的位置

1. A 这次 B 手术费 C 需要三万 D 元。　（差不多）
2. 我 A 看过 B 垃圾分类 C 方面的 D 节目。　（正好）
3. 腹腔镜手术 A 身体 B 的伤害 C 不算大 D。　（对）
4. A 你 B 好好儿 C 检查一下 D 需要带的材料。　（再）
5. A 出院 B 时间 C 大夫 D 决定。　（由）

五、用所给词语完成对话

1. 病人：护士，我什么时候能做手术？

   护士：________________________________。（由）

2. 妈妈：再买点儿水果吧。

   儿子：________________________________（剩），不用买了。

3. 妻子：我今天五点半下班。

丈夫：________________________________。（正好）

4. 病人：我做完手术后接着就能出院吗？

医生：____________________________。（尽管……可是/但是……）

5. 王晨：外面很冷，你还要出去跑步吗？

朋友：________________________________。（无论……都……）

六、根据课文内容回答问题

1. 做胃部腹腔镜手术，手术费大概需要多少钱？
2. 病人有保险吗？有什么保险？
3. 护士建议病人家属做什么？
4. 病人做完手术后为什么不能直接出院？
5. 病人什么时候可以出院？

七、根据课文内容填空

病人明天要做胃部腹腔镜手术，________大概需要两万元，________他的医保卡里还________两万多，但护士建议家属________多准备点儿钱，因为手术后的________也不少。做完手术，病人不能________就出院。________腹腔镜手术对身体________小，可是________还需要一段时间。什么时候出院，这要________大夫________。

课文（二）
Text（II）

（金龙和马大为在聊天儿。）

金龙：毕业以后，你打算工作还是考研究生？

马大为：我不想当穷学生了，我要工作赚钱，你呢？

金龙：我想考研。读硕士和博士一直是我的目标。

马大为：你适合做研究，应该读研究生。父母支持你吗？

金龙：他们很支持我，可是现在我父亲公司的生意不太好，我们家的收入减少了很多，经济条件不如以前了。

马大为：你可以申请奖学金。

金龙：我也想申请，不知道能不能申请到。

马大为：你的成绩一直都很优秀，你要有信心。

生词 New words

1. 研究生	yánjiūshēng	*n.*	graduate student
2. 穷	qióng	*adj.*	poor
3. 赚钱	zhuànqián	*v.*	to make money
赚	zhuàn	*v.*	to earn/make (money)
4. 考研	kǎoyán	*v.*	to take part in the postgraduate entrance examinations
5. 硕士	shuòshì	*n.*	master
6. 博士	bóshì	*n.*	doctor (Dr.)
7. 目标	mùbiāo	*n.*	target
8. 支持	zhīchí	*v.*	to support
9. 减少	jiǎnshǎo	*v.*	to reduce, to decrease
10. 经济	jīngjì	*n.*	financial condition
11. 不如	bùrú	*v.*	not as good as
12. 奖学金	jiǎngxuéjīn	*n.*	scholarship
13. 优秀	yōuxiù	*adj.*	excellent

语言点 Language Points

比较句（4）

比较句“A 不如 B（这么/那么）+ 形容词”表示 A 在某方面性状上比不上 B。例如：

1. 现在我父亲公司的生意不太好，我们家的收入减少了很多，经济条件不如以前了。
2. 我觉得扫地机打扫得不如自己干净。
3. 哥哥喜欢自己在家里做饭，他觉得在饭馆吃饭不如自己做健康。

※ 练习：请用“A 不如 B（这么/那么）+ 形容词”改写句子

1. 这家饭馆的菜不好吃，妈妈做的菜很好吃。

____

2. 今天很热，昨天不太热。

____

3. 姐姐成绩很优秀，我的成绩不太优秀。

____

4. 她做整形手术以前比现在更漂亮。

____

综合练习 Comprehensive Exercises

一、根据拼音写汉字

1. zhīchí ________　　3. jīngjì ________　　5. yōuxiù ________

2. jiǎnshǎo ________　　4. mùbiāo ________　　6. zhuànqián ______

二、辨字组词

1. 如________　　3. 秀________

　好________　　　季________

2. 持________　　4. 穷________

　特________　　　空________

三、选词填空

赚　支持　减少　申请　当

1. 我丈夫个子非常高，以前是打篮球的，现在在学校（　　）老师。

2. 我想报名，请问参加这次会议有什么（　　　）条件？

3. 现在什么工作最（　　　）钱？

4. 父母都（　　　）我考研究生，所以我打算试试。

5. 饭店的生意不太好，收入比去年（　　　）了十分之一。

四、选出下列词语在句子中的位置

1. 你毕业后 A 打算 B 考研 C 工作 D？（还是）
2. 当 A 汉语老师 B 是 C 我的 D 目标。（一直）
3. 在饭店 A 吃饭 B 在家做饭 C 放心 D。（不如）
4. 我 A 不想 B 出国留学，C 可是爸爸 D 坚持让我去国外读书。（本来）
5. 车刚走，我们要是 A 早一点儿 B 到 C 好了 D。（就）

五、用所给词语完成对话

1. 病人：每天睡觉前吃安眠药可以帮助睡眠吗？

   医生：________________________________。（不如）

2. 医生：除了头疼，还有什么地方不舒服吗？

   病人：________________________________。（稍微）

3. 大为：怎样能提高口语水平？

   同学：________________________________。（也许）

4. 美丽：你为什么要来中国学习医学？

   朋友：________________________________。（一直）

5. 朋友：________________________________？（还是）

   月亮：我想考研究生。

六、根据课文内容回答问题

1. 马大为毕业后要做什么？
2. 金龙的目标是什么？
3. 马大为觉得金龙适合做什么？
4. 金龙家怎么了？
5. 马大为觉得金龙能申请到奖学金吗？为什么？

七、根据课文内容填空

马大为不想当________了，他毕业以后要工作________。金龙想考研，读________和________一直是他的________。马大为也觉得金龙________做研究。金龙的父母也________他。可是最近金龙父亲的公司________不太好，他们家的收入________了很多，经济条件________以前了。金龙想________奖学金，马大为认为金龙的成绩一直都很________，希望他对自己有________。

课文（三）
Text（III）

我爸爸是一家公司的经理，妈妈在银行工作。他们虽然不是富人，但收入也不低，所以我和哥哥、姐姐才能有条件去留学。可是最近两年，由于公司生意不好，爸爸的收入减少了很多。我本来打算大学毕业以后继续读硕士、博士，可是现在我不得不重新考虑这个问题。马大为鼓励我申请奖学金，我也有这个想法。我要更努力，因为只有更努力，才能实现自己的理想。

生词 New words

1. 经理	jīnglǐ	*n.*	manager
2. 银行	yínháng	*n.*	bank
3. 富	fù	*adj.*	wealthy
4. 由于	yóuyú	*conj.*	because
5. 大学	dàxué	*n.*	university
6. 继续	jìxù	*v.*	to continue
7. 不得不	bùdébù		have to
8. 重新	chóngxīn	*adv.*	re-, again
9. 实现	shíxiàn	*v.*	to realize, to come true
10. 理想	lǐxiǎng	*n.*	ideal

语言点 Language Points

一、固定结构"由于……（因此）……"

固定结构"由于……（因此）……"连接表因果关系的分句，前一分句表示原因，后一分句表示结果，且后一分句中常有"因此"。例如：

1. 最近两年，由于公司生意不好，爸爸的收入减少了很多。
2. 由于自动体外除颤器可以用于心脏病病人的急救，因此越来越多的公共场合都安装了这一设备。
3. 由于上班的医院离家太远，哥哥就在医院附近租了一套房子。

※ 练习：请用固定结构"由于……（因此）……"完成对话

1. A：为什么这么多人冬天都去三亚旅游？

   B：________________________________。

2. A：金龙家的经济条件为什么不如以前了？

   B：________________________________。

3. A：为什么很多留学生来中国学习医学？

B：________________。

4. A：医生，为什么我爷爷的记忆力越来越差了？有时候连家人的名字也想不起来。

B：________________。

二、固定结构“只有……才……”

固定结构“只有……才……”连接表条件关系的分句，前一分句表示实现某一结果的唯一条件，后一分句表示这个条件下产生的结果。例如：

1. 只有更努力，才能实现自己的理想。
2. 只有多听、多说、多写，才能学好汉语。
3. 只有坚持锻炼，才能有一个好身体。

※ 练习：连线组句

A. 只有来中国留学　　　　a. 才能顺利度过更年期

B. 只有每天练习　　　　　b. 才能更好地了解中国社会

C. 只有使用助听器　　　　c. 才能打好球

D. 只有放松心情　　　　　d. 才能彻底解决老年性耳背的问题

综合练习 Comprehensive Exercises

一、根据拼音写汉字

1. jīnglǐ ________　　3. yóuyú ________　　5. chóngxīn ________

2. yínháng ________　　4. jìxù ________　　6. shíxiàn ________

二、辨字组词

1. 银________　　3. 想________
   很________　　　相________
2. 新________　　4. 实________
   亲________　　　买________

三、选词填空

由于　继续　不得不　不如　重新

1. 他的胆囊炎很严重，打了几天针也不好，（　　）住院治疗。
2. 医生（　　）给病人检查了一遍，开了新药。
3. 同学们先休息十分钟，然后回来（　　）上课。
4. （　　）天气不好，飞机晚点了。
5. 对我来说，坐公交车上班（　　）骑自行车方便。

四、选出下列词语在句子中的位置

1. 只有 A 放暑假 B，我 C 能回国 D 见父母。　（才）
2. 申请 A 奖学金的人 B 很多，我 C 更努力 D 学习。　（不得不）
3. 我 A 想做隆鼻手术 B，可是 C 父母反对，D 就没做。　（本来）
4. A 路上堵车 B，我不得不 C 下车 D 走到学校。　（由于）
5. A 走路 B 的话，C 十五分钟 D 就能到。　（大约）

五、用所给词语完成对话

1. 朋友：你怎么搬家了？
   佳乐：________________________________。（由于）

2. 病人：手术后我马上就能出院吗？

医生：________________________________。（由）

3. 月亮：我们常去吃饭的那家饭店为什么关门了？

朋友：________________________________。（不得不）

4. 大为：你不是做完作业了吗？

同屋：________________________________。（重新）

5. 病人：大夫，我怎样才能快点儿好起来？

医生：________________________________。（只有……才……）

六、根据课文内容回答问题

1. 金龙和哥哥、姐姐为什么可以去留学？
2. 爸爸的收入为什么减少了？
3. 金龙本来打算毕业以后做什么？
4. 马大为鼓励金龙做什么？
5. 金龙为什么要更努力？

七、根据课文内容填空

我爸爸是一家公司的________，妈妈在________工作。他们虽然不是________，但收入也不低，所以我和哥哥、姐姐才能有________去留学。可是________两年，________公司生意不好，爸爸的收入________了很多。我________打算________毕业以后继续读________、________，可是现在我________重新考虑这个问题。马大为鼓励我________奖学金，我也有这个想法。我要更努力，因为________更努力，才能________自己的理想。

语言任务 Language Tasks

一、阅读理解

很多人认为喝粥能养胃，也有“喝牛奶养胃”的说法。然而，胃不舒服，最主要的原因就是胃酸过多引发的慢性胃炎和胃溃疡。喝牛奶有时确实可以缓解胃痛，但最近的研究发现，牛奶中的蛋白质和钙会刺激胃酸分泌，从而进一步加重胃痛。不过，喝酒前喝些牛奶能减少酒精对胃黏膜的损伤。而喝粥确实可以让胃舒服，但并不能让胃炎减轻，也不能让溃疡愈合。

想要保护胃，我们在日常生活中就要养成良好的饮食习惯，饮食规律、清淡、营养、易消化，避免吃太烫或太凉的食物，减少对胃黏膜的刺激；还要注意用药安全，慎重服用刺激性药物。

来源：微信公众号“小大夫漫画”

补充词汇

1. 认为	rènwéi	*v.*	to think
2. 粥	zhōu	*n.*	gruel
3. 说法	shuōfǎ	*n.*	formulation, view
4. 然而	rán'ér	*conj.*	however
5. 胃酸	wèisuān	*n.*	gastric acid
6. 胃炎	wèiyán	*n.*	gastritis
7. 胃溃疡	wèikuìyáng	*n.*	gastric ulcer
溃疡	kuìyáng	*v.*	to have an ulcer
8. 胃痛	wèitòng	*n.*	stomachache
9. 钙	gài	*n.*	calcium
10. 分泌	fēnmì	*v.*	to secrete
11. 进一步	jìnyíbù	*adv.*	further, more
12. 加重	jiāzhòng	*v.*	to make or become more serious
13. 酒精	jiǔjīng	*n.*	alcohol
14. 黏膜	niánmó	*n.*	mucous membrane

15. 愈合	yùhé	*v.*	to coalesce
16. 日常	rìcháng	*adj.*	daily
17. 烫	tàng	*adj.*	very hot
18. 慎重	shènzhòng	*adj.*	cautious
19. 药物	yàowù	*n.*	pharmaceutical

回答问题

1. 胃不舒服的主要原因是什么？
2. 喝牛奶和喝粥对胃有什么好处和坏处？
3. 我们应该怎么保护胃？

二、口头表达

任务名称：了解腹腔镜手术后的注意事项。

任务背景：病人家属在护士站询问护士腹腔镜手术的费用，以及手术后什么时候可以出院。

任务要求：1. 两个学生一组，一个扮演病人家属，一个扮演护士。
2. 护士询问病人家属有什么问题。
3. 病人家属询问护士腹腔镜手术和一般手术的不同，以及手术费用和出院时间。

参考语言：手术费　正好　够　多　尽管……可是/但是……　由　不如　方便

三、书面表达

任务名称：我的理想。

任务要求：请向老师和同学介绍一下自己的理想，要求 200 字以上。

参考语言：小时候　理想　毕业　经济　申请　继续　支持　由于　实现
只有……才……

第七课 Lesson 7 会不会是骨折？

学习目标 Learning Objectives

1. 语言功能：能够打电话订包间，能够提出自己的要求。
2. 语言点：副词“只好”、副词“至少”、固定结构“再……也……”、副词“往往”、介词“对于”、动词“认为”。
3. 医学知识：初步了解骨质疏松症。
4. 社会文化：了解中餐礼仪。

热身活动 Warm-up

1. 你了解骨质疏松症吗？什么人容易得骨质疏松症？

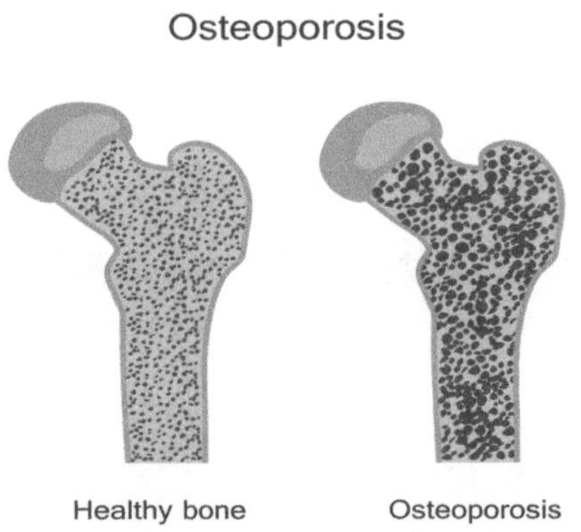

2. 你在中国餐厅订过餐吗？你对饭菜有什么要求？

课文（一）
Text（Ⅰ）

（李真陪奶奶在骨科门诊看病。）

李真：大夫，我奶奶最近后背很疼，躺着或坐着稍微好点儿，可是也坐不了太长时间。

医生：从什么时候开始的？

李真：上个月底，奶奶因为关窗户，后背疼了好几天，但是她坚持不来医院。昨天她抬胳膊拿一个很轻的盒子，后背又开始疼，疼得晚上睡不着，今天只好来医院了。

医生：我看一下。

（医生给奶奶做检查。）

医生：先做个 CT。老人走路不方便，你去服务台借个轮椅，推着她去做检查吧。

李真：谢谢您，我马上去。

生词 New words

1. 后背	hòubèi	*n.*	back (of the body)
背	bèi	*n.*	back (of the body)
2. 或	huò	*conj.*	or
3. 月底	yuèdǐ	*n.*	end of a month
底	dǐ		end
4. 抬	tái	*v.*	to lift up, to raise
5. 胳膊	gēbo	*n.*	arm
6. 轻	qīng	*adj.*	of little weight, light
7. 盒子	hézi	*n.*	box
8. 只好	zhǐhǎo	*adv.*	have to
9. 借	jiè	*v.*	to borrow
10. 轮椅	lúnyǐ	*n.*	wheelchair
11. 推	tuī	*v.*	to push

语言点 Language Points

副词“只好”

副词“只好”表示没有别的选择，不得不。例如：

1. 奶奶后背疼得晚上睡不着，今天只好来医院了。

2. 他感冒一直没有好，而且还越来越严重，只好再去看医生。

如果前面表示原因的分句和“只好”所在分句的主语不同，“只好”应放在所在分句的主语前。例如：

3. 他们都没有时间，只好你自己去了。

※ 练习：请用副词“只好”完成对话

1. A：你怎么没有开车？

   B：________________________________。

2. A：你不是最喜欢红色吗？为什么买了一个白色的手机？

B：________________________________。

3. A：美丽今天没来上课，她怎么了？

B：________________________________。

4. A：我上网看了一下，去云南的机票已经卖完了。

B：________________________________。

综合练习 Comprehensive Exercises

一、根据拼音写汉字

1. hòubèi ________　　3. hézi ________　　5. jiè ________

2. gēbo ________　　4. zhǐhǎo ________　　6. tuī ________

二、辨字组词

1. 底________　　3. 抬________

低________　　台________

2. 轻________　　4. 推________

经________　　准________

三、选词填空

或　月底　只好　重新　大约

1. 我爸爸的耳背已经持续（　　）半年了。

2. 快到（　　）了，我们要发工资了。

3. 你周四（　　）周五来医院复查吧。

4. 他的腿摔伤了，（　　）请假去医院。

5. 这部电影我第一次看时没看懂，所以昨天晚上又（　　）看了一遍。

四、选出下列词语在句子中的位置

1. 坐公交 A 骑自行车 B 都 C 能到 D 我们学校。（或）
2. 他 A 忘带 B 宿舍钥匙了，C 等同屋 D 回来开门。（只好）
3. 我怎么 A 也 B 找不 C 我刚买的 D 白大褂了。（着）
4. A 奶奶 B 关窗户，C 后背疼了 D 好几天。（因为）
5. 爸爸的 A 手术费很高，我们 B 只好向朋友 C 些钱 D。（借）

五、用所给词语完成对话

1. 艺文：外面下雨了，你打算怎么去上班？

   王东：________________________________。（或）

2. 病人：________________________________？（究竟）

   医生：现在还不好说，你先做个 CT 吧。

3. 病人家属：护士，我丈夫手术后在饮食上要注意什么？

   护士：________________________________。（或者）

4. 金龙：你怎么又喝了一杯咖啡？

   同学：________________________________。（只好）

5. 王晨：你认为钱是不是最重要的？

   朋友：________________________________。（只有……才……）

六、根据课文内容回答问题

1. 奶奶的身体有什么问题？
2. 奶奶的后背是什么时候开始疼的？

3. 昨天奶奶的后背为什么又开始疼了？

4. 奶奶今天为什么来医院了？

5. 李真为什么要借轮椅？

七、根据课文内容填空

我奶奶的________最近很疼，________或________稍微好点儿，可是也坐不了太长时间。上个________，奶奶因为关窗户，后背疼了________，但是她坚持不来医院。昨天她________胳膊拿一个很轻的________，后背又开始疼，疼得晚上________，今天________来医院了。医生让奶奶先做个CT，因为老人走路不________，所以我得去________个轮椅，________她去做检查。

课文（二）
Text（II）

（李真给饭店打电话订包间。）

李真：你好，我想订个礼拜天中午的大包间。

服务员：我们最大的包间可以坐15个人，您一共有多少位客人？

李真：至少16位。

服务员：这个包间很大，增加几个座位没问题。

李真：那就订这个吧。

服务员：您是订套餐还是点菜？

李真：订套餐吧。菜的味道要淡一点儿，汤里少放点儿盐。

服务员：好的。您还有别的要求吗？

李真：我们是家庭聚会，给老人祝贺80岁生日，你们能装饰一下房间吗？

服务员：如果要装饰房间，价格会更高一点儿。

李真：老人过生日，再贵也值得。

生词 New words

1. 包间	bāojiān	*n.*	private room
2. 礼拜天	lǐbàitiān	*n.*	Sunday
3. 客人	kèrén	*n.*	guest
4. 至少	zhìshǎo	*adv.*	at least
5. 增加	zēngjiā	*v.*	to increase
6. 座位	zuòwèi	*n.*	seat
7. 套餐	tàocān	*n.*	set meal
8. 味道	wèidao	*n.*	flavor, taste
9. 淡	dàn	*adj.*	tasteless
10. 汤	tāng	*n.*	soup
11. 盐	yán	*n.*	salt
12. 聚会	jùhuì	*n./v.*	meeting, gathering; to get together
13. 祝贺	zhùhè	*v.*	to congratulate
14. 装饰	zhuāngshì	*v.*	to decorate

语言点 Language Points

一、副词“至少”

副词“至少”表示最低的限度，后面常常有数量短语。例如：

1. 服务员：您一共有多少位客人？

   李真：至少 16 位。

2. A：今天来了多少人？

   B：至少一百人。

3. 金龙每天至少学习九个小时。

※ 练习：请用副词“至少”完成对话

1. A：你回国坐飞机要多长时间？

B：________________________________。

2. A：马大为的汉语说得真不错！他学了多长时间了？

B：________________________________。

3. A：五个人在外面吃饭，大概需要多少钱？

B：________________________________。

4. A：奶奶背疼了多长时间了？

B：________________________________。

二、固定结构“再……也……”

固定结构“再……也……”连接表让步和假设的分句。前一分句做出让步的假设，后一分句表示即使这样结果也不变。例如：

1. 老人过生日，再贵也值得。

2. 只要是你喜欢的工作，再累也不觉得辛苦。

3. 明天我一定要去跑步，天再冷我也要去。

※ 练习：请用固定结构“再……也……”改写句子

1. 我太喜欢这条裙子了，无论多贵，我都要买。

____

2. 医学很难，但我一定会坚持学习。

____

3. 虽然我牙疼得很，可是我就是不想去看牙医。

____

4. 这双鞋你穿不合适，虽然很便宜，但还是不要买了。

____

综合练习 Comprehensive Exercises

一、根据拼音写汉字

1. kèrén ________　　3. zuòwèi ________　　5. yán ________

2. zhìshǎo ________　　4. wèidao________　　6. zhùhè ________

二、辨字组词

1. 至________　　3. 座________

　到________　　　坐________

2. 祝________　　4. 味________

　礼________　　　妹________

三、选词填空

至少　座位　淡　祝贺　聚会

1. 昨天的（　　）你怎么没去呀？

2. 这个盒子非常重，（　　）有五十斤。

3.（　　）上的那件白大褂是金龙的还是大为的？

4. 听说你申请到了奖学金，（　　）你！

5. 给老人吃的菜味道上应该（　　）一点儿。

四、选出下列词语在句子中的位置

1. A 请问您 B 是 C 订套餐 D 点菜？　　（还是）

2. A 只要 B 病人需要，C 麻烦护士也会 D 帮忙。　　（再）

3. 窗外A那棵树B有C十米D高。（至少）

4. 服务员A李真B介绍了C饭店的D饭菜。（向）

5. A请注意B菜的味道C要淡D。（一点儿）

五、用所给词语完成对话

1. 病人：大夫，我的后背为什么一直疼？

   医生：________________________________。（由于）

2. 病人：大夫，我做完腹腔镜手术后能马上出院吗？

   医生：________________________________。（至少）

3. 大为：就要放假了，你打算什么时候回国？

   同学：________________________________。（或）

4. 美丽：这个西瓜很重，你拿得动吗？

   朋友：________________________________。（再……也……）

5. 艺文：我们今天都要加班，孩子怎么办？

   王东：________________________________。（只好）

六、根据课文内容回答问题

1. 李真要订哪一天的包间？
2. 这个包间可以坐多少人？
3. 李真想订套餐还是点菜？
4. 李真对菜有什么要求？
5. 李真家为什么要聚会？

七、根据课文内容填空

李真想________个礼拜天中午的大包间。饭店最大的包间可以坐________个人，李真他们________有16位，服务员说那个包间很大，________几个座位也没问题。李真订了________，希望菜的味道________一点儿，汤里少放点儿________。另外，他们是________，给老人________80岁生日，希望饭店能________一下房间。李真觉得，给________过生日，再________也________。

课文（三）
Text（III）

骨质疏松症是一种很常见的骨科疾病，多发生在中老年人身上。在性别方面，女性的骨质疏松症发病率比男性高。背部疼痛是骨质疏松症最常见的症状。很多患者往往会出现驼背，甚至骨折等更严重的症状，有些患者因为一个简单的动作就有可能骨折。对于骨质疏松症的预防，专家认为需要调整生活方式，增加体育锻炼。

生词 New words

1. 骨质疏松症	gǔzhì shūsōngzhèng	*n.*	osteoporosis
2. 常见	cháng jiàn	*VP*	common
3. 疾病	jíbìng	*n.*	disease
4. 性别	xìngbié	*n.*	sex
5. 发病率	fābìnglǜ	*n.*	incidence of a disease
率	lǜ	*suf.*	rate of
6. 男性	nánxìng	*n.*	male
7. 患者	huànzhě	*n.*	patient, sick person
8. 往往	wǎngwǎng	*adv.*	often
9. 驼背	tuóbèi	*v.*	to be hunchbacked
10. 骨折	gǔzhé	*v.*	to fracture
11. 动作	dòngzuò	*n.*	action, movement
12. 对于	duìyú	*prep.*	for, to
13. 预防	yùfáng	*v.*	to prevent
14. 认为	rènwéi	*v.*	to think

语言点 Language Points

一、副词“往往”

副词“往往”表示某种情况经常出现。例如：

1. 很多患者往往会出现驼背，甚至骨折等更严重的症状。
2. 外科医生很辛苦，一台大手术往往要做十几个小时。
3. 很多人往往是从很小就开始学习外语的。

往往 VS 常常

1. “往往”是对到目前为止的情况的总结，强调规律性，一般不用于主观意愿，不能用于将来；“常常”强调动作的重复性，可以用于主观意愿，也可以用于将来。例如：

以后你要常常锻炼。（√）　　　　以后你要往往锻炼。（×）

欢迎你常常来我家玩儿。（√）　　欢迎你往往来我家玩儿。（×）

2. 用“往往”的时候一般要指明与动作相关的情况、条件或结果，“常常”则没有这一要求。例如：

天气好的时候，我们往往去郊区爬山。（√）我们往往去郊区爬山。（×）

天气好的时候，我们常常去郊区爬山。（√）我们常常去郊区爬山。（√）

※ 练习：判断对错

1. 老师往往说英语。（　　）

2. 下个学期我要往往跑步。（　　）

3. 吃太多肉的人往往血压高。（　　）

4. 哥哥常常自己做饭。（　　）

二、介词“对于”

介词“对于”表示人与事物、行为之间的对待关系，后面往往接名词性成分；“对于……”可以用在主语前，也可以用在主语后。例如：

1. 对于骨质疏松症的预防，专家认为需要调整生活方式，增加体育锻炼。

2. 对于毕业以后的工作，我还没有想好。

3. 我对于这件事儿的看法和你一样。

关于VS对于

1. “关于”引出的是关联或涉及的事物，“对于”引出的是对象。例如：

（1）关于体检要注意的问题，您可以去我们的网站上了解一下。

（2）对于这个问题，我们要想办法解决。

两种意思都有的话，“关于”“对于”都可以用。例如：

（3）关于/对于这件事儿，我的看法和你一样。

2. “关于……”只能用在主语前，而“对于……”可以用在主语前，也可以用在主语后。例如：

关于中国历史，李真了解很多。（√）李真关于中国历史了解很多。（×）

对于中国历史，李真了解很多。（√）李真对于中国历史了解很多。（√）

3. “关于……”可以直接做文章标题，“对于……”后面必须再加名词才可以。例如：

《关于预防骨质疏松》

《对于预防骨质疏松的看法》

※ 练习：请用“关于”或“对于”填空

1. ＿＿＿＿＿篮球比赛的建议，我们大家要认真讨论一下。

2. 张大夫＿＿＿＿＿更年期综合征有很多研究。

3.《＿＿＿＿＿阿尔茨海默病的预防》是王医生写的。

4. ＿＿＿＿＿中国音乐的问题，我不太感兴趣。

三、动词“认为”

动词“认为”表示对人或事物有某种看法，做出某种判断。例如：

1. 对于骨质疏松症的预防，专家认为需要调整生活方式，增加体育锻炼。

2. 医生认为更年期女性应该注意放松心情。

3. 我认为夏天去哈尔滨旅行不如冬天去。

认为 VS 以为

“认为”和“以为”都可以用于做出某种判断，但是“以为”的语气比较轻。

1. “认为”后面一般是正确的判断，“以为”多用于不正确的判断。例如：

（1）我以为今天会下雪，可是没有下。

（2）很多人以为他是中国人，其实他是留学生。

2. “认为”前面可以用“被”，“以为”前面不能用“被”，但可以用“让”。例如：

（3）腹腔镜手术被认为是一种对人体伤害小的手术。

（4）阿尔茨海默病被认为是一种比较难以治疗的疾病。

（5）他刚才说的话让我以为他不高兴了。

※ 练习：请用“认为”或“以为”填空

1. 很多人__________这是他们看过的最好的电影。

2. 我__________这部电影一定很好看，可是看完以后，我觉得它并不好看。

3. 马大为刚开始__________金龙是中国人，后来才知道他也是留学生。

4. 专家__________应该在公共场合安装更多的自动体外除颤器。

综合练习 Comprehensive Exercises

一、根据拼音写汉字

1. wǎngwǎng __________
2. dòngzuò __________
3. duìyú __________
4. yùfáng __________
5. rènwéi __________
6. gǔzhé __________

二、辨字组词

1. 率__________
   摔__________
2. 防__________
   放__________
3. 往__________
   住__________
4. 疾__________
   病__________

三、选词填空

率　往往　对于　预防　认为

1. （　　）疾病的预防，我们每个人都应该重视。

2. 增加体育锻炼可以（　　）骨质疏松症。

3. 失眠（　　）跟压力有关系。

4. 我（　　）你这个季节去哈尔滨不如冬天去好。

5. 女性的骨质疏松症发病（　　）比男性高。

四、选出下列词语在句子中的位置

1. 骨质疏松症 A 患者 B 会出现 C 驼背 D 等症状。（往往）
2. A 骑自行车 B 坐公交车 C 方便 D 多了。（比）
3. A 你问的 B 这个问题，C 我们会 D 认真考虑的。（对于）
4. 他平时学习 A 十分 B 努力，C 放假期间都在 D 学习。（甚至）
5. A 他的病情 B 比我 C 想的 D 严重。（更）

五、用所给词语完成对话

1. 病人：大夫，女性是不是更容易得骨质疏松症啊？

   医生：________________________________。（在……方面）

2. 病人：________________________________？（对于）

   医生：放松心情，坚持锻炼身体，可以帮你顺利度过更年期。

3. 医生：你的骨质疏松症比较严重，平时做动作要小心点儿。

   病人：________________________________。（一定）

4. 艺文：工作忙的时候，你怎么放松自己？

   朋友：________________________________。（往往）

5. 王晨：听说你通过了 HSK 四级考试，祝贺你！

   大为：________________________________。（在……下）

六、根据课文内容回答问题

1. 骨质疏松症多发生在什么人身上？
2. 男性和女性，谁的骨质疏松症发病率更高？
3. 骨质疏松症最常见的症状是什么？

4. 除了背部疼痛，骨质疏松症还有什么症状？

5. 怎样预防骨质疏松症？

七、根据课文内容填空

骨质疏松症是一种很常见的骨科________，多发生在________身上。在________方面，女性的骨质疏松症________比男性高。________疼痛是骨质疏松症最常见的症状。很多患者________会出现驼背，甚至________等更严重的症状，有些患者因为一个简单的________就有可能骨折。________骨质疏松症的________，专家认为需要________生活方式，增加________锻炼。

语言任务 Language Tasks

一、阅读理解

骨质疏松症已成为困扰老年人的主要疾病，其发病率居于老年疾病第三位。骨质疏松症最大的危害是易导致骨折。一般人认为，预防骨质疏松症是老年人的事儿，其实这是一种片面的看法。骨质疏松症的危险在儿童时期就已经存在了，近年来在年轻的都市女性中，患骨质疏松症的越来越多，乱减肥、怕日晒、少运动是主要原因。

导致骨质疏松的原因包括遗传性因素、营养失衡、活动量不足、过度用药等。专业人士建议，人们平时在饮食上应多摄入含有丰富钙质和维生素 D 的食物，要养成进行户外运动的习惯和良好的生活方式，不抽烟，不酗酒，定期去医院做骨密度测试，并在医生的指导下服用防治骨质疏松症的药物。

来源：39 健康网《一定要告诉爸妈：骨质疏松日常要“紧一紧”》

补充词汇

1. 困扰　kùnrǎo　*v.*　to puzzle, to plague

2. 居于	jūyú	*v.*	to occupy (a certain position)
3. 片面	piànmiàn	*adj.*	one-sided
4. 看法	kànfǎ	*n.*	view, opinion
5. 儿童	értóng	*n.*	children
6. 存在	cúnzài	*v.*	to exist
7. 都市	dūshì	*n.*	city
8. 日晒	rì shài		to expose to the sun
9. 因素	yīnsù	*n.*	factor
10. 失衡	shīhéng	*v.*	to be out-of-balance
11. 活动量	huódòngliàng	*n.*	activity level
12. 不足	bùzú	*adj.*	insufficient
13. 人士	rénshì	*n.*	public figure, personage
14. 摄入	shèrù	*v.*	to take sth. in
15. 含有	hányǒu	*v.*	to contain
16. 丰富	fēngfù	*adj.*	abundant, rich
17. 钙质	gàizhì	*n.*	of calcium substance
18. 酗酒	xùjiǔ	*v.*	to indulge in excessive drinking
19. 骨密度	gǔmìdù	*n.*	bone mineral density
20. 防治	fángzhì	*v.*	to prevent and cure

回答问题

1. 骨质疏松症最大的危害是什么？
2. 导致骨质疏松的原因有哪些？
3. 专家建议怎么预防骨质疏松症？

二、口头表达

任务名称：如何预防骨质疏松症。

任务背景：病人最近常常感到背部疼痛，医生检查后说是骨质疏松症。病人询问医生骨质疏松症的发病原因、后果，以及预防方法。

任务要求：1. 两个学生一组，一个扮演病人，一个扮演医生。

2. 医生通过看检查结果诊断病人得了骨质疏松症。

3. 病人询问医生骨质疏松症的发病原因、后果，以及预防方法。

参考语言：后背　疼痛　关　抬　轻　胳膊　只好　疾病　发病率　动作　往往　对于　预防　认为　体育　调整　方式　运动

三、书面表达

任务名称：愉快的聚会。

任务要求：请介绍一次愉快的聚会，要求 200 字以上。

参考语言：礼拜天　包间　至少　套餐　淡　味道　聚会　祝贺　装饰

第八课 Lesson 8 怎么避免传染呢？

学习目标 Learning Objectives

1. 语言功能：能够列举事例或说明原因。
2. 语言点：固定结构“从……看”、动词“禁止”、介词“由”（2）。
3. 医学知识：了解流感和普通感冒的区别。
4. 社会文化：了解“世界地球日”。

热身活动 Warm-up

1. 你知道流感和普通感冒有哪些区别吗？

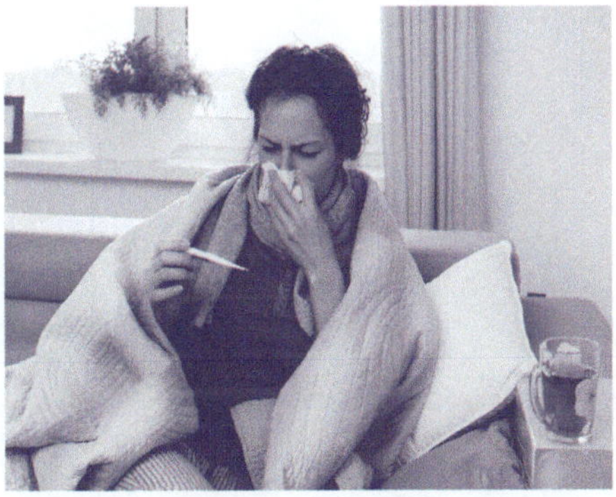

2. 你认为我们可以为保护环境做些什么？

课文（一）
Text（I）

（病人在发热门诊看病。）

病人：大夫，化验结果出来了，麻烦您看看。

医生：从化验结果看，是流感。你周围有人得流感吗？

病人：最近办公室里得流感的人很多，可是他们的症状都没有我严重。

医生：即使都是流感，每个人的症状也不相同，有的轻，有的重。

病人：大夫，我需要打针吗？

医生：暂时不需要。我给你开些药，你回家好好儿休息，出门戴口罩，减少跟别人的接触。

病人：在家里怎么避免传染呢？

医生：建议你与家人分开使用筷子、勺子、盘子、刀子、叉子等，毛巾也要分开；同时，经常接触的生活用品每天都要消毒。

生词 New words

1. 发热	fārè	*v.*	to have a fever
2. 流感	liúgǎn	*n.*	influenza (flu)
3. 相同	xiāngtóng	*adj.*	same
4. 暂时	zànshí	*adj.*	for the time being
5. 戴	dài	*v.*	to wear
6. 口罩	kǒuzhào	*n.*	gauze mask
7. 接触	jiēchù	*v.*	to contact, to touch
8. 避免	bìmiǎn	*v.*	to avoid
9. 传染	chuánrǎn	*v.*	to infect
10. 分开	fēnkāi	*v.*	to part, to separate
11. 筷子	kuàizi	*n.*	chopsticks
12. 勺子	sháozi	*n.*	spoon
13. 盘子	pánzi	*n.*	plate
14. 刀子	dāozi	*n.*	knife
15. 叉子	chāzi	*n.*	fork
16. 毛巾	máojīn	*n.*	towel

语言点 Language Points

固定结构“从……看”

介词“从”表示根据、凭借，固定结构“从……看”表示根据某个方面。例如：

1. 从化验结果看，是流感。

2. 从这件事情看，老王是一个好人。

3. 从他的考试成绩看，他一定是一个努力的学生。

※ 练习：请用固定结构“从……看”完成对话

1. A：医生，请问这种情况是骨折吗？

   B：________________________________。

2. A：你怎么知道她是更年期综合征？

   B：________________________________。

3. A：王大夫是一位好医生吗？

   B：________________________________。

4. A：孩子得的是普通感冒吗？

   B：________________________________。

综合练习 Comprehensive Exercises

一、根据拼音写汉字

1. xiāngtóng ________
2. zànshí ________
3. dài ________
4. chuánrǎn ________
5. kuàizi ________
6. máojīn ________

二、辨字组词

1. 暂________
   新________
2. 盘________
   盐________
3. 触________
   解________
4. 巾________
   帅________

三、选词填空

相同	暂时	戴	传染	毛巾

1. 戴口罩，多洗手，可以避免流感（　　）。
2. 出去旅行最好自己带一条（　　）。
3. 你（　　）不用打针，吃了药好好儿休息就行。
4. 办公室里得感冒的人症状各不（　　）。
5. 你今天怎么没（　　）眼镜啊？

四、选出下列词语在句子中的位置

1. 他们的 A 症状 B 没有 C 我 D 严重。（都）
2. A 即使都是流感，B 每个人的症状 C 不相同 D。（也）
3. 你 A 不 B 需要 C 打针 D。（暂时）
4. 服务员 A 笑 B 跟 C 我们 D 说话。（着）
5. 她 A 已经 B 医生 C 开的药 D 吃完了。（把）

五、用所给词语完成对话

1. 病人：大夫，这是我的检查结果，麻烦您看看。

   医生：________________________________。（从……看）

2. 月亮：你同学毕业以后都去医院工作吗？

   朋友：________________________________。（有的……有的……）

3. 病人：大夫，我们夫妻俩身体都很健康，可是为什么一直没孩子呢？

   医生：________________________________。（即使……也……）

4. 艺文：你住的地方离公司太远了，不打算换套房子吗？

   佳乐：________________________________。（暂时）

5. 病人：大夫，得了流感要注意什么？

医生：________________________________。（同时）

六、根据课文内容回答问题

1. 病人怎么了？
2. 得流感的人症状都一样吗？为什么？
3. 病人需要打针吗？
4. 医生让病人注意什么？
5. 在家里，怎么避免流感传染呢？

七、根据课文内容填空

从________看，病人得了流感。最近办公室里得流感的人很多，可是他们的________都没有这位病人________。医生说________都是流感，每个人的症状也不________，有的轻，有的________。病人________不需要打针。医生给他________了些药，让他回家好好儿休息，出门________，减少跟别人的________。医生还建议病人与家人分开使用________、勺子、________、刀子、叉子等，________也要分开；同时，经常________的生活用品每天都要消毒。这样在家里才可以________传染。

课文（二）
Text（II）

（同学们在聊天儿。）

王晨：周六是“世界地球日”，学校要举办三个活动，大家都知道吧？

美丽：听说了，不过不知道活动的具体内容。

王晨：第一个活动是关于节约资源的讲座，第二个是关于自然景色的绘画比赛，第三个——

金龙：是骑自行车去郊区，我已经报名了。

月亮：美丽，咱们参加绘画比赛吧，我想画森林。

美丽：那我画海洋。我常常回忆在三亚的旅行，那儿的海给我留下的印象太深了。

马大为：我要参加去郊区的活动，我打算骑我的新电动车去。

金龙：这是自行车比赛，禁止骑电动车！

生词 New words

1. 举办	jǔbàn	*v.*	to hold, to conduct
2. 活动	huódòng	*n.*	activity
3. 内容	nèiróng	*n.*	content
4. 节约	jiéyuē	*v.*	to save
5. 资源	zīyuán	*n.*	resource
6. 讲座	jiǎngzuò	*n.*	lecture
7. 自然	zìrán	*n.*	nature
8. 绘画	huìhuà	*v.*	to draw, to paint
9. 森林	sēnlín	*n.*	forest
10. 海洋	hǎiyáng	*n.*	sea, ocean
11. 回忆	huíyì	*v.*	to recall, to call to mind
12. 留下	liúxia	*VC*	to keep, to remain
留	liú	*v.*	to remain, to stay
13. 印象	yìnxiàng	*n.*	impression
14. 禁止	jìnzhǐ	*v.*	to prohibit

专名 Proper noun

世界地球日　Shìjiè Dìqiúrì　World Earth Day (April 22)

语言点 Language Points

动词“禁止”

动词“禁止”表示不允许做某事，常用在祈使句中，表达命令的语气。例如：

1. 这是自行车比赛，禁止骑电动车！
2. 病房里禁止抽烟！
3. 考试的时候，禁止带手机。

※ 练习：请用动词“禁止”完成对话

1. 王晨：哥哥，我们把车停在医院前面可以吗？

   王东：______________________。

2. 大为：我刚才给你打电话，你怎么一直不接？

   金龙：我在考试呢，__________。

3. 护士：这里是医院，________________！

   病人家属：对不起，我不抽了。

4. A：我能参观一下你们的实验室吗？

   B：不好意思，学校有规定，__________。

综合练习 Comprehensive Exercises

一、根据拼音写汉字

1. jǔbàn ________
2. jiéyuē ________
3. sēnlín ________
4. huíyì ________
5. yìnxiàng ________
6. jìnzhǐ ________

二、辨字组词

1. 约________
   绍________
2. 象________
   像________
3. 洋________
   样________
4. 禁________
   森________

三、选词填空

举办　节约　避免　回忆　禁止

1. 奶奶常常（　　）起自己小时候的事儿。

2. 卫生间的墙上写着“请（　　）用水”。

3. 学校（　　）这次活动是为了引起同学们对环境保护的重视。

4. 医院里（　　）抽烟。

5. 得了流感应该戴好口罩，（　　）传染。

四、选出下列词语在句子中的位置

1. 云南 A 游客 B 留下了 C 很深的 D 印象。（给）

2. 这是 A 一本 B 中国 C 文化 D 的书。（关于）

3. A 这个方面 B 看，保护环境 C 就是 D 保护我们自己。（从）

4. A 我也得了 B 流感，C 我的症状 D 不严重。（不过）

5. 有的人 A 把流感 B 当 C 普通 D 感冒了。（成）

五、用所给词语完成对话

1. 大为：金龙，这节课王老师讲的我怎么听不太懂呀？
   金龙：________________。（内容）

2. 朋友：你觉得三亚怎么样？
   月亮：太美了，________________。（留）

3. 刘一鸣：您好，请问体检前需要注意什么？
   护士：________________。（关于）

4. 大为：老师，午睡有什么好处？
   老师：________________。
   （第一……第二……第三……）

5. 朋友：等你出院以后，我请你喝酒。
   病人：________________。（禁止）

六、根据课文内容回答问题

1. 周六是“世界地球日”，学校要举办哪些活动？
2. 金龙参加什么活动？
3. 月亮要参加什么活动？
4. 美丽为什么要画海洋？
5. 马大为要参加什么活动？打算怎么参加？

七、根据课文内容填空

周六是“世界________日”，学校要________三个活动。活动的具体________是：第一个是关于节约________的讲座，第二个是关于________的绘画比赛，第三个是骑自行车去________。金龙已经报名参加了第三个活动。月亮想和美丽一起参加________比赛，她想画________，美丽想画________，因为美丽常常________在三亚的旅行，那儿的海给美丽________了很深的印象。马大为也要参加________的活动，他打算骑________去。金龙告诉他这是自行车比赛，________骑电动车。

课文（三）
Text（III）

流感是指一种由流感病毒引起的疾病。这种疾病一般在秋冬季节流行，主要通过空气中的飞沫、人与人之间的接触传染。常见的症状包括高烧、全身疼痛、没有力气等。

流感和普通感冒都有传染性，但是传染性强弱有区别。流感的传染性更强，更容易引起其他严重的疾病。对于流感，积极预防很重要，特别是老人和儿童。因此，专家建议每年流感季节到来前，易感人群要通过打流感疫苗进行预防。

生词 New words

1. 指	zhǐ	*v.*	to point, to indicate
2. 病毒	bìngdú	*n.*	virus
3. 流行	liúxíng	*v.*	to be widespread
4. 飞沫	fēimò	*n.*	flying particles of liquid
5. 之间	zhījiān	*n.*	between, among
6. 包括	bāokuò	*v.*	to include
7. 高烧	gāoshāo	*n.*	high fever
8. 普通	pǔtōng	*adj.*	common, ordinary
9. 强	qiáng	*adj.*	strong, powerful
10. 弱	ruò	*adj.*	weak
11. 区别	qūbié	*n./v.*	difference; to differentiate
12. 儿童	értóng	*n.*	children
13. 到来	dàolái	*v.*	to arrive
14. 人群	rénqún	*n.*	crowd
15. 疫苗	yìmiáo	*n.*	vaccine

语言点 Language Points

介词“由”（2）

介词“由”可以用来引出原因或来源。例如：

1. 流感是指一种由流感病毒引起的疾病。

2. 很多人想知道骨质疏松症到底是由什么引起的。

3. 流感主要是由飞沫、人与人之间的接触传染的。

在书面语中，我们还经常用“由此”表示“从这里”。例如：

4. 由此可知，预防感冒非常重要。

※ 练习：请用介词“由”完成对话

1. A：大夫，请问我为什么会得流感？

B：________________________________。

2. A：听说老李骨折了，这是怎么回事儿？

B：________________________________。

3. A：我妈妈最近非常容易生气，到底是因为什么？

B：________________________________。

4. A：高血压是由什么引起的？

B：________________________________。

综合练习 Comprehensive Exercises

一、根据拼音写汉字

1. liúxíng ________
2. zhījiān ________
3. bāokuò ________
4. qūbié ________
5. értóng ________
6. rénqún ________

二、辨字组词

1. 指________
   提________
2. 童________
   重________
3. 括________
   活________
4. 群________
   裙________

三、选词填空

指　包括　之间　区别　儿童

1. 流感和普通感冒的（　　）在哪儿？
2. 常见的流感症状（　　）发烧、咳嗽、头疼等。
3. 老人和（　　）更容易得流感，因此做好防护对他们来说很重要。
4. “吃不到葡萄就说葡萄酸”（　　）的是什么意思？
5. 分开使用筷子、毛巾等，可以避免流感在家人（　　）传染。

四、选出下列词语在句子中的位置

1. 流感 A 在 B 秋冬季节 C 流行 D。（一般）
2. A 这是 B 一种 C 流感病毒 D 引起的疾病。（由）
3. 朋友 A 最重要的 B 是 C 互相信任 D。（之间）
4. A 积极预防流感 B 很重要，C 是老人和 D 儿童。（特别）
5. 易感人群 A 要 B 打疫苗 C 来预防流感 D。（通过）

五、用所给词语完成对话

1. 病人：大夫，流感和普通感冒一样吗？

   医生：________________________。（由）

2. 月亮：你觉得那件红色的衣服怎么样？

   朋友：________________________。（就是）

3. 患者家属：大夫，流感的传染性这么强，那家里的孩子和老人该怎么办？

   医生：________________________。（通过）

4. 丈夫：我的血压一直都很正常，最近怎么变高了呢？

   妻子：________________________。（引起）

5. 朋友：大为，你平时早饭吃什么？

大为：________________________________。（一般）

六、根据课文内容回答问题

1. 流感一般在什么季节流行？
2. 流感主要通过什么方式传染？
3. 流感的常见症状有哪些？
4. 流感和普通感冒的区别是什么？
5. 老人和儿童应该怎么预防流感？

七、根据课文内容填空

流感是指一种________流感病毒________的疾病。这种疾病一般在________季节流行，主要________空气中的飞沫、人与人________的接触传染。常见的________包括高烧、全身________、没有力气等。

流感和普通感冒都有________，但是传染性________有区别。流感的传染性更________，更容易________其他严重的疾病。对于流感，积极________很重要，特别是老人和________。因此，专家建议每年流感季节________前，易感人群要通过________进行预防。

语言任务 Language Tasks

一、阅读理解

流感是一种疫苗可预防性疾病，每年接种流感疫苗是预防流感最有效的手段。但接种流感疫苗并不是唯一的手段，坚持健康的生活方式、养成良好的卫生习惯、做好个人日常防护对流感等呼吸道传染病的防控至关重要。个人防护措施主要包括：勤洗手；在流感流行季节，尽量避免去人群聚集的场所；咳嗽、打喷嚏时用纸巾遮住口鼻。有家人感染流感时，家中的老人与慢性病患者要尽量避免与其近距离接触。学校、托幼机构等集体单位中出现流感时，患者应居家休息，避免交叉感染，减少疾病传播。

来源：腾讯网《秋冬季控流感，接种疫苗并非唯一手段，做好个人防护至关重要！》

补充词汇

1. 接种	jiēzhòng	*v.*	to vaccinate
2. 手段	shǒuduàn	*n.*	means
3. 唯一	wéiyī	*adj.*	only
4. 个人	gèrén	*n.*	individual
5. 防护	fánghù	*v.*	to protect
6. 呼吸道传染病	hūxīdào chuánrǎnbìng		respiratory infectious disease
7. 防控	fángkòng	*v.*	to prevent and control
8. 至关重要	zhìguān-zhòngyào		crucial
9. 措施	cuòshī	*n.*	measure
10. 勤	qín	*adj.*	often, frequent
11. 洗手	xǐ shǒu	*VO*	to wash one's hand
12. 尽量	jǐnliàng	*adv.*	as far as possible
13. 聚集	jùjí	*v.*	to gather
14. 打喷嚏	dǎ pēntì	*VO*	to sneeze
15. 纸巾	zhǐjīn	*n.*	facial tissue
16. 遮住	zhēzhù	*VC*	to cover
17. 感染	gǎnrǎn	*v.*	to infect
18. 托幼机构	tuōyòu jīgòu		nursery
19. 集体单位	jítǐ dānwèi		collective working unit
20. 居家	jūjiā	*v.*	to be at home
21. 交叉感染	jiāochā gǎnrǎn	*VP*	cross infection
22. 传播	chuánbō	*v.*	to spread, to transmit

回答问题

1. 防控流感等呼吸道传染病的方法有哪些？

2. 预防流感的个人防护措施有哪些？

3. 学校、托幼机构等集体单位中出现流感时，要如何预防？

二、口头表达

任务名称：得了流感怎么办？

任务背景：病人很难受，去医院检查。医生说他得了流感，向他说明了流感与普通感冒的区别，并介绍了预防流感的方法。

任务要求：1. 两个学生一组，一个扮演病人，一个扮演医生。

2. 医生询问病人有什么症状。

3. 病人描述自己的病情并询问医生怎么避免家人之间的传染。

参考语言：流感　相同　戴口罩　避免　传染　筷子　毛巾　区别　疫苗

三、书面表达

任务名称：难忘的一次活动。

任务要求：请介绍一次难忘的活动，包括活动名称、活动时间和地点、活动的意义等，要求 200 字以上。

参考语言：举办　活动　内容　关于　讲座　比赛　尽管……可是/但是……　既……又……

第九课
Lesson 9

需要打狂犬病疫苗吗？

学习目标 Learning Objectives

1. 语言功能：能够对自己的观点进行解释，能够通过举例的方式对问题进行充分说明。
2. 语言点：形容词“及时”、副词“一旦”、固定结构“V来V去”、反问句（3）“疑问代词表反问”、连词“然而”、动词“例如”。
3. 医学知识：初步了解狂犬病疫苗的作用和注射方法。
4. 社会文化：了解中国家庭饲养宠物的情况。

热身活动 Warm-up

1. 你了解狂犬病吗？被猫、狗抓伤了应该怎么办？

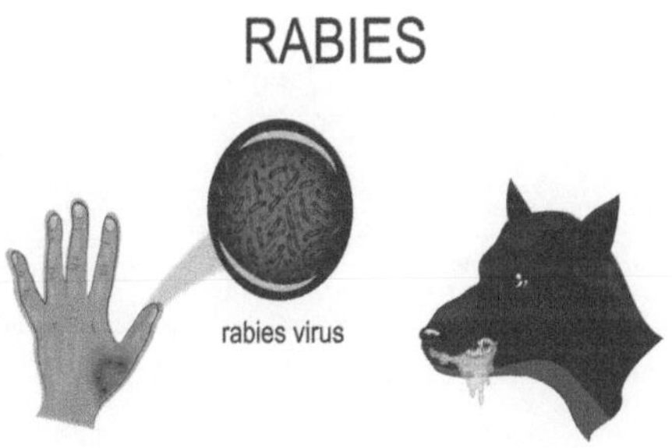

2. 你喜欢宠物吗？你家里有宠物吗？

课文（一）
Text（I）

（病人在防疫站咨询医生。）

病人：大夫，一个小时前，我被自己家的狗抓伤了。

医生：伤口处理了吗？

病人：我当时立刻用肥皂水仔细清洗了，并且擦了碘酒。

医生：你处理得很及时。让我看看伤口。

病人：大夫，我家的狗打过狂犬病疫苗，这种情况我还需要打吗？

医生：你这种情况感染狂犬病的可能性确实不大，但并不表示不会感染。一旦感染，死亡率是百分之百！

病人：太可怕了，那我必须得打。大夫，听说狂犬病疫苗要打好几针？

医生：对，要打五针，一会儿护士会告诉你具体怎么打。

生词 New words

1. 防疫站	fángyìzhàn	*n.*	epidemic prevention station
2. 抓	zhuā	*v.*	to scratch
3. 伤口	shāngkǒu	*n.*	wound
4. 处理	chǔlǐ	*v.*	to deal with, to handle
5. 立刻	lìkè	*adv.*	at once, immediately
6. 肥皂水	féizàoshuǐ	*n.*	soapsuds
肥皂	féizào	*n.*	soap
7. 仔细	zǐxì	*adj.*	careful
8. 清洗	qīngxǐ	*v.*	to wash, to clean
9. 碘酒	diǎnjiǔ	*n.*	tincture of iodine
10. 狂犬病疫苗	kuángquǎnbìng yìmiáo		rabies vaccine
狂犬病	kuángquǎnbìng	*n.*	rabies
11. 感染	gǎnrǎn	*v.*	to infect
12. 表示	biǎoshì	*v.*	to indicate, to mean
13. 一旦	yídàn	*adv.*	once, in case (sth. happens)
14. 死亡率	sǐwánglǜ	*n.*	death rate
死亡	sǐwáng	*v.*	to die

语言点 Language Points

一、形容词“及时”

形容词“及时”表示正赶上时候。例如：

1.（伤口）你处理得很及时。

2. 病人抢救得很及时，现在已经没有生命危险了。

3. 医生来得非常及时，否则病人就有危险了。

※ 练习：请用形容词“及时”和所给词语完成句子

1. 你的伤口________________________，现在已经没有问题了。（处理）

2. 这次的CT检查______________________，否则很难发现息肉变大了。（做）

3. 这次活动______________________，进一步引起了人们对环境保护的重视。（举办）

4. 这个包间______________________，没想到工作日这里客人这么多。（订）

二、副词“一旦”

副词“一旦”表示有一天，假设新情况的出现，后面常跟动词性成分。例如：

1. 一旦感染（狂犬病），死亡率是百分之百！
2. 一旦发现病人晕倒，要及时送往医院。
3. 病人一旦有什么情况，要立刻告诉医生。

※ 练习：请用副词“一旦”和所给词语完成句子

1. 你慢点儿跑，______________________。（摔倒）
2. 患有骨质疏松症的人运动时要小心，____________________。（骨折）
3. ______________________，所以老人和儿童要提前打流感疫苗。（感染）
4. 刘大夫，您刚做完手术，先好好儿休息，______________________。（有情况）

综合练习 Comprehensive Exercises

一、根据拼音写汉字

1. chǔlǐ ________	3. zǐxì ________	5. yídàn ________
2. lìkè ________	4. biǎoshì ________	6. sǐwáng ________

二、辨字组词

1. 处________　　3. 刻________

　外________　　　该________

2. 细________　　4. 清________

　备________　　　晴________

三、选词填空

及时　准时　同时　按时　时候

1. 今天下班的（　　），突然下起了大雨。
2. 更年期女性应该放松心情，（　　）也要坚持锻炼身体。
3. 医生告诉病人一定要（　　）吃药，不能想起来就吃，想不起来就不吃。
4. 汽车停得很（　　），避免了一场交通事故的发生。
5. 火车将（　　）到达北京南站，请做好下车准备。

四、选出下列词语在句子中的位置

1. 奶奶的手 A 家里 B 养的 C 小狗 D 抓伤了。（被）
2. A 这个问题 B 需要 C 我 D 再说一遍吗？（还）
3. 我 A 还没 B 去 C 北京，我打算明年申请去北京读 D 大学。（过）
4. A 这种病毒的传染性 B 不大，但一旦 C 被传染，后果就 D 很严重。（确实）
5. 孩子如果 A 被狗 B 咬伤，要 C 送到医院 D。（立刻）

五、用所给词语完成对话

1. 艺文：哎呀，高兴被狗抓伤了！

　王东：________________________。（立刻）

2. 月亮：你平时有什么爱好？

朋友：________________________。（并且）

3. 朋友：我家的狗都打过狂犬病疫苗，我是不是不需要打了？

王晨：________________________。（表示）

4. 病人：被猫、狗抓伤后为什么要马上去医院？

医生：________________________。（一旦）

5. 病人：我出院以后心脏再出问题怎么办？

护士：________________________。（一旦）

六、根据课文内容回答问题

1. 病人怎么了？
2. 病人自己是怎么处理伤口的？
3. 病人还需要打狂犬病疫苗吗？
4. 感染了狂犬病的后果是什么？
5. 狂犬病疫苗要打几针？

七、根据课文内容填空

一个小时前，病人被自己家的狗________了。他当时________用肥皂水仔细________伤口了，并且擦了碘酒。医生看了看他的伤口，认为他处理得很________。虽然病人家的狗打过狂犬病疫苗，这种情况下感染狂犬病的可能性________不大，但并不表示不会感染。________感染，________是百分之百！太可怕了，病人认为他必须________。狂犬病疫苗一般要打五针，一会儿护士会告诉他________怎么打。

课文（二）
Text（II）

（艺文和王东在家聊天儿。）

艺文：有件事儿，我想听听你的意见。

王东：什么事儿？

艺文：我想在家养只鸟，你同意吗？

王东：你不是一直反对在室内养小动物吗？

艺文：现在我的想法改变了。因为高兴特别喜欢小动物，看到小狗跑来跑去，小鸟飞来飞去，他就开心极了。

王东：那你打算在哪儿养？

艺文：我已经想好了，在阳台上。

王东：阳台太小了，不适合养鸟。而且，咱俩都这么忙，哪儿有时间照顾它呀？

艺文：你说得也有道理。

王东：高兴喜欢动物，咱们可以带他去动物园玩儿，还可以看老虎和大熊猫呢！

生词 New words

1. 意见	yìjiàn	*n.*	opinion, view
2. 只	zhī	*m.*	*a measure word for certain animals*
3. 鸟	niǎo	*n.*	bird
4. 内	nèi	*n.*	inside
5. 动物	dòngwù	*n.*	animal
6. 飞	fēi	*v.*	to fly
7. 阳台	yángtái	*n.*	balcony
8. 道理	dàolǐ	*n.*	reason
9. 动物园	dòngwùyuán	*n.*	zoo
10. 老虎	lǎohǔ	*n.*	tiger
11. 大熊猫	dàxióngmāo	*n.*	panda

语言点 Language Points

一、固定结构“V 来 V 去”

固定结构“V 来 V 去”表示动作的多次重复，前后两个动词一般是相同的，有时也可以是近义词。例如：

1. 高兴特别喜欢小动物，看到小狗跑来跑去，小鸟飞来飞去，他就开心极了。
2. 我们讨论来讨论去，也没有想出一个好办法。
3. 我思来想去，还是觉得这个办法有问题。

※ 练习：请用固定结构“V 来 V 去”和所给词语完成句子

1. 孩子很喜欢____________________。（跑）
2. 妻子正在做手术，丈夫在手术室外急得____________________。（走）
3. 我丈夫经常出差，总是世界各地____________________。（飞）
4. 快来看！好多小鱼在水里____________________。（游）

二、反问句（3）：疑问代词表反问

使用疑问代词“谁、什么、哪儿、怎么”等表示反问，语气比陈述句强烈，常表达说话人的不满意、不同意或不理解。例如：

1. 咱俩都这么忙，哪儿有时间照顾它呀？
2. 他每天工作都很忙，谁知道今天能不能回来吃饭呢？
3. A：你的汉语说得真好！

   B：好什么呀？跟你比差远了。

※ 练习：请用所给疑问代词完成对话

1. A：你很喜欢自己做饭吗？

   B：__________________________？附近没有好吃的饭馆，没办法。（谁）
2. A：听说上次考试你考得很好？

   B：__________________________？我才考了80多分。（什么）
3. A：咱们明天一起去爬山吧！

   B：__________________________？我们得准备考试了。（哪儿）
4. A：你最近打算去旅游吗？

   B：__________________________？我都快忙死了。（哪儿）

综合练习 Comprehensive Exercises

一、根据拼音写汉字

1. yìjiàn __________　　3. dòngwù__________　　5. lǎohǔ__________

2. niǎo __________　　4. yángtái __________　　6. dàolǐ__________

二、辨字组词

1. 内__________　　3. 鸟__________

   肉__________　　马__________

2. 虎________　　　　4. 熊________

虑________　　　　能________

三、选词填空

意见　内　阳台　道理　大熊猫

1. 他家的（　　）上放了很多纸盒子。
2. 是否需要做心脏支架手术，必须听医生的（　　）。
3. 冬天尤其要注意房间（　　）的通风换气。
4. 你说得很有（　　），我现在就打电话订餐。
5. （　　）长得圆圆的、胖胖的，特别可爱。

四、选出下列词语在句子中的位置

1. 明天 A 就到 B 预产期了，艺文今天 C 紧张 D。　（极了）
2. 周末我们就在 A 宿舍 B 做作业，C 也不去 D。　（哪儿）
3. A 哥哥喜欢 B 做饭，C 做得很好吃 D。　（而且）
4. 护士 A 已经把病人要吃的药 B 都准备 C 了 D。　（好）
5. 你 A 要 B 给我看 C 你以前的 D 照片吗？　（不是）

五、用所给词语完成对话

1. 病人：大夫，流感季节到了，家里的老人和孩子要注意什么？

   医生：应该做好个人防护，______________________。（而且）

2. 月亮：你决定假期去哪儿旅行了吗？

   朋友：______________________，还是不知道去哪儿好。（V 来 V 去）

3. 医生：你失眠持续多长时间了？

病人：________________________。（大约）

4. 艺文：________________________？（不是……吗）

爸爸：现在我的想法改变了，我觉得健康最重要，不能再抽烟了。

5. 王晨：你的工作看起来不错呀。

朋友：________________________，天天加班。（反问句：什么）

六、根据课文内容回答问题

1. 艺文想做什么？
2. 艺文以前同意在家养小动物吗？
3. 艺文为什么改变了想法？
4. 王东为什么不同意在家养鸟？
5. 王东有什么建议？

七、根据课文内容填空

艺文想在家养只________，王东觉得奇怪，因为艺文以前一直反对在________养小动物。现在艺文的想法________了，因为高兴特别喜欢小动物，看到小狗________，小鸟________，他就开心极了。艺文已经想好了，要在________上养。王东觉得阳台太小了，不适合养鸟。而且，他俩都这么忙，________有时间照顾它呀？艺文觉得王东说得有________。王东说高兴喜欢动物的话，他们可以带高兴去________玩儿，还可以看________和________。

课文（三）
Text（III）

很多人都喜欢在家里养几棵植物，这既可以美化室内环境，又可以放松心情。然而，想养好植物可不是件容易的事儿，需要耐心和经验。每种植物都有自己的特点，例如：有的植物适合室内的环境，有的植物适合室外的环境；有的喜阴，有的喜阳；有的需要多浇水，有的需要少浇水。我们只有充分了解每种植物的特点，才能把它们养得健健康康、漂漂亮亮的。

生词 New words

1. 棵	kē	*m.*	*a measure word for plants*
2. 植物	zhíwù	*n.*	plant
3. 美化	měihuà	*v.*	to beautify
4. 然而	rán'ér	*conj.*	however, but
5. 经验	jīngyàn	*n.*	experience
6. 特点	tèdiǎn	*n.*	characteristic, feature
7. 例如	lìrú	*v.*	for instance, for example
8. 喜	xǐ	*v.*	to have an inclination for
9. 阴	yīn		*yin*, shade
10. 阳	yáng		*yang*, sunshine
11. 浇	jiāo	*v.*	to water
12. 充分	chōngfèn	*adj.*	full, sufficient

语言点 Language Points

一、连词"然而"

连词"然而"表示转折，后面引出与上文相反的意思，书面色彩比较浓。例如：

1. 很多人都喜欢在家里养几棵植物，然而，想养好植物可不是件容易的事儿。
2. 很多人都觉得在家里养些植物很好，然而，卧室里养太多植物的话，并不一定对健康有好处。
3. 虽然狂犬病的死亡率极高，然而大家不用太担心，如果伤口处理得及时并且尽快打狂犬病疫苗的话，是可以避免感染的。

※ 练习：请用连词"然而"完成句子

1. 虽然手术做得很成功，________________________________。
2. 他学了两年汉语，________________________________。

3. 坐飞机又快又舒服，____。

4. 孩子一直想在家里养一只小狗，____。

二、动词“例如”

动词“例如”用来举例子，表示后面所说的就是说明前文观点的具体例子。例如：

1. 每种植物都有自己的特点，例如：有的植物适合室内的环境，有的植物适合室外的环境；有的喜阴，有的喜阳；有的需要多浇水，有的需要少浇水。
2. 有些工作需要晚上上班，例如医生、护士等。
3. 有很多方法对学习汉语有帮助，例如唱中国歌、看中国电影、读中文书等。

※ 练习：请用动词“例如”完成句子

1. 学习外语很有用，____。
2. 爸妈每个周末都过得很有意思，____。
3. 我对中国文化感兴趣，____。
4. 我认识很多有名的中国人，____。

综合练习 Comprehensive Exercises

一、根据拼音写汉字

1. rán'ér ________　　3. zhíwù ________　　5. yīn ________

2. jīngyàn ________　　4. tèdiǎn ________　　6. chōngfèn ________

二、辨字组词

1. 棵________　　3. 室________

课________　　宝________

2. 阴________　　　　4. 浇________

阳________　　　　烧________

三、选词填空

棵　然而　例如　经验　充分

1. 很多人都知道运动的好处，（　　）很少有人能坚持每天运动。
2. 我喜欢吃的菜很多，（　　）宫保鸡丁、北京烤鸭。
3. 医生办公室的窗外有一（　　）树。
4. 父母的生活（　　）比我们多多了。
5. 经过（　　）的准备，我顺利通过了 HSK 四级考试。

四、选出下列词语在句子中的位置

1. 北京 A 好吃的小吃 B 你 C 吃过 D 什么？（都）
2. 养花儿 A 既可以 B 美化室内环境，C 可以 D 放松心情。（又）
3. 想说好 A 汉语 B 不是 C 一件 D 容易的事儿。（可）
4. 动物园里 A 有很多 B 种动物，C 老虎、D 大熊猫。（例如）
5. 晚饭 A 以后 B 我 C 在房间里 D 做作业。（一直）

五、用所给词语完成对话

1. 艺文：我同事家都养花儿了，咱们也养几棵吧？

   王东：________________________________。（然而）

2. 月亮：________________________________？（AABB 的）

   朋友：那是我男朋友。

3. 病人：得了流感，除了戴好口罩，还要注意什么？

医生：____。（例如）

4. 李真：你为什么这么喜欢看中国电影？

大为：____。（既……又……）

5. 王晨：哥哥，你为什么每天都出去锻炼？

哥哥：____。（只有……才……）

六、根据课文内容回答问题

1. 人们为什么喜欢在家里养植物？
2. 养好植物需要什么？
3. 不同的植物各有什么特点？
4. 怎样才能养好植物？

七、根据课文内容填空

很多人都喜欢在家里养几棵________，这既可以________室内环境，又可以________心情。________，想养好植物可不是件容易的事儿，需要耐心和________。每种植物都有自己的________，________：有的植物适合室内的环境，有的植物适合________的环境；有的________，有的喜阳；有的需要多________，有的需要少________。我们只有________了解每种植物的特点，才能把它们养得________、漂漂亮亮的。

语言任务 Language Tasks

一、阅读理解

宝宝感冒期间，不建议打预防针。感冒期间，宝宝抵抗力比较低，免疫系统处于比较混乱的状态。预防针是外来的抗原，感冒期的患儿打预防针，容易引起抗原抗体反应，导致患儿发烧，甚至引发其他更严重的疾病。如果宝宝因气道过敏而咳嗽，打预防针可能导致交叉过敏，症状加重，还可能诱发其他过敏反应。因此，如果宝宝有流鼻涕、打喷嚏、咳嗽等症状，请不要打预防针。如果已经打了，应让其多喝热水，避免去人多的地方玩耍。

来源：薄荷医生《宝宝感冒能打预防针吗》

补充词汇

1. 预防针	yùfángzhēn	*n.*	immunization injection
2. 抵抗力	dǐkànglì	*n.*	immunity, resistance
3. 混乱	hùnluàn	*adj.*	disordered
4. 外来	wàilái	*adj.*	outside
5. 抗原	kàngyuán	*n.*	antigen
6. 患儿	huàn'ér	*n.*	pediatric patients
7. 抗体	kàngtǐ	*n.*	antibody
8. 气道	qìdào	*n.*	airway
9. 交叉过敏	jiāochā guòmǐn	*VP*	to have a cross allergy
10. 诱发	yòufā	*v.*	to cause to happen
11. 流鼻涕	liú bítì	*VO*	to have a runny nose
12. 玩耍	wánshuǎ	*v.*	to play, to have fun

回答问题

1. 宝宝感冒期间为什么不建议打预防针？
2. 宝宝感冒期间打了预防针可能会有什么后果？
3. 如果宝宝在感冒期间已经打了预防针，我们应该怎么做？

二、口头表达

任务名称：被狗抓伤了。

任务背景：孩子被家里的狗抓伤了，爸爸给医生打电话咨询，医生告诉他要及时处理伤口并打狂犬病疫苗。

任务要求：1. 两个学生一组，一个扮演孩子爸爸，一个扮演医生。

2. 孩子爸爸告诉医生孩子被狗抓伤了，询问应该怎么处理。

3. 医生指导孩子爸爸处理伤口并告知其打狂犬病疫苗的重要性。

参考语言：抓伤　处理　伤口　立刻　肥皂水　及时　仔细　清洗　感染　一旦　死亡

三、书面表达

任务名称：我喜欢的动物。

任务要求：请介绍一种自己喜欢的动物，要求200字以上。

参考语言：养　压力　放松　眼睛　鼻子　耳朵　嘴巴　照顾　可爱

不但……而且……　……，就是……

第十课 Lesson 10 孩子是不是近视了？

学习目标 Learning Objectives

1. 语言功能：能够逐步深入地论述自己的观点。
2. 语言点：助词“的话”、谦辞“哪里/哪里哪里”、副词“不过”、动词“受不了”。
3. 医学知识：初步了解近视及其防控方法。
4. 社会文化：初步了解中国中小学生的学习安排。

热身活动 Warm-up

1. 你的眼睛近视吗？什么原因可能导致近视？

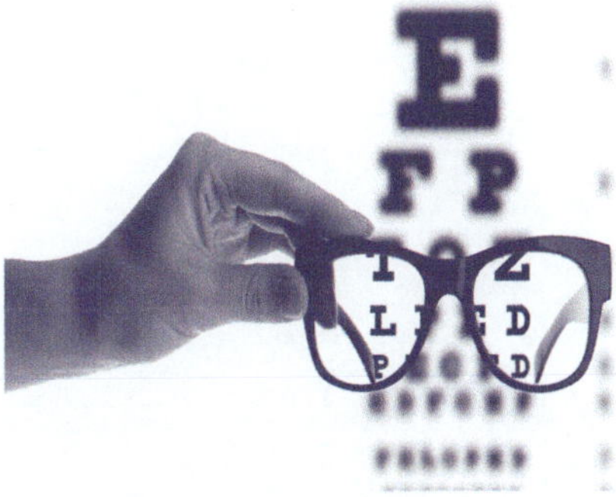

2. 请说一说你学过的才艺，例如画画儿、弹钢琴等。

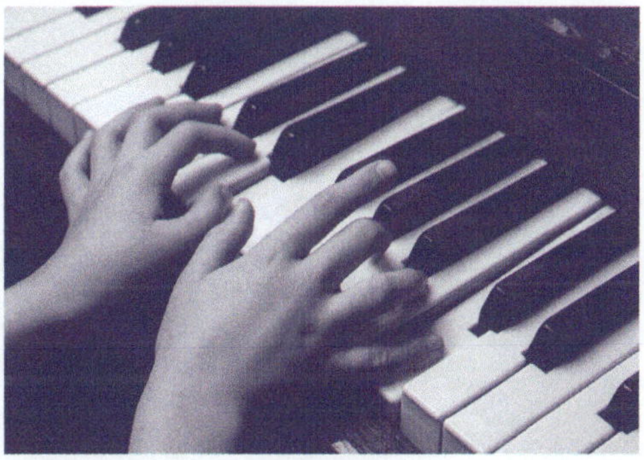

课文（一）
Text（Ⅰ）

（妈妈带孩子在眼科门诊检查视力。）

妈妈：大夫，孩子是不是近视了？

医生：从检查结果看，是假性近视。再不注意保护眼睛的话，就很可能变成真性近视。

妈妈：那需要配眼镜吗？

医生：暂时不需要。但是一定要养成良好的用眼习惯，平时读书、写字的姿势要正确，少使用电子产品。

妈妈：我们家孩子倒是不玩儿电子游戏，但是几乎每天都要上网课。

医生：孩子的眼睛还在发育过程中，一定要减少上网的时间，增加户外活动的时间，这是预防近视最简单、有效的方法。

生词 New words

1. 眼科	yǎnkē	*n.*	ophthalmology
2. 近视	jìnshì	*adj.*	nearsighted
3. 假性	jiǎxìng	*adj.*	pseudo-
假	jiǎ	*adj.*	fake, false
4. 的话	dehuà	*part.*	if
5. 真性	zhēnxìng	*adj.*	real
6. 良好	liánghǎo	*adj.*	good
7. 姿势	zīshì	*n.*	posture
8. 正确	zhèngquè	*adj.*	correct
9. 电子	diànzǐ	*n.*	electron
10. 产品	chǎnpǐn	*n.*	product
11. 网课	wǎngkè	*n.*	online course
12. 发育	fāyù	*v.*	to grow
13. 户外	hùwài	*n.*	outdoors
14. 有效	yǒuxiào	*v.*	to be effective

语言点 Language Points

助词“的话”

助词“的话”通常用在表示假设的分句句尾，可与表示假设的连词“如果、要是、假如”等合用，也可单独使用。例如：

1. 再不注意保护眼睛的话，就很可能变成真性近视。
2. 要是作息规律、心情放松的话，大部分女性都可以顺利度过更年期。
3. 要是养一只小狗的话，我们肯定要花很多时间照顾它，可是我们工作太忙了，哪儿有空儿呢？

※ 练习：请用助词“的话”完成句子

1. ________________________________，我就不去游泳了。

2. ________________________________，金龙就继续读研究生。

3. ________________________________，就可以避免感染狂犬病。

4. ________________________________，我就去全世界旅行。

综合练习 Comprehensive Exercises

一、根据拼音写汉字

1. jiǎxìng ________　3. zhèngquè ________　5. hùwài ________

2. zīshì ________　4. diànzǐ ________　6. yǒuxiào ________

二、辨字组词

1. 良________　3. 姿________

　很________　　资________

2. 产________　4. 效________

　户________　　较________

三、选词填空

的话	正确	户外	有效	电子

1. 周末有时间（　　），我们带孩子去动物园看大熊猫吧。

2. 孩子读书、写字的姿势一定要（　　），否则容易得近视。

3. 现在很多孩子从早到晚玩儿（　　）游戏，所以眼睛近视的很多。

4. 预防近视的（　　）方法是什么？

5. 很多年轻人喜欢（　　）运动，喜欢亲近大自然，呼吸新鲜空气。

四、选出下列词语在句子中的位置

1. 你 A 不努力 B，你的 C 汉语水平 D 就提高不了。（的话）
2. A 你 B 往 C 前走就 D 到眼科了。（一直）
3. 孩子 A 一定要 B 使用 C 电子 D 产品的时间。（减少）
4. A 这瓶牛奶 B 喝 C 就要 D 过期了。（再不）
5. A 我们家孩子 B 每天 C 都要 D 上网课。（几乎）

五、用所给词语完成对话

1. 艺文：我们已经两周没回去看父母了。

   王东：______________________________。（一定）

2. 病人：大夫，我这是得了流感吗？

   医生：这次不是，但现在是流感流行季节，______________。（再不）

3. 医生：孩子喜欢玩儿电子游戏吗？

   病人家属：______________________________。（倒是）

4. 病人：请问体检前需要注意什么？

   护士：______________________________。（的话）

5. 病人：大夫，这几天我总是咳嗽、打喷嚏。

   医生：______________________________。（从……看）

六、根据课文内容回答问题

1. 孩子的眼睛怎么了？
2. 假性近视会变成真性近视吗？为什么？
3. 平时怎么养成良好的用眼习惯？

4. 她家孩子为什么会得假性近视？

5. 预防近视最简单、有效的方法是什么？

七、根据课文内容填空

妈妈带孩子在________门诊检查视力，从________看，孩子得的是假性近视。医生说再不注意保护眼睛________，就很可能变成________近视。孩子现在还不需要配________，但是一定要养成________的用眼习惯，平时读书、写字的________要正确，少使用________产品。这个孩子________不玩儿电子游戏，但是________每天都要上________。医生说孩子的眼睛还在________过程中，一定要减少________的时间，增加________活动的时间，这是________近视最简单、________的方法。

课文（二）
Text（II）

（同学们在聊天儿。）

马大为：李真，昨天你在晚会上的表现太棒了！观众都被你的演奏吸引住了。

美丽：你的水平真高，就像是艺术专业的。

李真：哪里哪里！我不过是业余水平。

美丽：听说学钢琴挺苦的，每天都要坚持练习。

李真：对，所以刚开始的时候，我对弹钢琴并不感兴趣，甚至很讨厌。但是妈妈对我很严格，要求我每天写完作业就去弹琴。在我的记忆中，童年就是学习和弹琴。

马大为：我真同情你。

李真：尽管刚开始不喜欢，可是后来我发现弹钢琴能让自己放松，就越来越喜欢了。

马大为：那我开始羡慕你了。

美丽：大为，你也可以学！

马大为：我太笨了，学不会，还是放弃吧。

生词 New words

1. 晚会	wǎnhuì	*n.*	evening party
2. 表现	biǎoxiàn	*n./v.*	performance; to demonstrate
3. 观众	guānzhòng	*n.*	audience
4. 演奏	yǎnzòu	*v.*	to play a musical instrument in a performance
5. 吸引	xīyǐn	*v.*	to attract
6. 艺术	yìshù	*n.*	art
7. 业余	yèyú	*adj.*	amateur
8. 练习	liànxí	*v.*	to practice
9. 讨厌	tǎoyàn	*v.*	to hate, to dislike
10. 严格	yángé	*adj.*	strict
11. 童年	tóngnián	*n.*	childhood
12. 同情	tóngqíng	*v.*	to sympathize (with sb.)
13. 笨	bèn	*adj.*	stupid, silly
14. 放弃	fàngqì	*v.*	to give up

语言点 Language Points

一、谦辞"哪里/哪里哪里"

在汉语中，"哪里"在答句中单独用或重复用可以表示一种客气委婉的推辞，通常用来推辞别人对自己的称赞。例如：

1. 美丽：你（弹琴）的水平真高，就像是艺术专业的。

   李真：哪里哪里！我不过是业余水平。

2. A：你唱歌唱得太好了！

   B：哪里哪里！我不过是随便唱唱。

3. A：您家孩子长得太漂亮了！

   B：哪里！她就是个普通孩子。

※ 练习：请用谦辞“哪里”完成对话

1. A：大夫，您这伤口处理得太好了！

B：______________________________。

2. A：美丽，你今天在课上表现得太棒了！

B：______________________________。

3. A：你的新裙子也太好看了吧！

B：______________________________。

4. A：李大夫，这次手术您做得非常成功，怪不得大家都说你是医院里最受欢迎的医生呢。

B：______________________________。

二、副词“不过”

副词“不过”表示“仅仅”“只是”，用来将说话人所表达的意思往小处说或往轻里说。例如：

1. 我不过是业余水平。
2. 我不过是摔了一下，没有骨折，别担心。
3. 我不过是名医学生，还不是真正的医生。

※ 练习：请用副词“不过”完成对话

1. A：你的汉语说得太好了，就像中国人一样。

B：______________________________。

2. A：听说你是医学院学习最好的学生。

B：______________________________。

3. A：你怎么在医院？生病了吗？

B：______________________________。

4. A：听说你做手术了？严重吗？

B：______________________________。

综合练习 Comprehensive Exercises

一、根据拼音写汉字

1. guānzhòng ________　3. yángé ________　5. tóngqíng ________
2. xīyǐn ________　4. tóngnián ________　6. fàngqì ________

二、辨字组词

1. 观________　3. 吸________
   现________　　极________
2. 引________　4. 练________
   张________　　炼________

三、选词填空

表现　吸引　业余　严格　放弃

1. 一到秋天，西山公园的红叶就（　　）来很多游客。
2. 我常常在（　　）时间学习京剧。
3. 糖尿病病人应该（　　）控制血糖。
4. 他竟然（　　）了去国外留学的机会。
5. 因为感冒，今天的比赛她（　　）得不太好。

四、选出下列词语在句子中的位置

1. 她 A 学了半年 B 汉语，C 就说得 D 这么标准。　（不过）
2. 我发现 A 弹钢琴 B 能 C 自己 D 放松。　（让）

3. 你画得 A 真好 B，就 C 艺术品 D 一样。（像）

4. 老师 A 学生 B 要求 C 非常 D 严格。（对）

5. 大家 A 都 B 他的歌声 C 吸引住 D 了。（被）

五、用所给词语完成对话

1. 艺文：我们在家养一只鸟吧。

   王东：________________________________。（还是）

2. 月亮：你想考哪个专业的研究生？

   朋友：________________________________。（对……感兴趣）

3. 病人：大夫，做完支架手术后能运动吗？

   医生：________________________________。（不过）

4. 病人：大夫，糖尿病病人可以喝无糖饮料吗？

   医生：________________________________。（尽管……可是……）

5. 王晨：你画得真好！

   朋友：________________________________。（哪里哪里）

六、根据课文内容回答问题

1. 李真昨天在晚会上表现得怎么样？
2. 美丽觉得李真的演奏水平怎么样？
3. 美丽怎样看待学习钢琴这件事儿？
4. 请说说李真学钢琴的经历。
5. 马大为为什么放弃学钢琴？

七、根据课文内容填空

李真昨天在________上的________太棒了，观众都被她的演奏________住了。美丽觉得李真的演奏水平很高，就像是________专业的，李真却说自己不过是________水平。美丽听说学________挺苦的，每天都要坚持________。其实，刚开始的时候，李真对弹钢琴并不________，甚至很________。但是妈妈对她很________，要求她每天写完作业就去弹琴。在李真的________中，________就是学习和弹琴。马大为很________李真。________刚开始李真不喜欢，可是________她发现弹钢琴能让自己________，就越来越喜欢了。马大为又有点儿________李真了，可是他觉得自己太________了，学不会，还是________吧。

课文（三）
Text（III）

随着社会的发展，家长对孩子的教育更加重视。除了接受学校的教育，很多孩子业余时间还要上校外辅导班，学习任务很重。家长认为这样的安排对孩子的发展有利。

但记者通过采访发现，很多孩子的压力来自紧张的学习生活，这种压力让一些孩子受不了。因此，父母要根据孩子的实际情况，安排孩子的学习。而且，给孩子选择辅导班时，一定要跟孩子商量，尊重他们的意见和看法。真正适合孩子的教育才是最好的教育。

生词 New words

1. 社会	shèhuì	*n.*	society
2. 家长	jiāzhǎng	*n.*	parent or guardian of a child
3. 教育	jiàoyù	*n./v.*	education; to educate
4. 更加	gèngjiā	*adv.*	more, even more
5. 辅导班	fǔdǎobān	*n.*	tutorial class
辅导	fǔdǎo	*v.*	to coach, to tutor
班	bān	*n.*	class
6. 任务	rènwu	*n.*	task
7. 有利	yǒulì	*adj.*	beneficial
8. 记者	jìzhě	*n.*	reporter, journalist
9. 采访	cǎifǎng	*v./n.*	to interview; interview
10. 来自	láizì	*v.*	to be from
11. 受不了	shòubuliǎo	*v.*	cannot bear, to be unable to endure
12. 实际	shíjì	*n./adj.*	reality; realistic
13. 尊重	zūnzhòng	*v.*	to respect
14. 看法	kànfǎ	*n.*	opinion, view
15. 真正	zhēnzhèng	*adj.*	true, real

语言点 Language Points

动词“受不了”

动词“受不了”表示不能忍受，与其意义相反的是“受得了”。例如：

1. 很多孩子的压力来自紧张的学习生活，这种压力让一些孩子受不了。
2. 一次喝这么多啤酒，我可受不了。
3. 每天工作十小时，有的人受得了，有的人受不了。

※ 练习：请用“受得了/受不了”完成句子

1. 什么？早上五点就起床？________________________________。

2. 跑了两个小时步，我的腿________________。

3. 这个人总是和别人生气，________________。

4. 这家公司工作压力很大，________________。

综合练习 Comprehensive Exercises

一、根据拼音写汉字

1. shèhuì ________　　3. jìzhě ________　　5. zūnzhòng ________

2. jiàoyù ________　　4. cǎifǎng ________　　6. zhēnzhèng ________

二、辨字组词

1. 社________　　3. 尊________

   视________　　　酒________

2. 务________　　4. 际________

   条________　　　标________

三、选词填空

任务　有利　受不了　真正　实际

1. 大家以为无糖饮料里没有糖，（　　）上不是这样的。

2. 楼下吵架的声音太大了，真让人（　　）。

3. 放心吧，我一定按时完成（　　）。

4. 适当运动对顺利度过更年期（　　）。

5. 愿意在你困难时帮助你的朋友，才是（　　）的朋友。

四、选出下列词语在句子中的位置

1. 家长 A 孩子 B 的教育 C 越来越 D 重视。　　（对）
2. 现在 A 年轻人 B 的生活压力主要 C 买房的 D 压力。　　（来自）
3. 适合 A 自己的 B 工作 C 是真正的 D 好工作。　　（才）
4. 这本书 A 里 B 有很多 C 自然资源 D 的介绍。　　（关于）
5. 现在的 A 孩子 B 二十年前 C 的孩子 D 压力大多了。　　（比）

五、用所给词语完成对话

1. 佳乐：你怎么又换工作了？

   朋友：________________________________。（受不了）

2. 病人：大夫，我为什么经常头晕、头疼？

   医生：________________________________。（根据）

3. 月亮：为什么孩子从小就要学那么多东西？

   朋友：________________________________。（认为）

4. 王晨：你觉得京剧怎么样？

   金龙：________________________________。（但是）

5. 病人：大夫，孩子近视了怎么办？

   医生：________________________________。（除了……还……）

六、根据课文内容回答问题

1. 随着社会的发展，家长对孩子的教育态度发生了什么变化？
2. 除了接受学校的教育，孩子们业余时间还要做什么？
3. 家长为什么安排孩子上很多校外辅导班？
4. 孩子的压力主要来自哪里？
5. 什么样的教育才是最好的教育？

七、根据课文内容填空

随着________的发展，家长对孩子的教育________重视。________接受学校的教育，很多孩子________时间还要上校外辅导班，学习________很重。家长认为这样的安排对孩子的发展________。

但记者通过________发现，很多孩子的压力________紧张的学习生活，这种压力让一些孩子________。因此，父母要根据孩子的________情况，安排孩子的学习。而且，给孩子选择辅导班时，一定要跟孩子________，________他们的意见和看法。________适合孩子的教育才是________的教育。

语言任务 Language Tasks

一、阅读理解

现在青少年和低龄儿童的近视发病率越来越高。近视眼的防控，主要得从预防方面着手。公认的方法就是沐浴阳光，每天坚持 2 小时以上的户外活动。另外就是睡眠，每天保证 8—10 小时的睡眠，尤其是小学生。再就是坐姿和写字的姿势，平时读书、写字一定要注意姿势正确。此外就是得做眼保健操，少玩儿电脑、iPad 等，同时也要改掉不良的用眼习惯，如不能躺着看书、走路看书、坐车看书，也不能在强光下和暗淡的路灯下看书。要定期检查视力，一旦发现近视，一定要到专业的眼科医院验光配镜，配戴合适的眼镜或角膜塑形镜，防止眼镜度数快速增加。

补充词汇

1. 低龄	dīlíng	*adj.*	younger than usual
2. 近视眼	jìnshìyǎn	*n.*	myopia
3. 着手	zhuóshǒu	*v.*	to set about

4. 公认	gōngrèn	*v.*	to be generally acknowledged
5. 沐浴	mùyù	*v.*	to bathe
6. 以上	yǐshàng	*n.*	more than
7. 小学生	xiǎoxuéshēng	*n.*	schoolchild
8. 坐姿	zuòzī	*n.*	sitting position
9. 此外	cǐwài	*conj.*	besides
10. 眼保健操	yǎn bǎojiàncāo		eye exercises
11. 改掉	gǎidiào	*VC*	to give up
12. 强光	qiáng guāng		strong light
13. 暗淡	àndàn	*adj.*	dim
14. 路灯	lùdēng	*n.*	streetlight
15. 验光	yànguāng	*v.*	to have an examination of eyesight
16. 配镜	pèi jìng	*VO*	to get the right lenses for one's eyeglasses
17. 配戴	pèi dài	*VP*	to wear
18. 角膜塑形镜	jiǎomó sùxíngjìng	*n.*	orthokeratology
19. 防止	fángzhǐ	*v.*	to prevent, to avoid
20. 度数	dùshu	*n.*	number of degrees

回答问题

1. 防控近视的方法有哪些？
2. 哪些是不良的用眼习惯？
3. 一旦发现孩子近视，我们应该怎么做？

二、口头表达

任务名称：保护视力。

任务背景：妈妈带孩子在眼科门诊检查视力。孩子眼睛近视了，妈妈想知道怎么保护孩子的视力。

任务要求：1. 两个学生一组，一个扮演孩子妈妈，一个扮演医生。

2. 医生询问孩子平时的用眼习惯。

3. 妈妈询问医生保护视力的方法。

参考语言：从……看　近视　……的话　配眼镜　良好　姿势　正确　电子产品

减少　上网课　户外活动

三、书面表达

任务名称：最好的教育。

任务要求：请谈论一下你认为的“最好的教育”，要求 200 字以上。

参考语言：业余时间　辅导班　压力　学习任务　对……感兴趣　受不了

根据　实际　尊重　适合

第十一课 Lesson 11 少吃含糖的食物

学习目标 Learning Objectives

1. 语言功能：能够对食物的味道进行评价，能够对问题进行较为深入的论述。
2. 语言点：副词“反而”、固定结构“在……看来”、固定结构“像……一样”、介词“于”。
3. 医学知识：初步了解糖尿病的症状、危害及控制方法。
4. 社会文化：初步了解中国各地的饮食差异。

热身活动 Warm-up

1. 你了解糖尿病吗？糖尿病患者在饮食方面需要注意什么？

2. 你喜欢什么口味的菜？在餐厅点菜时需要注意什么？

课文（一）
Text（I）

（病人在内分泌科门诊看病。）

病人：大夫，这是我的体检报告，麻烦您看看。

医生：空腹血糖 9.1，挺高的。你以前查过餐后血糖吗？

病人：从来没查过。

医生：最近身体上有其他症状吗？

病人：吃得多，可是体重反而减轻了，力气也不如以前大。

医生：你得做个详细的检查。这是检查单，今天先交费，明天空腹来查吧。

病人家属：大夫，我丈夫特别喜欢吃饼干、喝果汁，这些都会让血糖变高吧？

医生：是的，平时应该少吃含糖的食物。

病人家属：顺便问一下，还有别的需要注意的吗？

医生：等全部检查结果出来以后再说吧。

生词 New words

1. 内分泌科	nèifēnmìkē	*n.*	endocrinology
内分泌	nèifēnmì	*n.*	internal secretion
2. 报告	bàogào	*n.*	report
3. 空腹	kōngfù	*v.*	on an empty stomach
4. 血糖	xuètáng	*n.*	blood sugar
5. 反而	fǎn'ér	*adv.*	instead, on the contrary
6. 详细	xiángxì	*adj.*	detailed
7. 饼干	bǐnggān	*n.*	biscuit
8. 果汁	guǒzhī	*n.*	fruit juice
9. 含	hán	*v.*	to contain
10. 糖	táng	*n.*	sugar
11. 食物	shíwù	*n.*	food
12. 顺便	shùnbiàn	*adv.*	incidentally, passingly
13. 全部	quánbù	*n.*	whole

语言点 Language Points

副词“反而”

副词“反而”表示转折，即后接成分所表达的意思跟前文意思相反或者超出预料。例如：

1. 吃得多，可是体重反而减轻了，力气也不如以前大。
2. 上次考试马大为没有好好儿准备，反而考得不错，真奇怪。
3. 由于经常去公园锻炼，七十岁的爷爷反而比四十岁的爸爸身体还好。

※ 练习：请用副词“反而”完成句子

1. 感冒以后他没有休息，________________________________。
2. 考上大学后我并没有觉得轻松，____________________________。

3. 我每天早上都出门锻炼，以为会变瘦，______________________________。

4. 虽然奶奶年纪大了，______________________________。

综合练习 Comprehensive Exercises

一、根据拼音写汉字

1. bàogào __________　　3. xiángxì __________　　5. shíwù __________

2. shùnbiàn __________　　4. xuètáng __________　　6. guǒzhī __________

二、辨字组词

1. 糖__________　　3. 腹__________

   糕__________　　　复__________

2. 含__________　　4. 详__________

   今__________　　　讲__________

三、选词填空

反而　因此　顺便　偶尔　也许

1. 失眠往往跟压力有关系，（　　）我们要想办法减轻生活压力。

2. 孩子们平时都在大城市里工作和生活，（　　）才能回家看看父母。

3. 我今天来医院拿体检报告，（　　）来看看你。

4. （　　）是因为工作压力太大，最近我总感觉心脏不太舒服。

5. 大夫，我坚持运动了一个星期了，为什么体重（　　）增加了？

四、选出下列词语在句子中的位置

1. A关于B病人的情况，医生C会给你做D的介绍。（详细）
2. A检查结果要B下个星期一才能C出来D。（全部）
3. A经过治疗，我的贫血B不但没C减轻，D越来越严重了。（反而）
4. A大夫，B问一下，我丈夫平时C在饮食上D要注意什么？（顺便）
5. A牛奶中B有很多C营养D。（含）

五、用所给词语完成对话

1. 病人：______________________________。（报告）

   医生：你的空腹血糖有点儿高。

2. 月亮：你是不是一会儿要去超市？能__________________？（顺便）

   朋友：没问题。

3. 留学生：老师，这个巧克力里有酒吗？

   老师：______________________________。（含）

4. 医生：你的体重有变化吗？

   病人：______________________________。（反而）

5. 客人：我刚刚点的菜要少放盐，不加糖。

   服务员：______________________________。（全部）

六、根据课文内容回答问题

1. 医生在病人的体检报告里发现了什么问题？
2. 病人最近身体上有什么症状？
3. 病人什么时候来做详细检查？
4. 哪些食物容易让血糖升高？
5. 医生建议病人平时在饮食上要注意什么？

七、根据课文内容填空

我的体检________出来了，空腹________9.1，挺高的。我最近吃得多，可是体重________减轻了，力气也________以前大。医生让我今天先交费，明天再做个________检查。我平时特别喜欢吃________、喝________，这些都会让血糖________。医生建议我少吃________的食物。

课文（二）
Text（II）

（马大为、王晨在饭店点菜。）

马大为：王东哥什么时候到？

王晨：他下午有个会议，一结束就赶过来，应该不会太晚。

马大为：他知道这家饭店吗？

王晨：我刚才发短信告诉他地址了。

马大为：那咱们看看菜单吧。

王晨：我们点个水煮鱼吧，这家饭店的水煮鱼很有名，又香又辣。

马大为：好。再来一份西红柿炒鸡蛋吧，酸酸甜甜的，特别好吃。

王晨：主食吃什么？

马大为：你是不是又想点饺子？

王晨：你猜错了，这次我想点包子。

马大为：在我看来，包子和饺子除了样子不一样，其他没什么区别。

生词 New words

1. 赶	gǎn	*v.*	to rush for
2. 短信	duǎnxìn	*n.*	text message
3. 地址	dìzhǐ	*n.*	address
4. 菜单	càidān	*n.*	menu
5. 水煮鱼	shuǐzhǔyú	*n.*	Fish Filets in Hot Chili Oil
6. 香	xiāng	*adj.*	appetizing
7. 份	fèn	*m.*	*a measure word for a set of things like meal, gift, newspaper, etc.*
8. 西红柿炒鸡蛋	xīhóngshì chǎo jīdàn	*n.*	Scrambled Egg with Tomato
9. 酸	suān	*adj.*	sour
10. 主食	zhǔshí	*n.*	staple food
11. 饺子	jiǎozi	*n.*	dumpling
12. 猜	cāi	*v.*	to guess
13. 包子	bāozi	*n.*	steamed stuffed bun
14. 样子	yàngzi	*n.*	appearance

语言点 Language Points

固定结构“在……看来”

固定结构“在……看来”中间通常是指人的代词或名词，整个结构常用于句首，后面所接成分表示前者发表的意见或看法。例如：

1. 在我看来，包子和饺子除了样子不一样，其他没什么区别。
2. 在爸爸妈妈看来，医学是很好的专业。
3. 在医生看来，骨质疏松症是中老年人的常见病。

※ 练习：请用固定结构“在……看来”和所给词语完成句子

1. ________________，睡前玩儿游戏不是一个好习惯。（妈妈）

2. ________________，更年期综合征是所有女性都会经历的一个特殊时期。（医生）

3. ________________，这并不是个大手术。（有经验的医生）

4. ________________，汉字很难学。（留学生）

综合练习 Comprehensive Exercises

一、根据拼音写汉字

1. zhǔshí ________
2. duǎnxìn ________
3. xiāng ________
4. dìzhǐ ________
5. cāi ________
6. suān ________

二、辨字组词

1. 酸________
   酒________
2. 猜________
   清________
3. 地________
   址________
4. 赶________
   起________

三、选词填空

香　酸　响　懒　饿

1. 昨晚打雷的声音太（　　）了，我一晚上都没睡好。
2. 你刚洗完头吗？头发怎么这么（　　）！
3. 医生让我空腹做检查，所以我一直没吃饭，这会儿觉得特别（　　）。

4. 自从怀孕以后，我就特别喜欢吃（　　）的东西。

5. 明天我要去医院体检，得早点儿起床，睡不了（　　）觉了。

四、选出下列词语在句子中的位置

1. A 在我 B，你暂时 C 不需要吃药，这些都是更年期 D 女性的常见症状。（看来）

2. A 我的那 B 西红柿炒鸡蛋 C 请不要放 D 糖。（份）

3. A 电影马上就要 B 开始了，C 你什么时候才能 D 过来？（赶）

4. 你 A 对了，B 我终于申请到了 C 国家奖学金 D！（猜）

5. A 看你的 B，昨晚 C 是不是又失眠 D 了？（样子）

五、用所给词语完成对话

1. 妈妈：这次买的苹果味道怎么样？

　女儿：________________________。（酸）

2. 送货员：________________________？（地址）

　客人：东山大学 3 号宿舍楼 401 房间。

3. 客人：________________________。（菜单）

　服务员：前面是我们的特色菜，后面是主食和饮料，您慢慢儿看。

4. 服务员：________________________？（主食）

　客人：请给我来一份饺子。

5. 孙女：________________________。（香）

　爷爷：你喜欢吃，爷爷下次再给你做。

六、根据课文内容回答问题

1. 王东什么时候到饭店？

2. 这家饭店有什么特色菜？

3. 马大为喜欢吃什么菜？

4. 王晨今天点了包子还是饺子？

5. 马大为觉得包子和饺子有什么区别吗？

七、根据课文内容填空

今天我和哥哥、马大为准备一起去外面的饭店吃饭。哥哥下午有个________，结束了以后才能________过来，所以我就先把饭店的________发________告诉他了。这家饭店我以前来过，他们家的________很有名，又________又辣。马大为想点一________西红柿炒鸡蛋，他觉得________甜甜的，特别好吃。马大为以为主食我要点________，但我今天想吃________。在马大为________，包子和饺子除了________不一样，其他没什么区别。

课文（三）
Text（III）

对于糖尿病患者来说，控制血糖的重点是不吃或少吃含糖的食物。因此，有些糖尿病患者会选择无糖食物，比如无糖饼干。其实，无糖饼干是含有淀粉的，食用太多的淀粉也会让血糖升高。并且，像普通饼干一样，无糖饼干也含有盐、油等，这些物质同样不利于控制血糖。所以，糖尿病患者在选择和食用无糖食物时，一定要进行控制。

生词 New words

1. 糖尿病	tángniàobìng	*n.*	diabetes
2. 控制	kòngzhì	*v.*	to control
3. 重点	zhòngdiǎn	*n.*	key point
4. 无	wú	*v.*	to not have, to be without
5. 含有	hányǒu	*v.*	to contain
6. 淀粉	diànfěn	*n.*	starch
7. 食用	shíyòng	*v.*	to eat
8. 升高	shēnggāo	*VC*	to rise
9. 油	yóu	*n.*	oil
10. 物质	wùzhì	*n.*	substance
11. 同样	tóngyàng	*adj./conj.*	same; in the same way
12. 不利于	búlì yú		adverse to
不利	búlì	*adj.*	unfavorable
于	yú	*prep.*	to, for

语言点 Language Points

一、固定结构“像……一样”

固定结构“像……一样”表示两种事物、感情、关系之间具有相同点，可以做等同比较。二者之间的相同点往往出现在其后接成分中。例如：

1. 像普通饼干一样，无糖饼干也含有盐、油等物质。
2. 像老年性耳背一样，阿尔茨海默病也一般多见于老年人。
3. 老师对我们像家人一样。

※ 练习：请用固定结构“像……一样”和所给词语完成句子

1. 美丽是我最好的朋友，______________________________。（姐妹）
2. 李护士对病人很有耐心，______________________________。（家人）

3. 我的宿舍又干净又舒服，________________。（家里）

4. 你的中文歌唱得太好了，________________。（中国人）

二、介词“于”

介词“于”后面可以引出对象、时间或处所。“有利于”是“对……有好处”，“不利于”是“对……有坏处”。例如：

1. 无糖饼干也含有盐、油等，这些物质同样不利于控制血糖。

2. 多吃水果有利于身体健康。

3. 喝酒、抽烟都不利于身体健康。

※ 练习：请用“有利于/不利于”完成句子

1. 不要太晚睡觉，________________。

2. 在中国，很多老人每天早上都去公园运动，________________。

3. 我从来不抽烟，________________。

4. 妈妈不让孩子玩儿电脑游戏，________________。

综合练习 Comprehensive Exercises

一、根据拼音写汉字

1. wùzhì ________　3. shíyòng ________　5. zhòngdiǎn ________

2. búlì ________　4. kòngzhì ________　6. shēnggāo ________

二、辨字组词

1. 升________　3. 淀________

介________　定________

2. 粉________　　　　4. 于________

份________　　　　　干________

三、选词填空

改变　吸引　无　控制　升高

1. 治疗糖尿病的关键是（　　）血糖。
2. 医生说我除了按时吃药，定期检查，还得（　　）饮食习惯。
3. 昨晚失眠，今天早上一检查，血压又（　　）了。
4. 你放心喝，这是（　　）糖饮料，不会影响健康的。
5. 观众都被她的演奏（　　）住了。

四、选出下列词语在句子中的位置

1. A 定期 B 体检 C 有利 D 身体健康。（于）
2. A 这件衣服 B 洗完 C 以后像新的 D。（一样）
3. A 食用太油、太甜、太辣、太咸 B 的食物对 C 身体健康 D。（不利）
4. A 水果 B 中含有 C 很多对人身体有益的 D。（物质）
5. A 医生说 B 下面的治疗 C 是控制 D 血糖。（重点）

五、用所给词语完成对话

1. 病人：为什么食用无糖食物也要控制？

   医生：________________________。（不利于）

2. 妈妈：听说你认识了很多新朋友？

   马大为：________________________。（像……一样）

3. 月亮：我想点一份西红柿炒鸡蛋。

朋友：________________________________。（不如）

4. 医生：________________________________。（有利于）

病人：那我以后每天都喝一杯牛奶。

5. 病人：大夫，这是我的体检报告，血糖 9.1，是不是高了？

医生：________________________________。（控制）

六、根据课文内容回答问题

1. 控制血糖的重点是什么？
2. 对于糖尿病患者来说，无糖食物可以随便吃吗？为什么？
3. 无糖饼干里含有哪些物质？
4. 无糖饼干中的盐、油对于控制血糖有什么影响？
5. 糖尿病患者在饮食中要注意哪些方面？

七、根据课文内容填空

对于________患者来说，________血糖的________是不吃或少吃________的食物。因此，有些糖尿病患者会选择________食物，比如无糖________。________，无糖饼干是含有________的，________太多的淀粉也会让血糖________。并且，________普通饼干________，无糖饼干也含有________、________等，这些________同样________控制血糖。所以，糖尿病患者在选择和食用无糖食物时，一定要进行________。

语言任务 Language Tasks

一、阅读理解

糖尿病是一种以高血糖为特征的代谢性疾病。很多人分不清糖尿病和高血糖有什么区别，于是根据血糖的高低判断自己是否患有糖尿病。

糖尿病是胰岛功能减退导致的代谢紊乱。除了血糖高之外，它还有其他特征，是一种比较明确的疾病状态，而且目前没有办法完全治愈。但高血糖则不一样，血糖本身就是一直在变化的。当我们摄入过多糖分时，血糖会较快地升高，促使胰腺在短时间内分泌大量胰岛素。长期高糖饮食会导致胰腺疲劳或功能衰退，使其无法及时调节血糖，进而形成高血糖状态。但如果注意饮食并加强锻炼，高血糖是完全可以控制的。

发现自己血糖过高，我们应先去医院做相关检查，然后根据情况进行治疗，而不是盲目地认定自己得了糖尿病。即使得了糖尿病，我们一样可以通过控制好血糖恢复正常生活。

补充词汇

1. 特征	tèzhēng	*n.*	characteristic, feature
2. 代谢性	dàixièxìng	*n.*	metabolic
3. 分清	fēnqīng	*v.*	to draw a clear distinction between
4. 胰岛	yídǎo	*n.*	pancreatic islet
5. 代谢紊乱	dàixiè wěnluàn		metabolic disorder
6. 明确	míngquè	*adj.*	clear and definite
7. 目前	mùqián	*n.*	at present
8. 治愈	zhìyù	*VC*	to cure
9. 本身	běnshēn	*pron.*	oneself, itself
10. 过多	guò duō	*AP*	too much, too many
过	guò	*adv.*	too, very

11. 糖分	tángfèn	*n.*	sugar
12. 促使	cùshǐ	*v.*	to impel
13. 胰腺	yíxiàn	*n.*	pancreas
14. 大量	dàliàng	*adj.*	a large number
15. 胰岛素	yídǎosù	*n.*	insulin
16. 疲劳	píláo	*adj.*	tired
17. 衰退	shuāituì	*v.*	to decline
18. 调节	tiáojié	*v.*	to adjust
19. 进而	jìn'ér	*conj.*	and then
20. 相关	xiāngguān	*v.*	to be bound up with
21. 盲目	mángmù	*adj.*	blind
22. 认定	rèndìng	*v.*	to firmly believe

回答问题

1. 糖尿病和高血糖是同一种病吗？它们之间是什么关系？
2. 如何区分糖尿病和高血糖？
3. 如果发现血糖过高，正确的做法是什么？

二、口头表达

任务名称：给住院的糖尿病病人订餐。

任务背景：病人因为糖尿病正在医院住院治疗。午饭时间到了，病人家属需要给病人订餐，事先询问病人在饮食上的喜好及注意事项。

任务要求：1. 两个学生一组，一个扮演病人，一个扮演病人家属。

2. 病人家属询问病人午饭想吃什么。

3. 病人描述自己的饮食喜好，并转述医生交代的饮食注意事项。

参考语言：不利　控制　血糖　重点　在……看来　像……一样　不利于　主食　份　含　反而

三、书面表达

任务名称：我最喜欢的一道菜。

任务要求：请介绍自己最喜欢的一道菜（包括名称、口味、所需材料、在哪里能吃到等），要求200字以上。

参考语言：酸　甜　辣　油　淀粉　含　糖　物质　在……看来　样子

第十二课 Lesson 12 孩子是不是有孤独症？

学习目标 Learning Objectives

1. 语言功能：能够对文章的主要内容进行概括并做出评价。
2. 语言点：固定结构“连……都/也……，更不用说……”、结构助词“地”、量词“遍”、方位名词“其中”、介词“由”（3）。
3. 医学知识：初步了解孤独症的表现和病因。
4. 社会文化：了解中国特殊教育的发展。

热身活动 Warm-up

1. 你看过下面这部电影吗？这部电影讲了一个什么故事？

2. 你认为孤独症群体应该如何适应社会？

课文（一）
Text（Ⅰ）

（父母带着孩子在儿童医院看病。）

医生：孩子怎么了？

孩子母亲：大夫，我家孩子快三岁了，可是不爱动，不爱笑，很害羞。

医生：孩子会说话吗？

孩子母亲：会说话，但是说得不多。

医生：喜欢跟小朋友玩儿吗？

孩子母亲：连我们跟他玩儿，他都常常拒绝，更不用说小朋友了。

孩子父亲：他只喜欢跟自己玩儿，最喜欢的游戏就是不停地给玩具排队，每次排列的顺序必须完全一样。

医生：他能跟你们正常对话吗？

孩子父亲：他不喜欢跟我们交流。我在网上看到一篇文章，说孤独症会有这样的表现。这不会是孤独症吧？

医生：你们别着急，先给孩子做个全面检查吧。

生词 New words

1. 动	dòng	*v.*	to move, to act
2. 害羞	hàixiū	*v.*	to be shy
3. 拒绝	jùjué	*v.*	to refuse, to reject
4. 不停	bù tíng	*VP*	to not stop
停	tíng	*v.*	to stop
5. 地	de	*part.*	*used after a word or phrase to modify the predicate*
6. 排队	páiduì	*v.*	to queue up
7. 排列	páiliè	*v.*	to arrange
8. 顺序	shùnxù	*n.*	order, sequence
9. 对话	duìhuà	*v.*	to have a dialogue
10. 篇	piān	*m.*	*a measure word for papers*
11. 文章	wénzhāng	*n.*	article, essay
12. 孤独症	gūdúzhèng	*n.*	autism
13. 全面	quánmiàn	*adj.*	overall

语言点 Language Points

一、固定结构"连……都/也……，更不用说……"

固定结构"连……都/也……，更不用说……"连接表递进关系的分句，有强调的意味。"连"后面可以带名词、动词、数量短语或小句，常与副词"都、也"合用，"更不用说……"有时可以省略。例如：

1. 连我们跟他玩儿，他都常常拒绝，更不用说小朋友了。
2. 这个字连中国人都不认识，更不用说留学生了。
3. 老王有糖尿病，连无糖饼干也不能吃，更不用说巧克力了。

※ 练习：请用固定结构“连……都/也……，更不用说……”完成对话

1. A：你去过哈尔滨吗？

   B：______________________________。（北京）

2. A：你经常去看电影吗？

   B：我工作太忙了，______________________________。（吃饭）

3. A：你平时都自己做饭吗？

   B：______________________________。（周末）

4. A：你血糖有点儿高，平时尽量不要喝果汁。

   B：我知道，______________________________。（水果）

二、结构助词“地”

结构助词“地”常用在动词性成分之前、状语之后，表示动作行为的状态或方式。例如：

1. 他最喜欢的游戏就是不停地给玩具排队。
2. 妈妈每天从早到晚不停地忙。
3. 这次考试非常重要，我们要认真地准备。

※ 练习：请用结构助词“的”“得”“地”填空

1. 听到我说的话，奶奶高兴____________笑了。
2. 张医生总是耐心____________听病人说话。
3. 这次考试我准备____________很充分。
4. 你____________血糖太高了，最近一定要严格控制饮食。

综合练习 Comprehensive Exercises

一、根据拼音写汉字

1. wénzhāng ________　　3. quánmiàn ________　　5. duìhuà ________

2. páiduì ________　　4. jùjué ________　　6. shùnxù ________

二、辨字组词

1. 篇________　　3. 羞________

　第________　　　差________

2. 章________　　4. 停________

　音________　　　得________

三、选词填空

动　拒绝　停　排队　排列

1. 为了方便老年人看病，医院新开了一个老年人（　　）窗口。
2. 我睡前喝了太多水，晚上不（　　）地去洗手间，影响了睡眠质量。
3. 病人（　　）做手术，坚持要吃药治疗。
4. CT 显示你的手部骨折，你先不要（　　），医生马上就给你治疗。
5. 请将下面的词语按照正确的顺序（　　）。

四、选出下列词语在句子中的位置

1. A 病人经常 B 接触的生活用品 C 每天都要进行 D 消毒。　（全面）
2. A 医生说我除了吃 B 药以外 C，还得不停 D 喝水。　（地）

3. A 爷爷得了阿尔茨海默病后，B 自己的亲人 C 都不认识了，D 更不用说邻居了。（连）

4. A 我最近 B 在 C 医学杂志上看了很多 D 文章。（篇）

5. 不要 A，你得把自己的病情 B 详细地 C 跟医生 D 说一说。（害羞）

五、用所给词语完成对话

1. 艺文：周末来医院看病的人太多了。

   王东：________________________。（连……都/也……，更不用说……）

2. 月亮：你觉得这条黄色的裙子怎么样？

   朋友：好看是好看，______________________________。（可是）

3. 病人：大夫，出院以后我还需要来复查吗？

   医生：______________________________。（地）

4. 家长：孩子现在学习太紧张了，每天 12 点以后才能睡觉。

   老师：______________________________。（不利于）

5. 王晨：你觉得南方的冬天和北方的有什么不一样？

   朋友：______________________________。（受不了）

六、根据课文内容回答问题

1. 孩子怎么了？
2. 孩子喜欢跟小朋友玩儿吗？
3. 孩子喜欢做什么游戏？
4. 孩子父亲担心什么？
5. 医生确定孩子得了孤独症吗？

七、根据课文内容填空

我的孩子快三岁了，可是不爱________，不爱笑，很________。平时话说得不多，也不喜欢跟小朋友玩儿，________我们跟他玩儿，他都常常________。他只喜欢跟自己玩儿，最喜欢的游戏就是________地给玩具________，每次________的顺序必须完全一样。孩子父亲在网上看到一________文章，说________会有这样的表现，他很担心。医生让我们别着急，先给孩子做个________检查。

课文（二）
Text（II）

（同学们在聊天儿。）

李真：美丽，你在看什么书？

美丽：《草房子》，你看过吗？

李真：我至少看过三遍了。这部小说很有名，作者是一位著名作家。

金龙：这本书没有英文翻译，你能看懂吗？

美丽：虽然很多句子很长，语法也很难，但是故事的主要内容我差不多能看懂。

金龙：遇到不懂的词语，你怎么办？

美丽：查词典。不过，查词典会影响阅读的速度。我看了一个多星期了，才看了三十多页。

李真：小说中的哪个人物给你留下的印象最深？

美丽：其中有一个总是戴着帽子的孩子，他给我留下的印象最深。

李真：这部小说很让人感动，越读越有意思。

生词 New words

1. 遍	biàn	*m.*	*a measure word denoting an action from beginning to end*
2. 小说	xiǎoshuō	*n.*	novel
3. 作者	zuòzhě	*n.*	author
4. 著名	zhùmíng	*adj.*	famous
5. 作家	zuòjiā	*n.*	writer
6. 翻译	fānyì	*n./v.*	translation; to translate
7. 句子	jùzi	*n.*	sentence
8. 语法	yǔfǎ	*n.*	grammar
9. 故事	gùshi	*n.*	story
10. 词语	cíyǔ	*n.*	word
11. 词典	cídiǎn	*n.*	dictionary
12. 页	yè	*m.*	page
13. 人物	rénwù	*n.*	figure, character
14. 其中	qízhōng	*n.*	among
15. 帽子	màozi	*n.*	cap, hat
16. 感动	gǎndòng	*adj./v.*	moved; to be moved

专名 Proper nouns

1.《草房子》	Cǎo Fángzi	*The Grass House*, a novel written by Cao Wenxuan
2. 英文	Yīngwén	English (language)

语言点 Language Points

一、量词"遍"

量词"遍"表示某个动作行为从开始到结束的整个过程。例如：

1. 这本书我至少看过三遍了。
2. 这部电影我都看了两三遍了。

3. 你唱得太好听了，再唱一遍吧！

※ 练习：请用量词“遍”和所给词语完成句子

1. 这件事儿很重要，老师________________。（说）
2. 这部电影太好看了，我想________________。（看）
3. 我忘记刚才医生说什么了，我再去________________。（问）
4. 学习汉字，你一定要多________________。（写）

二、方位名词“其中”

方位名词“其中”即“那里面”，指范围或处所。例如：

1.《草房子》里有很多人物，其中有一个总是戴着帽子的孩子，他给我留下的印象最深。
2. 医学院有五百多个学生，其中十分之一是留学生。
3. 我去过中国的很多城市，其中最喜欢的就是北京。

※ 练习：请用方位名词“其中”和所给词语完成句子

1. 不良的用眼习惯容易导致近视，________________。（电子游戏）
2. 很多疾病都与肥胖有关，________________。（高血压）
3. 月亮感兴趣的事情有很多，________________。（旅游）
4. 我们这个学期有很多课，________________。（外科学）

综合练习 Comprehensive Exercises

一、根据拼音写汉字

1. gǎndòng ________　　3. cíyǔ ________　　5. zuòzhě ________
2. rénwù ________　　4. xiǎoshuō ________　　6. qízhōng ________

二、辨字组词

1. 帽________　　3. 典________
   冒________　　 共________
2. 页________　　4. 译________
   贵________　　 详________

三、选词填空

翻译　其中　著名　页　感动

1. 这台自动体外除颤器是在国外买的，说明书没有中文(　　)，我看不懂。
2. 这篇文章的作者是来自东山医院的(　　)医生刘文。
3. 李医生治病救人的故事让人听了非常(　　)。
4. 医生开了三种药，(　　)一种一定要饭前吃。
5. 关于预防糖尿病的内容，在这本书的第 18 (　　)。

四、选出下列词语在句子中的位置

1. 这本书 A 一共 B 只有一百多 C，我一下午就看完 D 了。　(页)
2. A 患者接触过的 B 用品已经 C 消过两 D 毒了。　(遍)
3. A 流感和普通感冒 B 都有传染性，C 流感的 D 传染性更强。　(其中)
4. A 我被 B 医生和护士们的 C 工作热情所 D。　(感动)
5. A 椅子上的 B 那个 C 是不是 D 你的？　(帽子)

五、用所给词语完成对话

1. 邻居：________________________。(翻译)
   艺文：这是您儿子从国外给您带的营养品。

2. 病人：每天在病房里躺着实在太无聊了！

朋友：______________________________。（小说）

3. 大为：下周的考试你复习得怎么样了？书看完了吗？

同学：______________________________。（遍）

4. 美丽：你包里装了什么东西？这么重！

朋友：______________________________。（其中）

5. 学生：老师，您看看这个句子我写得对不对。

老师：______________________________。（语法）

六、根据课文内容回答问题

1. 李真看过《草房子》这部小说吗？
2. 没有翻译，美丽能看懂这部小说吗？
3. 遇到不懂的词语，美丽有什么办法？
4. 这部小说中谁给美丽留下了最深的印象？
5. 李真喜欢这部小说吗？

七、根据课文内容填空

我最近在看一部________，叫《草房子》，作者是一位著名________。李真说她也看过，而且看了至少________了。这部小说没有英文________，很多句子很长，________也很难，但是故事的主要内容我________能看懂。________不懂的词语，我就查________。不过，这会影响阅读的速度。一个多星期过去了，我才看了三十多________。这部小说中有一个________给我留下的印象最深，他是一个总是戴着________的孩子。这是一部很让人________的小说，越读越有意思。

课文（三）
Text（III）

《海洋天堂》这部电影讲了一位父亲和他孤独症儿子的故事。父亲是海洋馆的工作人员，每天由早到晚地工作，还要照顾孩子，非常辛苦。更不幸的是，父亲得了重病，剩下的时间已经不多了，于是想办法教儿子独立生活。电影中的亲情和友谊让观众非常感动。著名演员李连杰是这部电影的主演。李连杰的功夫电影很有名，在亲情电影《海洋天堂》里，他的表演也同样精彩。

生词 New words

1. 海洋馆	hǎiyángguǎn	*n.*	aquarium
2. 不幸	búxìng	*adj.*	unfortunate
3. 剩下	shèngxia	*VC*	to be left over
4. 独立	dúlì	*v.*	to be independent
5. 亲情	qīnqíng	*n.*	kinship
6. 友谊	yǒuyì	*n.*	friendship
7. 演员	yǎnyuán	*n.*	actor, actress
8. 主演	zhǔyǎn	*n.*	leading actor, leading actress
9. 功夫	gōngfu	*n.*	kung fu
10. 表演	biǎoyǎn	*n./v.*	performance; to perform
11. 精彩	jīngcǎi	*adj.*	wonderful, splendid

专名 Proper nouns

1.《海洋天堂》	Hǎiyáng Tiāntáng	*Ocean Heaven*, name of a film
2. 李连杰	Lǐ Liánjié	Jet Li

语言点 Language Points

介词"由"（3）

介词"由"可以表示时间或空间的起点或者经过的路线、场所。例如：

1. 父亲是海洋馆的工作人员，每天由早到晚地工作，还要照顾孩子，非常辛苦。
2. 我们这次旅行，由哈尔滨出发，一路向南，最后到三亚。
3. 由东往西走，大概500米就到了。

※ 练习：请用介词“由”和所给词语完成句子

1. A：听说你们暑假去旅行了？都去了哪些地方？

   B：________________________________。（上海）

2. A：这个公园有两个门，我们从哪儿进去呢？

   B：________________________________。（东门）

3. A：请问今年国庆节放假几天？

   B：________________________________。（10 月 1 日）

4. A：护士您好，请问洗手间在哪儿？

   B：________________________________。（医生办公室）

综合练习 Comprehensive Exercises

一、根据拼音写汉字

1. dúlì __________　　3. biǎoyǎn __________　　5. qīnqíng __________

2. yǒuyì __________　　4. jīngcǎi __________　　6. búxìng __________

二、辨字组词

1. 独__________　　3. 演__________

   猫__________　　油__________

2. 谊__________　　4. 彩__________

   姐__________　　采__________

三、选词填空

精彩　独立　不幸　稳定　安静

1. 手术后，病人的情况暂时比较（　　），不用担心。
2. 病人正在手术，请家属在手术室外保持（　　）。
3. 孩子还太小，家长不放心他一个人（　　）生活。
4. 观众被演员（　　）的表演吸引住了。
5. （　　）的是，患者的伤口感染了。

四、选出下列词语在句子中的位置

1. A 北京到上海 B 的高铁 C 每天都有 D 很多趟。（由）
2. A 在医院的病房里 B，每天都在发生着 C 各种各样的 D。（故事）
3. A 医生告诉他 B 平时要注意营养均衡，C 他开始学习自己 D 做饭。（于是）
4. A 病情严重的时候，她 B 连床都起不来，C 不用说 D 去上班了。（更）
5. A 医生和病人 B 有着 C 的目标——D 让病人/自己早日康复。（同样）

五、用所给词语完成对话

1. 朋友：你觉得今晚演员的表演怎么样？
   佳乐：________________________。（精彩）
2. 朋友：开车的话应该从医院哪个门进呀？
   艺文：________________________。（由）
3. 朋友：你回国以后别忘了经常跟我联系。
   月亮：________________________。（友谊）

4. 朋友：去医院体检得注意什么？

王东：________________________________。（要……还要……）

5. 朋友：你觉得这一年的留学经历怎么样？

大为：________________________________。（独立）

六、根据课文内容回答问题

1.《海洋天堂》是一部关于什么的电影？

2. 李连杰在这部电影中演的是谁？

3. 电影中的一家人遇到了什么不幸的事儿？

4. 李连杰在里面表演得怎么样？

5. 观众喜欢这部电影吗？为什么？

七、根据课文内容填空

《海洋天堂》这________电影讲了一位父亲和他孤独症儿子的________。父亲是________的工作人员，每天________到晚地工作，还要照顾孩子，非常辛苦。更________的是，父亲________重病，________的时间已经不多了，于是想办法教儿子________生活。电影中的________和________让观众非常________。著名演员李连杰是这部电影的________。李连杰的________电影很有名，在亲情电影《海洋天堂》里，他的________也同样________。

语言任务 Language Tasks

一、阅读理解

在普通人看来，孤独症就是自我封闭，因此很多家长发现孩子突然把自己关在房间里不出来，就怀疑孩子是不是得了孤独症。实际上，孤独症多在婴幼儿时期起病，主要表现为不同程度的社会交往障碍、语言发育障碍、兴趣狭窄和行为方式刻板。其中，75%—80% 的患者伴有不同程度的智力障碍。

孤独症的病因及发病机制暂不明确。多年研究表明，孤独症与遗传因素有密切关系；儿童大脑的器质性损害、结构异常，母亲孕龄高、先兆流产、抽烟、情绪刺激等各种不利因素，以及孩子出生时缺氧、难产、早产等都与孤独症发病有一定关系。由此我们可以看出，孤独症是一种遗传因素与环境因素相互作用导致的疾病。

来源：有来医生《自闭症是如何造成的》《什么叫自闭症》

补充词汇

1. 自我	zìwǒ	*pron.*	ego
2. 封闭	fēngbì	*v.*	to seal off
3. 起病	qǐbìng	*v.*	to begin, to start
4. 程度	chéngdù	*n.*	degree, level
5. 交往	jiāowǎng	*v.*	to contact
6. 行为	xíngwéi	*n.*	behavior
7. 刻板	kèbǎn	*adj.*	stereotyped
8. 伴有	bànyǒu	*v.*	to be accompanied by
9. 智力	zhìlì	*n.*	intelligence
10. 病因	bìngyīn	*n.*	cause of disease
11. 机制	jīzhì	*n.*	framework
12. 表明	biǎomíng	*v.*	to make known, to indicate

13. 器质性损害	qìzhìxìng sǔnhài		organic lesion
14. 结构	jiégòu	*n.*	structure
15. 异常	yìcháng	*adj.*	abnormal
16. 孕龄	yùnlíng	*n.*	gestational age
17. 先兆流产	xiānzhào liúchǎn	*VP*	to have a threatened miscarriage
18. 缺氧	quē yǎng	*VO*	to lack oxygen
19. 难产	nánchǎn	*v.*	to have a difficult labor
20. 早产	zǎochǎn	*v.*	to have a premature labor
21. 相互	xiānghù	*adv.*	mutually

回答问题

1. 孤独症多在什么时期起病？
2. 孤独症有哪些表现？
3. 研究表明，孤独症的发病原因有哪些？

二、口头表达

任务名称：我身边的好医生/好医院。

任务背景：向自己身边的朋友推荐你熟悉的医院和医生，包括介绍医院的位置、环境、医生的专业能力、护士的服务态度，讲述自己曾经的就诊经历。

任务要求：1. 两个学生一组，二人互为朋友，互相询问彼此最近的身体状况。

2. 向朋友推荐自己熟悉的医院和医生，并介绍医院和医生的详细信息。

3. 说明推荐原因并对医院和医生做出评价。

4. 讲述自己曾经的就诊经历。

参考语言：由　其中　独立　感动　遍　著名　全面　排队　拒绝

连……都/也……，更不用说……　地

三、书面表达

任务名称：我最喜欢的演员。

任务要求：请介绍自己最喜欢的演员(包括国籍、年龄、外貌、影视作品、喜爱的原因，并做出评价)，要求200字以上。

参考语言：个子　体重　千克　头发　眼睛　鼻子　耳朵　嘴巴　性格　表演　主演　精彩　遍　演员

第十三课 Lesson 13 孩子手背烫伤了

学习目标 Learning Objectives

1. 语言功能：能够对出行准备做出安排，能够对操作步骤进行讲解。
2. 语言点：连词“结果”、指示代词“另”、固定结构“首先……然后……最后……”、连词“以”。
3. 医学知识：初步了解烧伤、烫伤的处理办法。

热身活动 Warm-up

1. 你知道怎样处理烧伤、烫伤吗？

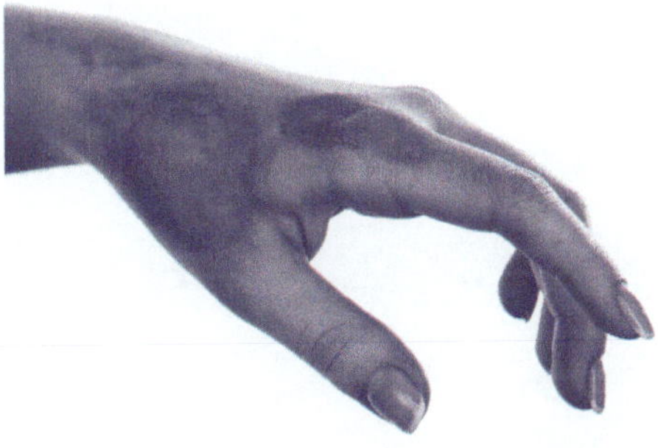

2. 旅行前，我们通常要做哪些准备？

课文（一）
Text（Ⅰ）

（奶奶和妈妈带孩子在烧伤科门诊看病。）

孩子妈妈：大夫，您快看看，刚才孩子手背烫伤了。

医生：除了手背，还有其他地方烫伤吗？

孩子妈妈：没有。

医生：是怎么烫的？

孩子奶奶：我正关火的时候，孩子拉我的胳膊，我一不小心碰倒了热水瓶，结果把孩子双手烫伤了。我实在是太粗心了！

孩子妈妈：妈，您不是故意的，别责备自己了。

孩子奶奶：孩子伤得这么严重，我不能原谅我自己。

医生：您不用太紧张，孩子的烫伤不严重。

孩子妈妈：大夫，需要打针吗？

医生：虽然烫伤不严重，但是为了预防感染，还得打几天针。

生词 New words

1. 烧伤科	shāoshāngkē	*n.*	Department of Burn
2. 手背	shǒubèi	*n.*	back of the hand
3. 烫	tàng	*v./adj.*	to scald, to burn; very hot
4. 火	huǒ	*n.*	fire
5. 拉	lā	*v.*	to pull
6. 倒	dǎo	*v.*	to fall
7. 热水瓶	rèshuǐpíng	*n.*	thermos (bottle)
8. 结果	jiéguǒ	*conj.*	as a result
9. 双	shuāng	*adj./m.*	dual, twin; pair
10. 粗心	cūxīn	*adj.*	careless
11. 故意	gùyì	*adv.*	deliberately
12. 责备	zébèi	*v.*	to blame
13. 原谅	yuánliàng	*v.*	to forgive

语言点 Language Points

连词"结果"

连词"结果"常用在下半句，表示在某种条件或情况下产生了某种结局。例如：

1. 我正关火的时候，孩子拉我的胳膊，我一不小心碰倒了热水瓶，结果把孩子双手烫伤了。
2. 我们周末去爬山的时候突然下雨了，我们都没带伞，结果都感冒了。
3. 上次考试马大为没有好好儿复习，结果考得很差，没有通过。

※ 练习：请用连词"结果"完成句子

1. 早上九点的飞机，我们八点多才出发，________________。
2. 上个星期我就开始牙疼，但一直没去看医生，________________。
3. 踢足球的时候他摔倒了，开始以为不严重，________________。
4. 妈妈血糖一直很高，她也没重视，________________。

综合练习 Comprehensive Exercises

一、根据拼音写汉字

1. gùyì ________
2. jiéguǒ ________
3. shuāng ________
4. cūxīn ________
5. zébèi ________
6. dǎo ________

二、辨字组词

1. 谅________
   凉________
2. 粗________
   姐________
3. 责________
   贵________
4. 烫________
   汤________

三、选词填空

烫　拉　倒　责备　原谅

1. 虽然考试没考好，但他已经做了最大的努力，你不要（　　）他了。
2. 小孩子过马路的时候一定要（　　）着爸爸妈妈的手。
3. 我拿热水瓶的时候不小心把手（　　）伤了。
4. 他做错了事情却不道歉，我怎么可能（　　）他呢？
5. 大夫，我踢足球的时候不小心摔（　　），把腿摔骨折了。

四、选出下列词语在句子中的位置

1. A 我看到 B 她的 C 手在电脑 D 上敲来敲去。（双）
2. A 今天路上 B 大堵车，C 我上班迟到了 D 二十分钟。（结果）

3. A 我不是 B 把你 C 生病的事情告诉 D 别人的。（故意）

4. A 考试的时候要冷静 B，多看几遍题，别 C 像以前那么 D 了。（粗心）

5. A 病人的父母 B 病人的丈夫 C 没有及时 D 打 120。（责备）

五、用所给词语完成对话

1. 艺文：孩子怎么突然发烧了？

   王东：____________________________。（结果）

2. 月亮：你的体检结果出来了吗？怎么样？

   朋友：____________________________。（跟……相比）

3. 病人家属：大夫，我丈夫做完手术后就能下床走路吗？

   医生：____________________________。（倒）

4. 王晨：哥，我不小心把你的电脑弄坏了，我错了。

   王东：____________________________。（原谅）

5. 王晨：你的手背怎么了？

   朋友：____________________________。（烫）

六、根据课文内容回答问题

1. 孩子哪里烫伤了？
2. 孩子是怎么烫伤的？
3. 孩子的奶奶为什么责备自己？
4. 孩子的烫伤严重吗？
5. 医生打算怎么给孩子治疗？

七、根据课文内容填空

孩子今天在家不小心把________烫伤了，原来孩子奶奶在________的时候，孩子________她的胳膊，她一不小心碰________了热水瓶，________把孩子双手烫伤了。孩子奶奶一直在________自己，认为是自己太________了。医生检查了孩子的伤口说烫伤并不________，但为了________感染，还得打几天针。

课文（二）
Text（II）

（王东一家要去旅行，他们正在收拾行李。）

王东：出去玩儿两天，不需要带两个行李箱吧？

艺文：一个行李箱是我们的，另一个是高兴的。孩子需要的东西，再多也得带。

王东：勺子和筷子也要带吗？饭店里都有，也很卫生。

艺文：饭店里的虽然不脏，但是不一定适合小孩子用。

王东：宾馆提供牙膏、牙刷和毛巾，咱们就不用带了吧？

艺文：刷牙、洗脸的东西，我还是习惯用自己的。

王东：导游提醒要带着雨伞，你带了吗？

艺文：已经放在我们的行李箱里了。对了，还带照相机吗？

王东：当然要带了。手机照相虽然很方便，但还是不如照相机。

艺文：行李箱里已经没地方了，你自己背着吧。

王东：没问题。

生词 New words

1. 行李	xíngli	*n.*	luggage, baggage
2. 行李箱	xínglixiāng	*n.*	suitcase
3. 另	lìng	*pron.*	another
4. 脏	zāng	*adj.*	dirty
5. 宾馆	bīnguǎn	*n.*	hotel
6. 牙膏	yágāo	*n.*	toothpaste
7. 牙刷	yáshuā	*n.*	toothbrush
8. 刷牙	shuā yá	*VO*	to brush one's teeth
9. 洗脸	xǐ liǎn	*VO*	to wash one's face
洗	xǐ	*v.*	to wash
10. 导游	dǎoyóu	*n.*	tourist guide
11. 雨伞	yǔsǎn	*n.*	umbrella
12. 照相机	zhàoxiàngjī	*n.*	camera
照相	zhàoxiàng	*v.*	to take a photo
13. 背	bēi	*v.*	to carry on the back

语言点 Language Points

指示代词“另”

指示代词“另”指上文所说之外的人或事物，后面经常带数量短语。例如：

1. 一个行李箱是我们的，另一个是高兴的。

2. 这件白大褂是我的，另一件是马大为的。

3. 明天我们有两门考试，一门是数学，另一门是汉语。

“另”还可以做副词，指上文所说的范围之外。例如：

4. 这个手机你不喜欢，我再另给你买一个。

5. 去年冬天我们去了三亚，今年咱们另去一个地方。

※ 练习：请用“另”完成句子

1. 马大为有两个好朋友，一个是王晨，________________。

2. 我有两双运动鞋，一双是白色的，________________。

3. 左边的房间是我的，________________。

4. 对不起，明天下午我没有空儿，________________。

综合练习 Comprehensive Exercises

一、根据拼音写汉字

1. yǔsǎn ________　　3. xíngli ________　　5. dǎoyóu ________

2. yáshuā ________　　4. bīnguǎn ________　　6. zhàoxiàngjī ________

二、辨字组词

1. 伞________　　3. 刷________

　 苹________　　 到________

2. 导________　　4. 膏________

　 易________　　 高________

三、选词填空

洗　关　抬　背　刷牙

1. 昨天忙了一天，今天累得胳膊都（　　）不起来了。

2. 孩子腿受伤了，爸爸只好（　　）着他去医院。

3. 牙医提醒我每次吃完东西后都得（　　）。

4. 太晚了，等我赶到的时候，药店已经（　　）门了。

5. 为了避免传染，病人接触的用品我都已经消毒并（　　）干净了。

四、选出下列词语在句子中的位置

1. A 她不在这间病房，B 你去 C 一间病房 D 看看吧。（另）
2. A 这家宾馆的 B 卫生情况不太好，沙发看上去 C 有点儿 D。（脏）
3. A 父亲去旅游的时候总是背着一台 B，走到 C 哪儿拍到哪儿 D。（照相机）
4. A 一定要 B 保持伤口的 C，以避免 D 感染。（卫生）
5. A 别忘了 B 我两个星期以后 C 去医院 D 复查。（提醒）

五、用所给词语完成对话

1. 医生：伤口怎么样？还疼吗？

   病人：这个伤口已经不疼了，____________________________。（另）

2. 艺文：东西这么多，怎么拿呀？

   王东：____________________________。（背）

3. 月亮：美丽，你的牙看起来又白又健康，你平时是怎么保护的？

   美丽：____________________________。（刷牙、洗牙）

4. 美丽：这件白大褂是谁的？怎么放在桌子上了？

   朋友：____________________________。（粗心）

5. 护士：请不要随便按呼叫铃。

   病人：____________________________。（故意）

六、根据课文内容回答问题

1. 王东和艺文打算做什么？
2. 艺文为什么要带两个行李箱？

3. 艺文为什么不想用宾馆提供的用品？

4. 导游提醒他们要带什么？

5. 王东为什么要带照相机？

七、根据课文内容填空

我和艺文打算出去玩儿两天。艺文收拾了两个________，一个是我们的，________是高兴的。孩子吃饭时用的________和________艺文都带了，她说饭店里的虽然不________，但是不一定适合________用。宾馆会提供的________、________和毛巾她也带了，因为她还是________用自己的。导游提醒要带的________，艺文也已经放在我们那个________里了。行李箱里放了这么多东西，已经没有地方放我的________了，于是艺文让我自己________着。

课文（三）
Text（III）

在生活中，孩子被烫伤是比较常见的。这往往不是因为家人马虎，而是因为有的孩子特别好动，几秒钟的时间就可能出现安全问题。如果孩子被烫伤，家人应该怎么处理呢？首先，应该赶快用冷水冲洗伤口，这样既可以减轻痛苦，也可以降低烫伤带来的危害。然后，要给烫伤的部位涂上烫伤药。最后，一定要保持伤口的卫生，以避免感染。当然，如果烫伤非常严重，要马上带孩子去医院。

生词 New words

1. 马虎	mǎhu	*adj.*	careless
2. 好	hào	*v.*	to like, to be fond of
3. 秒钟	miǎozhōng	*m.*	second
秒	miǎo	*m.*	second
4. 首先	shǒuxiān	*adv.*	first
5. 赶快	gǎnkuài	*adv.*	quickly, at once
6. 冲洗	chōngxǐ	*v.*	to wash, to flush
7. 痛苦	tòngkǔ	*adj.*	painful
8. 危害	wēihài	*n./v.*	harm; to harm
9. 部位	bùwèi	*n.*	(particularly the human body) position, location
10. 涂	tú	*v.*	to spread on
11. 保持	bǎochí	*v.*	to keep, to maintain
12. 以	yǐ	*conj.*	in order to, so as to

语言点 Language Points

一、固定结构“首先……然后……最后……”

固定结构“首先……然后……最后……”连接表承接关系的分句，表示按照先后顺序列举。“最后……”有时可省略。例如：

1. 如果孩子被烫伤，家人应该怎么处理呢？首先，应该赶快用冷水冲洗伤口，这样既可以减轻痛苦，也可以降低烫伤带来的危害。然后，要给烫伤的部位涂上烫伤药。最后，一定要保持伤口的卫生，以避免感染。
2. 如果被狗抓伤怎么办？首先要用大量的肥皂水清洗，然后尽快去医院打狂犬病疫苗。
3. 你先去挂号，然后去看医生，最后再去拿药。

※ 练习：请用固定结构“首先……然后……最后……”完成对话

1. A：如果身边的人突然骨折了，我们应该怎么办？

   B：________________________________。

2. A：你是怎么申请来中国留学的？

   B：________________________________。

3. A：突然感到心脏不舒服，应该怎么办？

   B：________________________________。

4. A：我的手受伤流血了！怎么办？

   B：________________________________。

二、连词“以”

连词“以”表示目的，常用在两个动词性短语之间，后面的动词性短语表目的。例如：

1. 最后，一定要保持伤口的卫生，以避免感染。
2. 糖尿病病人一定要注意少吃或不吃含糖的食物，以控制血糖。
3. 被狗抓伤一定要及时打狂犬病疫苗，以避免感染狂犬病毒。

※ 练习：请用连词“以”完成句子

1. 很多人买了扫地机，________________________________。
2. 很多机场、车站都安装了自动体外除颤器，__________________________。
3. 更年期女性生活要规律，________________________________。
4. 骨质疏松症是中老年常见病，中老年人要注意调整生活方式，增加锻炼，________________________________。

综合练习 Comprehensive Exercises

一、根据拼音写汉字

1. bùwèi ________　　3. shǒuxiān ________　　5. tòngkǔ ________

2. bǎochí ________　　4. gǎnkuài ________　　6. wēihài ________

二、辨字组词

1. 涂________　　3. 危________

　添________　　　包________

2. 秒________　　4. 苦________

　种________　　　草________

三、选词填空

首先　赶快　顺便　仍然　好

1. 在生活中，很多孩子被烫伤是因为孩子特别（　　）动。

2. 大夫，我吃了三天药了，可是伤口（　　）感到疼痛。

3. 去医院看病（　　）得预约挂号。

4. 你下楼的时候（　　）把家里的垃圾拿出去扔了。

5. 如果感到心脏不舒服，一定要（　　）去医院。

四、选出下列词语在句子中的位置

1. 首先 A 做一个听力 B 测试，C 根据测试结果 D 治疗。　（然后）

2. A 我们得 B 把 C 病人送到医院 D 抢救。　（赶快）

3. A做检查的时候B一定不能C，要认认真真D地仔细检查。 （马虎）

4. A更年期女性更B应该注意营养均衡，C提高身体D免疫力。（以）

5. 大夫，A请问您开的B这个药一天需要C几次D？ （涂）

五、用所给词语完成对话

1. 病人：大夫，女性怎么顺利度过更年期啊？

   医生：______________________________。（首先……然后……最后……）

2. 医生：每天要给伤口换药，______________________________。（以）

   病人：好的，我一定多注意。

3. 月亮：孩子被烫伤一定是因为父母太粗心了。

   朋友：______________________________。（不是……而是……）

4. 病人：最近办公室里得流感的人很多，我也被传染了。

   医生：______________________________。（往往）

5. 朋友：你打算继续读研究生吗？

   金龙：______________________________。（如果）

六、根据课文内容回答问题

1. 在生活中，为什么孩子被烫伤是很常见的事儿？
2. 处理烫伤，为什么首先要用冷水冲洗伤口？
3. 冲洗完伤口，下一步做什么？
4. 为什么要保持伤口的卫生？
5. 如果烫伤比较严重，应该怎么办？

七、根据课文内容填空

在生活中，孩子________烫伤是比较________的。这往往________因为家人马虎，________因为有的孩子特别________，几秒钟的时间就可能出现安全问题。如果孩子被烫伤，家人应该怎么________呢？________，应该赶快用冷水________伤口，这样既可以减轻________，也可以降低烫伤带来的________。________，要给烫伤的部位________烫伤药。最后，一定要________伤口的卫生，以________感染。当然，如果烫伤非常严重，要________带孩子去医院。

语言任务 Language Tasks

一、阅读理解

很多人在遇到烧、烫伤后的第一反应是涂抹牙膏、碘酒等，其实这是不正确的。在创面上擅自涂抹药物，不仅不会起到治疗烧、烫伤的作用，反而会掩盖创面，使医生无法立刻确定创面的大小和深度，甚至会导致细菌滋生和创面感染。

烧伤请记住急救“四字诀”：“脱”“冲”“裹”“送”。“脱”指的是烧伤后第一时间脱离致伤物，立即扑灭火焰，脱去燃烧衣物。“冲”指的是用自来水冲洗伤口，并持续用冷水湿敷，这样能快速散热，减轻疼痛和炎症。“裹”指的是用干净毛巾湿敷并包裹创面，预防创面污染及再次伤害。“送”指的是及时送到医院。

来源：科普中国《烧伤的紧急救护措施》

补充词汇

1. 涂抹	túmǒ	*v.*	to daub, to paint
2. 创面	chuāngmiàn	*n.*	surface of a wound
3. 擅自	shànzì	*adv.*	do sth. without authorization
4. 起作用	qǐ zuòyòng	*VO*	to take effect
5. 掩盖	yǎngài	*v.*	to cover
6. 无法	wúfǎ	*v.*	to be unable to
7. 确定	quèdìng	*v.*	to determine
8. 深度	shēndù	*n.*	depth
9. 细菌	xìjūn	*n.*	bacterium
10. 滋生	zīshēng	*v.*	to breed
11. 诀	jué		rhymed formula
12. 脱离	tuōlí	*v.*	to separate oneself from
13. 致伤物	zhìshāngwù	*n.*	the causing trauma
14. 立即	lìjí	*adv.*	immediately, at once
15. 扑灭	pūmiè	*v.*	to put out
16. 火焰	huǒyàn	*n.*	flame
17. 燃烧	ránshāo	*v.*	to burn
18. 衣物	yīwù	*n.*	clothing and other articles of daily use
19. 自来水	zìláishuǐ	*n.*	running water
20. 湿敷	shīfū	*v.*	to have a hydropathic compress treatment
21. 散热	sànrè	*v.*	to lose heat
22. 炎症	yánzhèng	*n.*	inflammation
23. 包裹	bāoguǒ	*v.*	to wrap up
24. 再次	zàicì	*adv.*	once more

回答问题

1. 为什么烧、烫伤后不能立刻涂抹牙膏或碘酒？
2. 烧伤急救“四字诀”中的“脱”是什么意思？
3. 烧伤急救“四字诀”中的“裹”是什么意思？

二、口头表达

任务名称：我是宣传员。

任务背景：医院要策划一期以烧、烫伤为主题的展览。你和同事要一起商量确定活动步骤、内容和呈现方式等。

任务要求：1. 两个学生一组，二人商量确定宣传内容。

2. 安排分工，设定工作截止时间。

3. 讨论展览的注意事项。

参考语言：首先……然后……最后……　以　结果　另　涂　冲洗　痛苦　保持　伤口　赶快　部位　烫

三、书面表达

任务名称：我的旅行清单。

任务要求：请介绍自己的旅行清单（包括携带的物品及携带原因、打包注意事项等），要求 200 字以上。

参考语言：行李箱　雨伞　首先……然后……最后……　马虎　粗心　牙刷　保持　背　另

第十四课 Lesson 14 我想来你们医院应聘

学习目标 Learning Objectives

1. 语言功能：能够对应聘事宜进行咨询和讨论，能够对穿着打扮进行讨论。
2. 语言点：连词“以及”、介词“至于”、固定结构“首先……其次……”。
3. 医学知识：初步了解主要的医学学科及方向。
4. 社会文化：了解医学生去医院求职的基本要求，以及成为合格医生的职业条件。

热身活动 Warm-up

1. 你对哪个医学方向感兴趣？请说明原因。

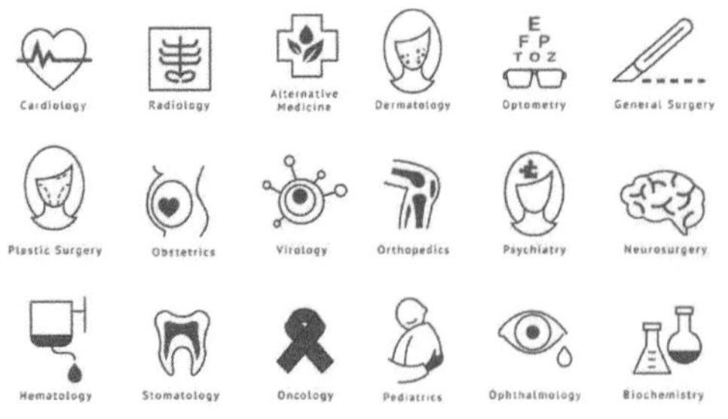

2. 一名合格的医生应当具备哪些能力？请说说你的理解。

课文（一）
Text（Ⅰ）

（医院人事科的工作人员正在接电话。）

工作人员：您好！这里是东山医院。

应聘者：您好！我是外科学骨科方向的博士研究生，我看到了你们医院的招聘信息，想来应聘。

工作人员：欢迎您来应聘，您可以去我们的网站上了解具体的应聘要求，准备好材料。

应聘者：我已经把填好的表格和简历发过去了。

工作人员：那您等通知就可以了。

应聘者：我的电子邮件已经发出去十几天了，可是现在还没有收到你们的答复。

工作人员：下周一我们会在网站上公布面试名单，以及面试的时间、地点等具体安排，请您及时查看。

生词 New words

1. 人事科	rénshìkē	*n.*	personnel section
人事	rénshì	*n.*	personnel matters
2. 应聘者	yìngpìnzhě	*n.*	applicant
应聘	yìngpìn	*v.*	to apply for a job
者	zhě	*suf.*	person or thing
3. 外科学	wàikēxué	*n.*	surgery
4. 方向	fāngxiàng	*n.*	direction
5. 招聘	zhāopìn	*v.*	to recruit
6. 表格	biǎogé	*n.*	form, table
7. 简历	jiǎnlì	*n.*	resume, CV
8. 通知	tōngzhī	*n.*	notice
9. 电子邮件	diànzǐ yóujiàn		e-mail
10. 答复	dáfù	*n./v.*	reply; to reply
11. 公布	gōngbù	*v.*	to announce
12. 面试	miànshì	*v.*	to interview
13. 名单	míngdān	*n.*	name list
14. 以及	yǐjí	*conj.*	and, as well as
15. 地点	dìdiǎn	*n.*	location, place
16. 查看	chákàn	*v.*	to check

语言点 Language Points

连词"以及"

连词"以及"用来连接并列的词或短语。"以及"前面连接的并列成分往往是主要的，且"以及"前面可以有语音停顿。例如：

1. 下周一我们会在网站上公布面试名单，以及面试的时间、地点等具体安排。
2. 现在很多家长让孩子在业余时间上很多辅导班以及兴趣班。
3. 爷爷很喜欢给我们讲他年轻时候的工作经历，以及他认识奶奶的过程。

※ 练习：请用连词“以及”完成对话

1. A：要申请奖学金，需要什么材料？

B：________________________________。

2. A：来中国留学之前，都需要做哪些准备？

B：________________________________。

3. A：孩子应该如何预防近视？

B：________________________________。

4. A：冬天是流感高发季，我们应该注意什么？

B：________________________________。

综合练习 Comprehensive Exercises

一、根据拼音写汉字

1. gōngbù ________
2. jiǎnlì ________
3. biǎogé ________
4. fāngxiàng ________
5. dìdiǎn ________
6. tōngzhī ________

二、辨字组词

1. 招________
   拾________
2. 及________
   圾________
3. 聘________
   聪________
4. 邮________
   抽________

三、选词填空

招聘　应聘　公布　涂　保持

1. 昨天医院已经在网站上（　　）了假期门诊安排。
2. 请问在哪里可以了解到医院的（　　）信息？
3. 你的胳膊烫得严重不严重？（　　）烫伤药了吗？
4. 医生让我（　　）这个姿势十秒钟，不要动。
5. 你也是来口腔医院（　　）的吗？

四、选出下列词语在句子中的位置

1. A 王东医生的门诊时间 B 是星期一下午、星期三 C 上午 D 星期五下午。（以及）
2. A 被狗抓伤了 B 以后一定要 C 去医院打 D 狂犬病疫苗。（及时）
3. A 我暂时 B 还没有收到 C 医院人事科的 D。（答复）
4. A 情况得等 B 检查结果 C 出来以后才能 D 知道。（具体）
5. A 您的 B 结果将会通过 C 电子邮件通知 D 您。（面试）

五、用所给词语完成对话

1. 病人：大夫，流感有哪些常见症状？

   医生：______________________________。（以及）

2. 病人：______________________________？（具体）

   护士：你先把东西收拾好，医生查房的时候会告诉你出院时间。

3. 大为：______________________________？（公布）

   同学：听老师说是下个星期二。

4. 金龙：您好，我想要办理居留许可证延期。

警察：________________________。（表格）

5. 王晨：我发给你的邮件你收到了吗？

朋友：________________________。（查看）

六、根据课文内容回答问题

1. 应聘者为什么给医院人事科打电话？
2. 在哪里可以了解到东山医院的具体招聘要求？
3. 应聘者准备好材料了吗？
4. 下周一东山医院的网站上将要公布哪些信息？
5. 工作人员提醒应聘者什么？

七、根据课文内容填空

我是外科学________方向的博士研究生，半个月前我看到了东山医院的________信息，想去________。我按照东山医院网站上的要求，准备好了________和________，用________发了出去。可是十几天过去了，我还没有收到________。我有点儿着急，于是今天给医院________打了电话，他们的工作人员告诉我下周一他们会在网站上________面试名单，________面试的时间、________等具体安排，并提醒我要及时________。

课文（二）
Text（II）

（张佳乐的弟弟要去面试，姐姐在给他一些建议。）

张佳乐：明天的面试，你准备得怎么样了？

弟弟：材料已经准备好，都放到信封里了。

张佳乐：面试一定要好好儿打扮打扮。

弟弟：我现在这样不好看吗？

张佳乐：你误会了。我的意思是面试时第一印象尤其重要，你要穿得正式一些。

弟弟：我已经准备好了西装、衬衫、皮鞋和袜子，可以了吧？

张佳乐：你的头发太长了，快去理理发吧。

弟弟：又要穿西装，又要去理发，面试比约会还麻烦！

张佳乐：那你觉得工作重要，还是爱情重要？

弟弟：对现在的我来说，工作重要；至于爱情，我现在很难回答，咱们以后再谈吧。我现在马上去理发店。

张佳乐：快去吧，小伙子！

生词 New words

1. 信封	xìnfēng	*n.*	envelope
2. 打扮	dǎban	*v.*	to dress up
3. 误会	wùhuì	*v.*	to misunderstand
4. 正式	zhèngshì	*adj.*	formal
5. 西装	xīzhuāng	*n.*	Western-style clothes
6. 衬衫	chènshān	*n.*	shirt
7. 皮鞋	píxié	*n.*	leather shoes
鞋	xié	*n.*	shoes
8. 袜子	wàzi	*n.*	socks
9. 理发	lǐfà	*v.*	to have a haircut
10. 约会	yuēhuì	*n./v.*	date; to have a date
11. 爱情	àiqíng	*n.*	love (between man and woman)
12. 至于	zhìyú	*prep.*	as to, with regard to
13. 回答	huídá	*v.*	to answer
14. 理发店	lǐfàdiàn	*n.*	barbershop
15. 小伙子	xiǎohuǒzi	*n.*	lad, young fellow

语言点 Language Points

介词"至于"

介词"至于"表示另提起一件事。例如：

1. 张佳乐：那你觉得工作重要，还是爱情重要？

   弟弟：对现在的我来说，工作重要；至于爱情，我现在很难回答，咱们以后再谈吧。

2. 爸爸：你希望孩子以后成为什么样的人？

   妈妈：我只希望他健康快乐。至于别的方面，我没有太多要求。

3. 朋友：你毕业以后想去哪家医院工作？

王晨：我最近忙着准备考试呢。至于毕业以后去哪儿工作，我还没想过。

※ 练习：请用介词“至于”和所给词语完成对话

1. 同事：佳乐，你想租个什么样的房子？

张佳乐：最好在医院附近，________________。（租金）

2. 妈妈：你对孩子以后的教育有什么想法？

爸爸：我觉得让孩子接受学校教育就够了，____________。（辅导班）

3. 马大为：金龙，今天我请客，想吃什么随便点。

金龙：那我就不客气了。先来一个宫保鸡丁，一个西红柿炒鸡蛋，____________。（主食）

4. 美丽：你毕业以后有什么打算？

月亮：我想留在大城市，____________。（压力）

综合练习 Comprehensive Exercises

一、根据拼音写汉字

1. zhìyú ________　　3. zhèngshì ________　　5. wùhuì ________

2. dǎban ________　　4. xìnfēng ________　　6. àiqíng ________

二、辨字组词

1. 式________　　3. 误________

或________　　语________

2. 袜________　　4. 封________

衬________　　对________

三、选词填空

理发　打扮　至于　正式　回答

1. 我已经半年没有（　　）了，现在头发长得特别长。
2. 这个问题让我很难（　　）。
3. 去参加面试，应该穿得（　　）一些。
4. 现在看来这次的手术很成功，（　　）后面的治疗，我们得等专家们开会后确定。
5. 你是去做体检，又不是去约会，不用（　　）得这么好看吧？

四、选出下列词语在句子中的位置

1. A 今天我们 B 先谈工作计划，C 假期安排，我们 D 等会儿再说。（至于）
2. A 请不要 B 我的意思，我当然希望你 C 能成为一名 D 医生。（误会）
3. A 这个问题比较 B 复杂，我暂时 C 不 D 了（liǎo）。（回答）
4. A 今天 B 只是练习，C 演出定在下星期一 D 晚上。（正式）
5. A 每天早上我 B 都要花 C 半个小时 D 自己。（打扮）

五、用所给词语完成对话

1. 医生：伤口还疼吗？

   病人：____________________________。（尤其）

2. 朋友：你觉得这里的环境怎么样？气候适应吗？

   月亮：____________________________。（至于）

3. 马大为：我觉得有点儿头晕。

   同学：____________________________。（好好儿 + v.）

4. 王晨：爷爷，您觉得我穿这套西装怎么样？

爷爷：________________________________。（打扮）

5. 朋友：你想买件什么样的衣服？

月亮：________________________________。（正式）

六、根据课文内容回答问题

1. 明天的面试，弟弟准备得怎么样了？
2. 张佳乐认为面试应该注意什么？
3. 弟弟打算穿什么去参加面试？
4. 弟弟认为现在爱情和工作哪个更重要？
5. 弟弟要去做什么？

七、根据课文内容填空

明天的面试，我已经准备好了。面试需要的材料，我都放到__________里了。为了能有一个好的第一印象，我打算穿得__________一些。我准备好了__________、__________、__________和袜子。当我以为一切都准备好了的时候，姐姐却说我的头发太__________了，让我去__________。又要穿西装，又要去理发，面试比约会还__________！

课文（三）
Text（III）

在很多国家和地区，医生是让人羡慕的职业。要想成为一名合格的医生，医学专业的学生在学习阶段就要做好充分的准备。首先，要努力学习基础知识，提高专业能力。其次，要提升学历水平。本科学历已经不能满足时代的需要，很多医院对医生的学历要求是博士。同时，还要积累工作经验。经验越丰富的人，越能适应工作环境。只有努力丰富和提高自己，才能有竞争力。

生词 New words

1. 地区	dìqū	*n.*	region
2. 职业	zhíyè	*n.*	profession, occupation
3. 合格	hégé	*adj.*	qualified
4. 阶段	jiēduàn	*n.*	stage
5. 其次	qícì	*pron.*	secondly, next
6. 提升	tíshēng	*v.*	to promote
7. 学历	xuélì	*n.*	educational background
8. 本科	běnkē	*n.*	undergraduate course
9. 满足	mǎnzú	*v.*	to meet, to satisfy
10. 时代	shídài	*n.*	age, times
11. 积累	jīlěi	*v.*	to accumulate
12. 丰富	fēngfù	*adj./v.*	abundant; to enrich
13. 竞争力	jìngzhēnglì	*n.*	competitiveness
竞争	jìngzhēng	*v.*	to compete

语言点 Language Points

固定结构"首先……其次……"

固定结构"首先……其次……"连接表承接关系的分句，前一分句指次序在前的、主要的人或事物，后一分句指次序在后的、次要的人或事物。例如：

1. 要想成为一名合格的医生，首先，要努力学习基础知识，提高专业能力；其次，要提升学历水平。
2. 王主任是我们医院最受欢迎的外科医生，这是因为：首先，他手术做得好；其次，他对病人很有耐心。
3. 学习什么专业首先要看自己的兴趣是什么，其次才看父母的意见。

※ 练习：请用固定结构“首先……其次……”完成对话

1. A：你觉得什么样的医生是好医生？

B：______________________________。

2. A：你觉得什么样的老师是好老师？

B：______________________________。

3. A：你想找什么样的工作？

B：______________________________。

4. A：你为什么想做医生呢？

B：______________________________。

综合练习 Comprehensive Exercises

一、根据拼音写汉字

1. mǎnzú ________
2. tíshēng ________
3. fēngfù ________
4. jīlěi ________
5. jiēduàn ________
6. jìngzhēng ______

二、辨字组词

1. 阶________
   介________
2. 竞________
   境________
3. 升________
   生________
4. 合________
   会________

三、选词填空

竞争　合格　满足　积累　提升

1. 医院要全面（　　）医疗水平和服务质量。
2. 我在医院的急诊室（　　）了很多工作经验。
3. 为了（　　）糖尿病病人的特殊需要，食堂提供了很多无糖食品。
4. 体检（　　）以后才能办理居留许可证。
5. 从面试名单来看，五个医学博士在同时（　　）一份工作。

四、选出下列词语在句子中的位置

1. A 一般来说，糖尿病的 B 治疗至少 C 需要三个 D。（阶段）
2. A 首先 B 要打好医学基础，C 要积累 D 丰富的工作经验。（其次）
3. 在家里养几棵 A 植物既可以 B 美化室内环境，C 又可以 D 生活质量。（提升）
4. 我们国家 A 大部分 B 不下雪，只有南方有时 C 会下点儿 D 小雪。（地区）
5. A 面试 B 的人员名单将会在医院网站上 C 公布，请您及时查看 D。（合格）

五、用所给词语完成对话

1. 朋友：听说我们学校附近要修地铁了！

   月亮：______________________________。（满足）

2. 佳乐：假期我打算去参加培训。

   朋友：______________________________。（积累）

3. 朋友：听说你假期打算去西安？

金龙：________________________。（丰富）

4. 病人：大夫，怎么避免流感传染呢？

医生：________________________。（首先……其次……）

5. 病人：大夫，我妻子的更年期症状特别严重，有没有缓解的办法呀？

医生：________________________。（同时）

六、根据课文内容回答问题

1. 为什么不少人都想当医生？
2. 想要成为一名合格的医生，医学生需要做什么样的准备？
3. 本科毕业可以当医生吗？
4. 为什么医院要求应聘者有丰富的工作经验？
5. 对一名医学生来说，怎样才能在未来应聘工作时获得竞争力？

七、根据课文内容填空

在很多国家和________，医生是让人羡慕的________。要想成为一名________的医生，医学专业的学生在________阶段就要做好充分的准备。________，要努力学习基础知识，提高专业能力。________，要________学历水平。本科学历已经不能________时代的需要，很多医院对医生的学历要求是________。同时，还要________工作经验。经验越________的人，越能适应工作环境。只有努力丰富和提高自己，才能有________。

语言任务 Language Tasks

一、阅读理解

AI医生，又叫“人工智能医生”。它不但能“看”影像、“读”病历、“动”手术、“做”检查，还能给出临床诊断建议。机器不仅可以当医生，而且可以进行科研、教学和管理，帮助医生提升科研水平，提高诊疗能力。

目前，医疗人工智能行业的发展还面临一个突出问题：医疗各个领域的数据没有实现互通。因涉及个人隐私保护，我们还需要界定医疗数据的知识产权。但可以预见，未来人类将离不开“人工智能医生”。那时的医疗不再是“排队医疗”，而是“秒医疗”“精准医疗”。

来源：科普中国《“人工智能医生”来了》

补充词汇

1. 人工智能	réngōng-zhìnéng		artificial intelligence
2. 影像	yǐngxiàng	*n.*	icon
3. 临床诊断	línchuáng zhěnduàn		clinical diagnosis
4. 机器	jīqì	*n.*	machine
5. 科研	kēyán	*v./n.*	to make scientific researches; scientific research
6. 诊疗	zhěnliáo	*v.*	to make a diagnosis and give treatment
7. 行业	hángyè	*n.*	trade
8. 面临	miànlín	*v.*	to be confronted with
9. 领域	lǐngyù	*n.*	field
10. 数据	shùjù	*n.*	data
11. 互通	hùtōng	*v.*	to interflow
12. 涉及	shèjí	*v.*	to involve, to relate to
13. 隐私	yǐnsī	*n.*	privacy
14. 界定	jièdìng	*v.*	to define
15. 知识产权	zhīshi chǎnquán		intellectual property
16. 预见	yùjiàn	*v.*	to predict

17. 未来　wèilái　*n.*　future
18. 人类　rénlèi　*n.*　human
19. 精准　jīngzhǔn　*adj.*　precise

回答问题

1. 人工智能医生除了能够“看”影像、“读”病历，还能做什么？
2. 人工智能除了能够给病人看病，还有什么用途？
3. 目前，医疗人工智能的发展面临着什么问题？

二、口头表达

任务名称：我也想当医生。

任务背景：讨论如何成为一名合格的医生，介绍不同国家对医学专业学生从业的学历要求，谈论如何获取招聘信息，等等。

任务要求：1. 四个学生一组，分别介绍自己国家对医生从业的要求，包括教育经历、学历、工作经验等。

2. 分别介绍自己未来的就业打算。

3. 讨论如何获取招聘信息。

参考语言：首先……其次……　学历　提升　积累　丰富　以及　地区　时代　合格　满足　竞争　招聘　应聘　表格　方向

三、书面表达

任务名称：第一印象。

任务要求：请谈论一下第一印象的重要性，以及如何给别人留下好的第一印象，要求200字以上。

参考语言：首先……其次……　以及　打扮　积累　提升　丰富　满足　竞争　时代　招聘　应聘

第十五课 Lesson 15 医院也贴“福”字

学习目标 Learning Objectives

1. 语言功能：能够向别人表示祝贺，能够叙述事情发展的经过。
2. 语言点：固定结构“不但不/没……反而……”、固定结构“为了……而……”、连词“并”、介词“趁”。
3. 医学知识：了解手术前的流程。
4. 社会文化：了解丰富多彩的春节习俗。

热身活动 Warm-up

1. 去医院看望病人，你会选择带什么礼物？

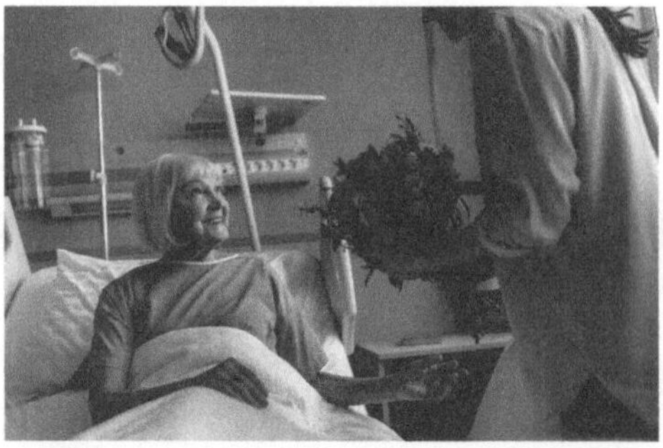

2. 你知道下图中的这个女孩儿在做什么吗？关于中国的春节习俗，你了解多少？

课文（一）
Text（I）

（护士在外科病房查房。）

护士：这么漂亮的花儿！

病人：是我男朋友送的。

护士：你男朋友真浪漫！

病人：他昨天还带来了很多小吃，您尝尝。

护士：谢谢你。不过医院有规定，上班时间不能吃东西。

病人：那好吧。对了，卫生间的灯坏了，麻烦您找工人来看一下。

护士：好，我一会儿就给修理工打电话。

病人：马上到春节了，我看到医院也贴上了春联、“福”字。过年的时候，医院食堂关门吗？

护士：食堂不但不会关门，反而会给工作人员和住院病人免费提供饺子。

病人：太棒了！

生词 New words

1. 浪漫	làngmàn	*adj.*	romantic
2. 小吃	xiǎochī	*n.*	snack
3. 灯	dēng	*n.*	light
4. 工人	gōngrén	*n.*	worker
5. 修理工	xiūlǐgōng	*n.*	repairman
修理	xiūlǐ	*v.*	to repair
6. 贴	tiē	*v.*	to stick
7. 春联	chūnlián	*n.*	Spring Festival couplets
8. 福	fú	*n.*	blessing, good fortune
9. 过年	guònián	*v.*	to celebrate the Chinese New Year
10. 关门	guānmén	*v.*	to close
11. 免费	miǎnfèi	*v.*	to be free of charge

语言点 Language Points

固定结构“不但不/没……反而……”

固定结构“不但不/没……反而……”连接表递进关系的分句，后一分句的意思跟前一分句意思相反或者跟预期相反，是一种反向递进。例如：

1. 食堂不但不会关门，反而会给工作人员和住院病人免费提供饺子。
2. 爷爷今年快七十岁了，身体不但没变差，反而更好了。
3. 吃了药以后，我的感冒不但没好，反而更严重了。

※ 练习：请用固定结构“不但不/没……反而……”完成句子

1. 只吃水果不吃主食不但不能减肥，____________________。
2. ____________________，反而更差了。
3. 运动一周后，她的体重不但没有减轻，____________________。
4. ____________________，反而比以前更忙了。

综合练习 Comprehensive Exercises

一、根据拼音写汉字

1. làngmàn ________　　3. dēng ________　　5. xiūlǐ ________

2. miǎnfèi ________　　4. guònián ________　　6. tiē ________

二、辨字组词

1. 浪________　　3. 漫________

　很________　　　慢________

2. 免________　　4. 贴________

　决________　　　硕________

三、选词填空

反而　浪漫　修理　贴　免费

1. 医院本周给老年人（　　）提供了测血糖、血压的服务。

2. 我的自行车坏了，你知道哪里有（　　）店吗？

3. 我吃得多，可是体重不但没增加，（　　）减轻了。

4. 我能想到的最（　　）的事儿就是和你一起慢慢儿变老。

5. 你知道应该把春联（　　）在哪儿吗？

四、选出下列词语在句子中的位置

1. A 有的植物不喜欢水，B 水浇多了不但 C 不能帮助它，D 对它不利。

（反而）

2. A 中心医院的网站 B 上提供 C 咨询服务 D。（免费）

3. A 给你开的 B 这两种药 C 请按照说明书的 D 使用。（规定）

4. A 可能是我昨晚吃的 B 不卫生，C 导致了 D 急性肠胃炎。（小吃）

5. A 请把 B 邮票 C 在信封的 D 右上角。（贴）

五、用所给词语完成对话

1. 小刘：爸爸，我觉得我的鼻子不好看，我想做整形手术。

   父亲：________________。（不但不/没……反而……）

2. 病人家属：吃完药以后，疼痛有没有减轻一些？

   病人：________________。（不但不/没……反而……）

3. 佳乐：别人的男朋友都送女朋友花儿和巧克力，我男朋友竟然送我一台扫地机。

   朋友：________________。（浪漫）

4. 朋友：大为，给你打电话你怎么不接？

   大为：________________。（修理）

5. 朋友：伤口什么时候能拆线？

   吉米：________________。（不过）

六、根据课文内容回答问题

1. 这些漂亮的花儿是哪儿来的？
2. 护士为什么不接受病人给的小吃？
3. 如果病房卫生间的灯坏了，病人应该怎么办？
4. 马上到春节了，医院里有哪些改变？
5. 过年的时候，医院食堂关门吗？

七、根据课文内容填空

昨天男朋友来医院看我，给我带了________和________。我想把小吃送给护士尝尝，但是她说医院有规定，________时间不能吃东西。卫生间的________坏了，我让护士找________来看一下。

马上到春节了，我看到医院也________了春联和________字。护士说过年的时候医院的食堂________不会关门，________会给工作人员和住院病人免费提供________，这真是太棒了！

课文（二）
Text（II）

（金龙申请到了研究生奖学金，同学们在饭店给他庆祝。）

马大为：告诉大家一个好消息，金龙申请到了研究生奖学金！今天邀请大家来给他庆祝一下。

李真：祝贺你，金龙！

金龙：谢谢大家的帮助和支持！

李真：来，大家干杯，祝贺金龙！

所有人：干杯！

月亮：金龙一直在为了理想而努力。

王晨：对，他经常受到老师的表扬。对了，金龙，你什么时候回国？

金龙：我已经订好机票了，下周回国。回国以前，我想去一趟北京。

美丽：你还没去过北京吗？这可太让我吃惊了。那可是中国的首都！

马大为：他当然去过。他去过首都国际机场。

金龙：大为就爱开玩笑。不过，说实话，来中国五年了，除了去过大使馆，我哪儿都没去过。这次我一定要去天安门，还要去爬长城。

王晨：不到长城非好汉！长城你一定要去！

生词 New words

1. 庆祝	qìngzhù	*v.*	to celebrate
2. 邀请	yāoqǐng	*v.*	to invite
3. 干杯	gānbēi	*v.*	cheers, to toast
4. 受到	shòudào	*VC*	to be given
5. 表扬	biǎoyáng	*v.*	to praise
6. 吃惊	chījīng	*v.*	to be shocked
7. 首都	shǒudū	*n.*	capital
8. 国际	guójì	*n.*	international
9. 开玩笑	kāi wánxiào	*VO*	to make a joke
玩笑	wánxiào	*n.*	joke
10. 大使馆	dàshǐguǎn	*n.*	embassy
11. 非	fēi	*v.*	not to be
12. 好汉	hǎohàn	*n.*	true man

专名 Proper nouns

1. 首都国际机场	Shǒudū Guójì Jīchǎng	Beijing Capital International Airport
2. 天安门	Tiān'ān Mén	Tian'anmen, the Gate of Heavenly Peace of the Imperial Palace of Beijing
3. 长城	Chángchéng	the Great Wall

语言点 Language Points

固定结构"为了……而……"

固定结构"为了……而……",前一部分表示的是后一部分的目的。例如:

1. 金龙一直在为了理想而努力。

2. 马大为前几个月换工作了,最近他一直为了新工作而努力学习。

3. 金龙一直在为了成为一名合格的医生而努力。

※ 练习：请用固定结构“为了……而……”和所给词语完成句子

1. 快毕业了，同学们________________________________。（找工作）

2. 她的理想是当一名作家，____________________________。（实现理想）

3. 弟弟最近非常忙，________________________________。（申请研究生）

4. 姐姐每天早上跑步，______________________________。（减肥）

综合练习 Comprehensive Exercises

一、根据拼音写汉字

1. yāoqǐng ________　　3. biǎoyáng ________　　5. chījīng ________

2. guójì ________　　4. shǒudū ________　　6. qìngzhù ________

二、辨字组词

1. 扬________　　3. 首________

场________　　自________

2. 受________　　4. 庆________

爱________　　床________

三、选词填空

吃惊　受到　庆祝　邀请　赶

1. 你的身体恢复能力太让人（　　）了，才几天就可以出院了。

2. 120 已经在（　　）来的路上了，你再坚持一下。

3. 这次会议我们（　　）到了来自首都医科大学的专家。

4. 一边看书，一边查词典，阅读速度会（　　）影响。

5. 为了（　　）春节，每家每户都在大门上贴了春联和“福”字。

四、选出下列词语在句子中的位置

1. A 我不是在跟你 B，我 C 洗澡的时候真的 D 晕倒了。　（开玩笑）
2. 马大为 A 最近学习 B 非常努力，C 得到了老师的 D。　（表扬）
3. A 我要为了 B 成为一名合格的 C 医生 D 努力。　（而）
4. A 即使 B 是为了 C，也不能 D 喝酒。　（庆祝）
5. 学期快 A 结束了 B，老师准备 C 同学们到家里 D 做客。　（邀请）

五、用所给词语完成对话

1. 朋友：我最近每天都能看到马大为在图书馆学习。

   金龙：________________________。（为了……而……）

2. 儿子：爸爸，这次考试我考了 100 分！

   爸爸：________________________。（表扬）

3. 刘一鸣：从上个月到现在，我的体重减了 32 斤！

   同事：________________________。（吃惊）

4. 朋友：你不是说想去做个隆鼻手术吗？

   小刘：________________________。（受到）

5. 王晨：大为，我爬不动了，咱们回去吧！

   病人：________________________。（不到长城非好汉）

六、根据课文内容回答问题

1. 大家今天为什么会聚在一起？

2. 金龙打算什么时候回国？

3. 回国之前，金龙想去哪儿？为什么？

4. 美丽为什么感到吃惊？

5. 王晨建议金龙去哪里？为什么？

七、根据课文内容填空

金龙申请到了研究生________，今天他和马大为________同学们一起庆祝一下。这么多年，金龙一直在________理想而________，他经常________老师的表扬。我们都为他感到高兴。金龙说他已经________好机票了，打算下周回国。回国以前，他想去________北京。美丽听到这个消息感到很________，北京是中国的________，她以为金龙早就去过了。金龙说他来中国五年了，除了去过________，他哪儿都没去过。这次他一定要去________，还要去爬________。

课文（三）
Text（III）

上周三，我坐高铁到了北京。我去了天安门，爬了长城，逛了王府井，并趁这次机会参观了北京大学和清华大学。这两所大学不仅在亚洲很有名，而且在全世界也很有名。北京给我留下了深刻的印象。

三天以后，我乘航班回国。在机场，换登机牌、托运行李、安全检查等都很顺利，可是因为天气不好，飞机起飞推迟了。十几个小时以后，飞机平安降落。全家人都在机场迎接我，我和家人都非常激动。最让家人高兴的是，我申请到了研究生奖学金。他们都为我感到骄傲。

生词 New words

1. 趁	chèn	*prep.*	take advantage of, while
2. 机会	jīhuì	*n.*	opportunity
3. 所	suǒ	*m.*	*a measure word for houses, schools, etc.*
4. 深刻	shēnkè	*adj.*	profound
5. 乘	chéng	*v.*	to travel by (plane, car, ship, etc.)
6. 航班	hángbān	*n.*	flight
7. 登机牌	dēngjīpái	*n.*	boarding pass
8. 托运	tuōyùn	*v.*	to consign
9. 起飞	qǐfēi	*v.*	(of aircraft) to take off
10. 推迟	tuīchí	*v.*	to postpone
11. 平安	píng'ān	*adj.*	safe and sound
12. 降落	jiàngluò	*v.*	to land
13. 迎接	yíngjiē	*v.*	to welcome
14. 骄傲	jiāo'ào	*adj.*	proud

专名 Proper nouns

1. 王府井	Wángfǔjǐng	Wangfujing, a commercial street in Beijing
2. 北京大学	Běijīng Dàxué	Peking University
3. 清华大学	Qīnghuá Dàxué	Tsinghua University
4. 亚洲	Yàzhōu	Asia

语言点 Language Points

一、连词“并”

连词“并”表示更进一层，相当于“并且”。它可以连接并列的双音节动词，也可以连接小句。连接小句时，后一小句的主语往往省略。“并”一般用于书面语。

例如：

1. 我去了天安门，爬了长城，逛了王府井，并趁这次机会参观了北京大学和清华大学。
2. 我同意并支持你考研究生。
3. 医生让病人查了血，并做了 CT。
4. 哥哥去年顺利毕业并考上了研究生。

※ 练习：请用连词“并”和所给词语完成句子

1. 一旦被狗抓伤，为了避免感染狂犬病，我们需要马上清洗伤口，____________。（狂犬病疫苗）
2. 爸爸是 1990 年毕业________________________。（参加工作）
3. 爸爸总是无条件地支持________________________。（帮助）
4. 医生给我开了药________________________。（建议）

二、介词“趁”

介词“趁”表示利用某一个有利的机会、条件或时间做某事。例如：

1. 去了天安门，爬了长城，逛了王府井，并趁这次机会参观了北京大学和清华大学。
2. 我们要趁年轻努力学习。
3. 我想趁这个假期出国旅游。

※ 练习：请用介词“趁”和所给词语完成句子

1. ________________________，我们去北京玩儿吧。（放假）
2. ________________________，我想好好儿休息休息。（没课）
3. ________________________，我们一起去爬山吧。（风景好）
4. ________________________，我们一起去踢球吧。（天气好）

综合练习 Comprehensive Exercises

一、根据拼音写汉字

1. hángbān ________　　3. yíngjiē ________　　5. shēnkè ________

2. jīhuì ________　　4. jiāo'ào ________　　6. tuīchí ________

二、辨字组词

1. 骄________　　3. 托________

骑________　　指________

2. 傲________　　4. 航________

做________　　船________

三、选词填空

推迟　迎接　趁　骄傲　逛

1. 手术时间（　　）到星期五上午八点。
2. 我们全家为了（　　）小宝宝的出生已经做好了充分的准备。
3. 我打算（　　）这次出差的机会见见朋友。
4. 医生说你必须等伤口养好了才能出去（　　）。
5. 听说我考上了博士研究生，全家人都为我感到（　　）。

四、选出下列词语在句子中的位置

1. A 我完全 B 同意 C 支持 D 你的想法。　（并）
2. 金龙 A 打算 B 着假期好好儿 C 准备 HSK 五级考试 D。　（趁）

3. 这次 A 经历告诉了我一个 B 的道理：C 做事一定 D 不能粗心、马虎！（深刻）

4. A 飞机 B 马上要 C 了，我得 D 关机了。（起飞）

5. A 飞机 B 地降落 C 在首都国际机场 D。（平安）

五、用所给词语完成对话

1. 朋友：你周末去哪儿了？

   佳乐：________________________________。（并）

2. 朋友：今天天气可真好！

   月亮：________________________________。（趁）

3. 病人：减肥也能引起贫血，是吧？

   医生：________________________________。（不仅……而且……）

4. 金龙：飞机怎么还不起飞？

   工作人员：________________________________。（推迟）

5. 艺文：这么大的行李箱能带上飞机吗？

   王东：________________________________。（托运）

六、根据课文内容回答问题

1. 金龙是坐飞机去的北京吗？
2. 金龙去了北京的哪些地方？
3. 金龙回国的航班遇到了什么问题？
4. 金龙回国坐了多久的飞机？
5. 金龙的家人为什么为他感到骄傲？

七、根据课文内容填空

上周三，我坐________到了北京。我去了天安门，________了长城，________了王府井，并________这次机会参观了北京大学和清华大学。这两所大学不仅在________很有名，而且在________也很有名。北京给我留下了________的印象。

三天以后，我乘________回国。在机场，换________、________行李、安全检查等都很________，可是因为天气不好，飞机起飞________了。十几个小时以后，飞机平安________。全家人都在机场________我，我和家人都非常激动。最让家人高兴的是，我________到了研究生________。他们都为我感到________。

语言任务 Language Tasks

一、阅读理解

手术前一天，医生会和患者家属谈话，告知家属手术的必要性、操作过程、术后的预期效果、手术风险等事项，并请家属签《知情同意书》。这是术前的必要程序。

其实，《知情同意书》并不是医生的免责声明，它只是用于保障患者和家属的知情权。如果术中真的发生了医疗事故，医生还是要负责任的。现在主要的争议在于，术中发生了并发症，个别患者家属无法理解。即使《知情同意书》上写清楚了，他们也要状告医生没有在术前谈话中跟他们讲明白。为了防止这种情况出现，现在很多医院都会对术前谈话进行录音和录像。

来源：好大夫在线《带你揭秘手术完整流程：多一些了解，少一点误会》

补充词汇

1. 谈话	tánhuà	*v.*	to have a conversation
2. 必要性	bìyàoxìng	*n.*	necessity
必要	bìyào	*adj.*	necessary
3. 预期	yùqī	*v.*	to expect
4. 事项	shìxiàng	*n.*	item
5. 签	qiān	*v.*	to sign
6.《知情同意书》	Zhīqíng Tóngyìshū		Informed Consent
7. 程序	chéngxù	*n.*	procedure
8. 免责声明	miǎnzé shēngmíng		disclaimer
9. 保障	bǎozhàng	*v.*	to assure
10. 知情权	zhīqíngquán	*n.*	right to learn the truth
11. 医疗事故	yīliáo shìgù		medical accident
12. 负责任	fù zérèn	*VO*	to be responsible for
13. 争议	zhēngyì	*v.*	to dispute
14. 并发症	bìngfāzhèng	*n.*	complication
15. 个别	gèbié	*adj.*	rare
16. 状告	zhuànggào	*v.*	to sue
17. 录音	lùyīn	*v.*	to be recorded on tape
18. 录像	lùxiàng	*v.*	to record a video of

回答问题

1. 手术前，医生和患者家属主要谈些什么？
2. 为什么医生要求患者家属签《知情同意书》？
3. 如果手术中发生了医疗事故，医生需要负责任吗？

二、口头表达

任务名称：祝贺病人身体恢复。

任务背景：病人一个月前做了手术，今天来医院复查。复查结果很理想，医生为病人感到高兴并向他表示祝贺。病人在感谢医生的同时提出了一个小小的请求。

任务要求：1. 两个学生一组，一个扮演医生，一个扮演病人。

2. 病人和医生打招呼，医生询问并检查病人的身体恢复情况。

3. 检查结果很好，医生向病人表示祝贺。

4. 病人很高兴，向医生表示感谢并提出一个请求。

参考语言：为了……而……　趁　复查　不但不/没……反而……　改变　提　恢复　吃惊　或者　随着　经过　大约　跟……相比

三、书面表达

任务名称：难忘的旅行。

任务要求：请介绍一次难忘的旅行经历（包括地点、时间、交通工具、事件等），要求200字以上。

参考语言：乘　深刻　机会　印象　航班　行李箱　趟　花　价格　另　导游　为了……而……　趁　提醒

词汇总表

A				
阿尔茨海默病	ā'ěrcíhǎimòbìng	*n.*	Alzheimer's disease	5
爱情	àiqíng	*n.*	love (between man and woman)	14
安眠药	ānmiányào	*n.*	sleeping pill	3
安慰	ānwèi	*v.*	to console	5
安装	ānzhuāng	*v.*	to install	1
B				
班	bān	*n.*	class	10
包间	bāojiān	*n.*	private room	7
包括	bāokuò	*v.*	to include	8
包子	bāozi	*n.*	steamed stuffed bun	11
保持	bǎochí	*v.*	to keep, to maintain	13
保护	bǎohù	*v.*	to protect	3
保险	bǎoxiǎn	*n.*	insurance	6
报告	bàogào	*n.*	report	11
报纸	bàozhǐ	*n.*	newspaper	1
背	bēi	*v.*	to carry on the back	13
背	bèi	*n.*	back (of the body)	7
本科	běnkē	*n.*	undergraduate course	14
笨	bèn	*adj.*	stupid, silly	10
彼此	bǐcǐ	*pron.*	each other	5
避免	bìmiǎn	*v.*	to avoid	8
变	biàn	*v.*	to change	1
变化	biànhuà	*n./v.*	change; to change	1

遍	biàn	*m.*	*a measure word denoting an action from beginning to end*	12
表格	biǎogé	*n.*	form, table	14
表示	biǎoshì	*v.*	to indicate, to mean	9
表现	biǎoxiàn	*n./v.*	performance; to demonstrate	10
表演	biǎoyǎn	*n./v.*	performance; to perform	12
表扬	biǎoyáng	*v.*	to praise	15
宾馆	bīnguǎn	*n.*	hotel	13
饼干	bǐnggān	*n.*	biscuit	11
病毒	bìngdú	*n.*	virus	8
博士	bóshì	*n.*	doctor (Dr.)	6
不利	búlì	*adj.*	unfavorable	11
不利于	búlì yú		adverse to	11
不幸	búxìng	*adj.*	unfortunate	12
不得不	bùdébù		have to	6
不如	bùrú	*v.*	not as good as	6
不停	bù tíng	*VP*	to not stop	12
部	bù	*m.*	*a measure word for books, movies, etc.*	4
部位	bùwèi	*n.*	(particularly the human body) position, location	13
			C	
擦	cā	*v.*	to wipe, to scrub	2
猜	cāi	*v.*	to guess	11
采访	cǎifǎng	*v./n.*	to interview; interview	10
菜单	càidān	*n.*	menu	11
测试	cèshì	*v.*	to test	2
叉子	chāzi	*n.*	fork	8
查看	chákàn	*v.*	to check	14
产品	chǎnpǐn	*n.*	product	10
常见	cháng jiàn	*VP*	common	7
场所	chǎngsuǒ	*n.*	place	1
超过	chāoguò	*v.*	to exceed	1
衬衫	chènshān	*n.*	shirt	14

趁	chèn	*prep.*	take advantage of, while	15
成为	chéngwéi	*v.*	to become	3
乘	chéng	*v.*	to travel by (plane, car, ship, etc.)	15
吃惊	chījīng	*v.*	to be shocked	15
持续	chíxù	*v.*	to continue	3
充分	chōngfèn	*adj.*	full, sufficient	9
冲洗	chōngxǐ	*v.*	to wash, to flush	13
重新	chóngxīn	*adv.*	re-, again	6
出发	chūfā	*v.*	to set off	3
出现	chūxiàn	*v.*	to appear	3
除颤器	chúchànqì	*n.*	defibrillator	1
处理	chǔlǐ	*v.*	to deal with, to handle	9
传染	chuánrǎn	*v.*	to infect	8
传真	chuánzhēn	*n.*	fax	2
春联	chūnlián	*n.*	Spring Festival couplets	15
词典	cídiǎn	*n.*	dictionary	12
词语	cíyǔ	*n.*	word	12
粗心	cūxīn	*adj.*	careless	13
猝死	cùsǐ	*v.*	to die suddenly	1
错误	cuòwù	*adj./n.*	wrong; error	5
		D		
答复	dáfù	*n./v.*	reply; to reply	14
打扮	dǎban	*v.*	to dress up	14
打雷	dǎléi	*v.*	to thunder	2
打招呼	dǎ zhāohu	*VO*	to greet (sb.)	2
大使馆	dàshǐguǎn	*n.*	embassy	15
大型	dàxíng	*adj.*	large	1
大熊猫	dàxióngmāo	*n.*	panda	9
大学	dàxué	*n.*	university	6
大约	dàyuē	*adv.*	approximately	2
戴	dài	*v.*	to wear	8
淡	dàn	*adj.*	tasteless	7

蛋白质	dànbáizhì	*n.*	protein	4
刀子	dāozi	*n.*	knife	8
导游	dǎoyóu	*n.*	tourist guide	13
倒	dǎo	*v.*	to fall	13
到来	dàolái	*v.*	to arrive	8
道理	dàolǐ	*n.*	reason	9
道歉	dàoqiàn	*v.*	to apologize	4
地	de	*part.*	*used after a word or phrase to modify the predicate*	12
的话	dehuà	*part.*	if	10
灯	dēng	*n.*	light	15
登机牌	dēngjīpái	*n.*	boarding pass	15
底	dǐ		end	7
地点	dìdiǎn	*n.*	location, place	14
地区	dìqū	*n.*	region	14
地铁站	dìtiězhàn	*n.*	subway station	1
地址	dìzhǐ	*n.*	address	11
碘酒	diǎnjiǔ	*n.*	tincture of iodine	9
电池	diànchí	*n.*	battery	1
电视剧	diànshìjù	*n.*	TV series	4
电子	diànzǐ	*n.*	electron	10
电子邮件	diànzǐ yóujiàn		e-mail	14
淀粉	diànfěn	*n.*	starch	11
调查	diàochá	*v./n.*	to investigate; investigation	3
动	dòng	*v.*	to move, to act	12
动物	dòngwù	*n.*	animal	9
动物园	dòngwùyuán	*n.*	zoo	9
动作	dòngzuò	*n.*	action, movement	7
独立	dúlì	*v.*	to be independent	12
度过	dùguò	*v.*	to spend	4
短信	duǎnxìn	*n.*	text message	11
段	duàn	*m.*	*used to indicate time or distance*	4

对话	duìhuà	*v.*	to have a dialogue	12
对于	duìyú	*prep.*	for, to	7
		E		
饿	è	*adj.*	hungry	5
儿童	értóng	*n.*	children	8
耳背	ěrbèi	*adj.*	hard of hearing	2
耳鼻喉科	ěr-bí-hóukē	*n.*	Department of ENT (ear-nose-throat)	2
		F		
发病率	fābìnglǜ	*n.*	incidence of a disease	7
发热	fārè	*v.*	to have a fever	8
发生	fāshēng	*v.*	to happen	4
发育	fāyù	*v.*	to grow	10
发展	fāzhǎn	*v.*	to develop	2
法律	fǎlǜ	*n.*	law	3
翻译	fānyì	*n./v.*	translation; to translate	12
反而	fǎn'ér	*adv.*	instead, on the contrary	11
方法	fāngfǎ	*n.*	method	1
方式	fāngshì	*n.*	way, mode	2
方向	fāngxiàng	*n.*	direction	14
防疫站	fángyìzhàn	*n.*	epidemic prevention station	9
放弃	fàngqì	*v.*	to give up	10
飞	fēi	*v.*	to fly	9
飞沫	fēimò	*n.*	flying particles of liquid	8
非	fēi	*v.*	not to be	15
肥皂	féizào	*n.*	soap	9
肥皂水	féizàoshuǐ	*n.*	soapsuds	9
分开	fēnkāi	*v.*	to part, to separate	8
分类	fēnlèi	*v.*	to classify	1
份	fèn	*m.*	*a measure word for a set of things like meal, gift, newspaper, etc.*	11
丰富	fēngfù	*adj./v.*	abundant; to enrich	14
服务区	fúwùqū	*n.*	service zone	1

福	fú	*n.*	blessing, good fortune	15
辅导	fǔdǎo	*v.*	to coach, to tutor	10
辅导班	fǔdǎobān	*n.*	tutorial class	10
妇科	fùkē	*n.*	gynaecology	4
富	fù	*adj.*	wealthy	6
腹腔镜	fùqiāngjìng	*n.*	laparoscope	6
		G		
干杯	gānbēi	*v.*	cheers, to toast	15
赶	gǎn	*v.*	to rush for	11
赶快	gǎnkuài	*adv.*	quickly, at once	13
感动	gǎndòng	*adj./v.*	moved; to be moved	12
感染	gǎnrǎn	*v.*	to infect	9
感谢	gǎnxiè	*v.*	to thank	5
高烧	gāoshāo	*n.*	high fever	8
高速公路	gāosù gōnglù		expressway	1
胳膊	gēbo	*n.*	arm	7
更年期	gēngniánqī	*n.*	menopause	4
更加	gèngjiā	*adv.*	more, even more	10
工人	gōngrén	*n.*	worker	15
公布	gōngbù	*v.*	to announce	14
公共场所	gōnggòng chǎng-suǒ		public place	1
公司	gōngsī	*n.*	company	3
功夫	gōngfu	*n.*	kung fu	12
孤独症	gūdúzhèng	*n.*	autism	12
骨折	gǔzhé	*v.*	to fracture	7
骨质疏松症	gǔzhì shūsōng-zhèng	*n.*	osteoporosis	7
故事	gùshi	*n.*	story	12
故意	gùyì	*adv.*	deliberately	13
关门	guānmén	*v.*	to close	15
关系	guānxì	*n.*	relationship, relevance	3

关注	guānzhù	*v.*	to pay attention to, to follow with interest	3
观众	guānzhòng	*n.*	audience	10
广播	guǎngbō	*n./v.*	broadcast; to broadcast	2
规律	guīlǜ	*n.*	law, regularity	4
国际	guójì	*n.*	international	15
果汁	guǒzhī	*n.*	fruit juice	11
过年	guònián	*v.*	to celebrate the Chinese New Year	15
			H	
海洋	hǎiyáng	*n.*	sea, ocean	8
海洋馆	hǎiyángguǎn	*n.*	aquarium	12
害怕	hàipà	*v.*	to be afraid	1
害羞	hàixiū	*v.*	to be shy	12
含	hán	*v.*	to contain	11
含有	hányǒu	*v.*	to contain	11
航班	hángbān	*n.*	flight	15
好处	hǎochù	*n.*	benefit, advantage	3
好汉	hǎohàn	*n.*	true man	15
好用	hǎoyòng	*adj.*	easy to use	2
好	hào	*v.*	to like, to be fond of	13
合格	hégé	*adj.*	qualified	14
盒子	hézi	*n.*	box	7
后背	hòubèi	*n.*	back (of the body)	7
互联网	hùliánwǎng	*n.*	(the) Internet	2
互相	hùxiāng	*adv.*	mutually	5
户外	hùwài	*n.*	outdoors	10
怀疑	huáiyí	*v.*	to doubt	5
坏	huài	*adj.*	bad	3
患者	huànzhě	*n.*	patient, sick person	7
回答	huídá	*v.*	to answer	14
回收	huíshōu	*v.*	to recycle	1
回忆	huíyì	*v.*	to recall, to call to mind	8
绘画	huìhuà	*v.*	to draw, to paint	8

活动	huódòng	*n.*	activity	8
火	huǒ	*n.*	fire	13
火车站	huǒchēzhàn	*n.*	railway station	1
或	huò	*conj.*	or	7
获得	huòdé	*v.*	to obtain	2
			J	
机会	jīhuì	*n.*	opportunity	15
鸡蛋	jīdàn	*n.*	egg	5
积极	jījí	*adj.*	active	4
积累	jīlěi	*v.*	to accumulate	14
急救	jíjiù	*v.*	to give first aid treatment	1
疾病	jíbìng	*n.*	disease	7
记忆	jìyì	*v./n.*	to remember; memory	5
记忆力	jìyìlì	*n.*	faculty of memory	5
记者	jìzhě	*n.*	reporter, journalist	10
既	jì	*adv.*	both ... and ..., as well as	2
既……又……	jì…yòu…		both ... and ...	2
继续	jìxù	*v.*	to continue	6
寄	jì	*v.*	to mail, to send	2
加油站	jiāyóuzhàn	*n.*	gas station	5
家务	jiāwù	*n.*	housework	4
家用	jiāyòng	*adj.*	household	1
家长	jiāzhǎng	*n.*	parent or guardian of a child	10
假	jiǎ	*adj.*	fake, false	10
假性	jiǎxìng	*adj.*	pseudo-	10
减少	jiǎnshǎo	*v.*	to reduce, to decrease	6
简历	jiǎnlì	*n.*	resume, CV	14
讲	jiǎng	*v.*	to tell	5
讲座	jiǎngzuò	*n.*	lecture	8
奖学金	jiǎngxuéjīn	*n.*	scholarship	6
降低	jiàngdī	*v.*	to lower	3
降落	jiàngluò	*v.*	to land	15

浇	jiāo	*v.*	to water	9
骄傲	jiāo'ào	*adj.*	proud	15
焦虑	jiāolǜ	*adj.*	worried	4
饺子	jiǎozi	*n.*	dumpling	11
脚	jiǎo	*n.*	foot	5
教育	jiàoyù	*n./v.*	education; to educate	10
阶段	jiēduàn	*n.*	stage	14
接触	jiēchù	*v.*	to contact, to touch	8
接受	jiēshòu	*v.*	to accept	4
接着	jiēzhe	*adv.*	then	6
街道	jiēdào	*n.*	street	5
节约	jiéyuē	*v.*	to save	2
结果	jiéguǒ	*conj.*	as a result	13
解释	jiěshì	*v.*	to explain	5
借	jiè	*v.*	to borrow	7
尽管	jǐnguǎn	*conj.*	although	6
进入	jìnrù	*v.*	to enter	2
近视	jìnshì	*adj.*	nearsighted	10
禁止	jìnzhǐ	*v.*	to prohibit	8
京剧	jīngjù	*n.*	Beijing opera	3
经过	jīngguò	*v.*	to go through	1
经济	jīngjì	*n.*	financial condition	6
经理	jīnglǐ	*n.*	manager	6
经历	jīnglì	*v./n.*	to experience; experience	4
经验	jīngyàn	*n.*	experience	9
精彩	jīngcǎi	*adj.*	wonderful, splendid	12
精力	jīnglì	*n.*	energy, vigor	3
精神	jīngshén	*n.*	spirit, mind	3
竞争	jìngzhēng	*v.*	to compete	14
竞争力	jìngzhēnglì	*n.*	competitiveness	14
举办	jǔbàn	*v.*	to hold, to conduct	8
句子	jùzi	*n.*	sentence	12

拒绝	jùjué	*v.*	to refuse, to reject	12
聚会	jùhuì	*n./v.*	meeting, gathering; to get together	7
均衡	jūnhéng	*adj.*	balanced	4
			K	
开玩笑	kāi wánxiào	*VO*	to make a joke	15
看法	kànfǎ	*n.*	opinion, view	10
考研	kǎoyán	*v.*	to take part in the postgraduate entrance examinations	6
科技	kējì	*n.*	science and technology	2
科学	kēxué	*n.*	science	1
棵	kē	*m.*	*a measure word for plants*	9
客人	kèrén	*n.*	guest	7
空腹	kōngfù	*v.*	on an empty stomach	11
恐怕	kǒngpà	*adv.*	maybe, *indicating an estimation*	1
控制	kòngzhì	*v.*	to control	11
口罩	kǒuzhào	*n.*	gauze mask	8
筷子	kuàizi	*n.*	chopsticks	8
狂犬病	kuángquǎnbìng	*n.*	rabies	9
狂犬病疫苗	kuángquǎnbìng yìmiáo		rabies vaccine	9
矿泉水	kuàngquánshuǐ	*n.*	mineral water	1
			L	
垃圾桶	lājītǒng	*n.*	trash can	1
拉	lā	*v.*	to pull	13
来自	láizì	*v.*	to be from	10
懒	lǎn	*adj.*	lazy	3
浪漫	làngmàn	*adj.*	romantic	15
老虎	lǎohǔ	*n.*	tiger	9
老年	lǎonián	*n.*	old age	2
老年性	lǎoniánxìng	*n.*	senile	2
乐观	lèguān	*adj.*	optimistic	4
雷	léi	*n.*	thunder	2

冷静	lěngjìng	*adj.*	calm	4
礼拜天	lǐbàitiān	*n.*	Sunday	7
理发	lǐfà	*v.*	to have a haircut	14
理发店	lǐfàdiàn	*n.*	barbershop	14
理想	lǐxiǎng	*n.*	ideal	6
立刻	lìkè	*adv.*	at once, immediately	9
例如	lìrú	*v.*	for instance, for example	9
联系	liánxì	*v.*	to contact	5
练习	liànxí	*v.*	to practice	10
良好	liánghǎo	*adj.*	good	10
另	lìng	*pron.*	another	13
另外	lìngwài	*conj.*	in addition	3
留	liú	*v.*	to remain, to stay	8
留下	liúxia	*VC*	to keep, to remain	8
流感	liúgǎn	*n.*	influenza (flu)	8
流行	liúxíng	*v.*	to be widespread	8
率	lǜ	*suf.*	rate of	7
轮椅	lúnyǐ	*n.*	wheelchair	7
			M	
马虎	mǎhu	*adj.*	careless	13
卖	mài	*v.*	to sell	2
满足	mǎnzú	*v.*	to meet, to satisfy	14
慢	màn	*adj.*	slow	2
毛巾	máojīn	*n.*	towel	8
矛盾	máodùn	*n.*	contradiction	4
帽子	màozi	*n.*	cap, hat	12
美化	měihuà	*v.*	to beautify	9
迷路	mílù	*v.*	to lose one's way	5
免费	miǎnfèi	*v.*	to be free of charge	15
免疫力	miǎnyìlì	*n.*	immunity	3
面试	miànshì	*v.*	to interview	14
面条儿	miàntiáor	*n.*	noodles	5

秒	miǎo	*m.*	second	13
秒钟	miǎozhōng	*m.*	second	13
名单	míngdān	*n.*	name list	14
目标	mùbiāo	*n.*	target	6
目的	mùdì	*n.*	purpose	3
			N	
耐心	nàixīn	*n./adj.*	patience; patient	4
男性	nánxìng	*n.*	male	7
难道	nándào	*adv.*	used in a rhetorical question for emphasis	1
内	nèi	*n.*	inside	9
内分泌	nèifēnmì	*n.*	internal secretion	11
内分泌科	nèifēnmìkē	*n.*	endocrinology	11
内容	nèiróng	*n.*	content	8
能力	nénglì	*n.*	ability	5
年级	niánjí	*n.*	grade	4
年纪	niánjì	*n.*	age (*used to refer to the elderly*)	2
鸟	niǎo	*n.*	bird	9
			O	
偶尔	ǒu'ěr	*adv.*	occasionally	3
			P	
排队	páiduì	*v.*	to queue up	12
排列	páiliè	*v.*	to arrange	12
盘子	pánzi	*n.*	plate	8
培训	péixùn	*v.*	to train	1
配	pèi	*v.*	to match	2
批评	pīpíng	*v.*	to criticize	4
皮鞋	píxié	*n.*	leather shoes	14
脾气	píqi	*n.*	temper	3
篇	piān	*m.*	*a measure word for papers*	12
平安	píng'ān	*adj.*	safe and sound	15
普遍	pǔbiàn	*adj.*	common	2
普通	pǔtōng	*adj.*	common, ordinary	8

Q				
其次	qícì	*pron.*	secondly, next	14
其中	qízhōng	*n.*	among	12
起飞	qǐfēi	*v.*	(of aircraft) to take off	15
千米	qiānmǐ	*m.*	kilometer	2
强	qiáng	*adj.*	strong, powerful	8
抢救	qiǎngjiù	*v.*	to rescue	1
敲门	qiāo mén	*VO*	to knock at a door	2
亲情	qīnqíng	*n.*	kinship	12
青春期	qīngchūnqī	*n.*	puberty	4
轻	qīng	*adj.*	of little weight, light	7
轻松	qīngsōng	*adj.*	easy	2
清洗	qīngxǐ	*v.*	to wash, to clean	9
庆祝	qìngzhù	*v.*	to celebrate	15
穷	qióng	*adj.*	poor	6
区别	qūbié	*n./v.*	difference; to differentiate	8
全部	quánbù	*n.*	whole	11
全面	quánmiàn	*adj.*	overall	12
缺点	quēdiǎn	*n.*	disadvantage	2
缺少	quēshǎo	*v.*	to lack	4
确实	quèshí	*adv.*	indeed	1
R				
然而	rán'ér	*conj.*	however, but	9
热水瓶	rèshuǐpíng	*n.*	thermos (bottle)	13
人群	rénqún	*n.*	crowd	8
人事	rénshì	*n.*	personnel matters	14
人事科	rénshìkē	*n.*	personnel section	14
人物	rénwù	*n.*	figure, character	12
认为	rènwéi	*v.*	to think	7
任务	rènwu	*n.*	task	10
入口	rùkǒu	*n.*	entrance	5
弱	ruò	*adj.*	weak	8

S				
扫地机	sǎodìjī	*n.*	sweeper	2
森林	sēnlín	*n.*	forest	8
伤害	shānghài	*v.*	to hurt	6
伤口	shāngkǒu	*n.*	wound	9
伤心	shāngxīn	*v.*	to be sad	4
商店	shāngdiàn	*n.*	shop, store	2
烧伤科	shāoshāngkē	*n.*	Department of Burn	13
稍微	shāowēi	*adv.*	slightly	5
勺子	sháozi	*n.*	spoon	8
设备	shèbèi	*n.*	equipment	1
设立	shèlì	*v.*	to establish	3
社会	shèhuì	*n.*	society	10
深刻	shēnkè	*adj.*	profound	15
什么的	shénmede	*part.*	and the like	1
升高	shēnggāo	*VC*	to rise	11
生命	shēngmìng	*n.*	life	3
生气	shēngqì	*v.*	to get angry	4
生意	shēngyi	*n.*	business	4
声音	shēngyīn	*n.*	sound	2
省	shěng	*v.*	to save	8
剩	shèng	*v.*	to be left	6
剩下	shèngxia	*VC*	to be left over	12
失眠	shīmián	*v.*	to suffer from insomnia	3
时代	shídài	*n.*	age, times	14
时期	shíqī	*n.*	period, stage	4
实话	shíhuà	*n.*	truth	1
实际	shíjì	*n./adj.*	reality; realistic	10
实现	shíxiàn	*v.*	to realize, to come true	6
实行	shíxíng	*v.*	to implement	1
食物	shíwù	*n.*	food	11
食用	shíyòng	*v.*	to eat	11

使	shǐ	*v.*	to make, to cause	2
世纪	shìjì	*n.*	century	2
手背	shǒubèi	*n.*	back of the hand	13
手表	shǒubiǎo	*n.*	(wrist) watch	5
手术费	shǒushùfèi	*n.*	cost of surgery	6
手续	shǒuxù	*n.*	procedure	1
首都	shǒudū	*n.*	capital	15
首先	shǒuxiān	*adv.*	first	13
受不了	shòubuliǎo	*v.*	cannot bear, to be unable to endure	10
受到	shòudào	*VC*	to be given	15
熟悉	shúxi	*v.*	to be familiar with	5
数量	shùliàng	*n.*	quantity	1
数字	shùzì	*n.*	figure, numeral	5
刷牙	shuā yá	*VO*	to brush one's teeth	13
双	shuāng	*adj./m.*	dual, twin; pair	13
水煮鱼	shuǐzhǔyú	*n.*	Fish Filets in Hot Chili Oil	11
睡懒觉	shuì lǎnjiào	*VO*	to sleep late	3
睡眠	shuìmián	*n.*	sleep	3
顺便	shùnbiàn	*adv.*	incidentally, passingly	11
顺序	shùnxù	*n.*	order, sequence	12
说明	shuōmíng	*v.*	to explain, to demonstrate	1
硕士	shuòshì	*n.*	master	6
死亡	sǐwáng	*v.*	to die	9
死亡率	sǐwánglǜ	*n.*	death rate	9
酸	suān	*adj.*	sour	11
算	suàn	*v.*	to count as	2
所	suǒ	*m.*	*a measure word for houses, schools, etc.*	15
所有	suǒyǒu	*adj.*	all	4
			T	
台	tái	*m.*	*a measure word for machines and instruments*	1
抬	tái	*v.*	to lift up, to raise	7
态度	tàidù	*n.*	attitude	4

汤	tāng	*n.*	soup	7
糖	táng	*n.*	sugar	11
糖尿病	tángniàobìng	*n.*	diabetes	11
烫	tàng	*v./adj.*	to scald, to burn; very hot	13
讨厌	tǎoyàn	*v.*	to hate, to dislike	10
套餐	tàocān	*n.*	set meal	7
特点	tèdiǎn	*n.*	characteristic, feature	9
特殊	tèshū	*adj.*	special	4
提高	tígāo	*v.*	to increase	2
提升	tíshēng	*v.*	to promote	14
体力	tǐlì	*n.*	physical strength	3
体外	tǐwài	*n.*	in vitro	1
添	tiān	*v.*	to add, to get or give more	5
贴	tiē	*v.*	to stick	15
停	tíng	*v.*	to stop	12
通知	tōngzhī	*v.*	to inform, to notify	1
通知	tōngzhī	*n.*	notice	14
同情	tóngqíng	*v.*	to sympathize (with sb.)	10
同时	tóngshí	*conj.*	at the same time	4
同样	tóngyàng	*adj./conj.*	same; in the same way	11
童年	tóngnián	*n.*	childhood	10
痛苦	tòngkǔ	*adj.*	painful	13
涂	tú	*v.*	to spread on	13
推	tuī	*v.*	to push	7
推迟	tuīchí	*v.*	to postpone	15
托运	tuōyùn	*v.*	to consign	15
驼背	tuóbèi	*v.*	to be hunchbacked	7
W				
袜子	wàzi	*n.*	socks	14
外科学	wàikēxué	*n.*	surgery	14
完成	wánchéng	*v.*	to finish	2
玩笑	wánxiào	*n.*	joke	15

晚会	wǎnhuì	*n.*	evening party	10
万	wàn	*num.*	ten thousand	1
网课	wǎngkè	*n.*	online course	10
网友	wǎngyǒu	*n.*	net friend	5
往往	wǎngwǎng	*adv.*	often	7
忘记	wàngjì	*v.*	to forget	5
危害	wēihài	*n./v.*	harm; to harm	13
卫生	wèishēng	*n./adj.*	hygiene; sanitary	2
位置	wèizhì	*n.*	location	5
味道	wèidao	*n.*	flavor, taste	7
文件	wénjiàn	*n.*	document, file	2
文章	wénzhāng	*n.*	article, essay	12
稳定	wěndìng	*adj.*	stable	4
无	wú	*v.*	to not have, to be without	11
无论	wúlùn	*conj.*	no matter (what, where, how, etc.)	5
午睡	wǔshuì	*n./v.*	afternoon nap; to have a nap after lunch	3
物质	wùzhì	*n.*	substance	11
误会	wùhuì	*v.*	to misunderstand	14
			X	
西红柿炒鸡蛋	xīhóngshì chǎo jīdàn	*n.*	Scrambled Egg with Tomato	11
西装	xīzhuāng	*n.*	Western-style clothes	14
吸引	xīyǐn	*v.*	to attract	10
洗	xǐ	*v.*	to wash	13
洗脸	xǐ liǎn	*VO*	to wash one's face	13
洗澡	xǐzǎo	*v.*	to take a shower	3
喜	xǐ	*v.*	to have an inclination for	9
相同	xiāngtóng	*adj.*	same	8
相信	xiāngxìn	*v.*	to believe	5
香	xiāng	*adj.*	appetizing	11
详细	xiángxì	*adj.*	detailed	11
响	xiǎng	*adj.*	loud	2

小吃	xiǎochī	*n.*	snack	15
小伙子	xiǎohuǒzi	*n.*	lad, young fellow	14
小说	xiǎoshuō	*n.*	novel	12
笑话儿	xiàohuar	*n.*	joke	5
鞋	xié	*n.*	shoes	14
心脏病	xīnzàngbìng	*n.*	heart disease	1
信封	xìnfēng	*n.*	envelope	14
行李	xíngli	*n.*	luggage, baggage	13
行李箱	xínglixiāng	*n.*	suitcase	13
性别	xìngbié	*n.*	sex	7
修理	xiūlǐ	*v.*	to repair	15
修理工	xiūlǐgōng	*n.*	repairman	15
学历	xuélì	*n.*	educational background	14
血糖	xuètáng	*n.*	blood sugar	11
		Y		
牙膏	yágāo	*n.*	toothpaste	13
牙刷	yáshuā	*n.*	toothbrush	13
严格	yángé	*adj.*	strict	10
研究	yánjiū	*v./n.*	to research; research	1
研究生	yánjiūshēng	*n.*	graduate student	6
盐	yán	*n.*	salt	7
眼镜	yǎnjìng	*n.*	glasses	5
眼科	yǎnkē	*n.*	ophthalmology	10
演出	yǎnchū	*n./v.*	performance; to perform	3
演员	yǎnyuán	*n.*	actor, actress	12
演奏	yǎnzòu	*v.*	to play a musical instrument in a performance	10
阳	yáng		*yang*, sunshine	9
阳台	yángtái	*n.*	balcony	9
养成	yǎngchéng	*v.*	to form, to develop	3
样子	yàngzi	*n.*	appearance	11
邀请	yāoqǐng	*v.*	to invite	15
钥匙	yàoshi	*n.*	key	5

也许	yěxǔ	*adv.*	maybe	4
业余	yèyú	*adj.*	amateur	10
页	yè	*m.*	page	12
医保卡	yībǎokǎ	*n.*	medical card	6
医疗	yīliáo	*v.*	(to provide) medical treatment	6
医疗保险	yīliáo bǎoxiǎn		medical insurance	6
一旦	yídàn	*adv.*	once, in case (sth. happens)	9
以	yǐ	*conj.*	in order to, so as to	13
以及	yǐjí	*conj.*	and, as well as	14
艺术	yìshù	*n.*	art	10
疫苗	yìmiáo	*n.*	vaccine	8
意见	yìjiàn	*n.*	opinion, view	9
因此	yīncǐ	*conj.*	therefore	1
阴	yīn		*yin*, shade	9
银行	yínháng	*n.*	bank	6
印象	yìnxiàng	*n.*	impression	8
迎接	yíngjiē	*v.*	to welcome	15
应聘	yìngpìn	*v.*	to apply for a job	14
应聘者	yìngpìnzhě	*n.*	applicant	14
优点	yōudiǎn	*n.*	advantage	2
优秀	yōuxiù	*adj.*	excellent	6
由	yóu	*prep.*	by (sb.)	6
由于	yóuyú	*conj.*	because	6
邮局	yóujú	*n.*	post office	2
油	yóu	*n.*	oil	11
友好	yǒuhǎo	*adj.*	friendly	5
友谊	yǒuyì	*n.*	friendship	12
有害	yǒu hài		harmful	1
有利	yǒulì	*adj.*	beneficial	10
有效	yǒuxiào	*v.*	to be effective	10
于	yú	*prep.*	to, for	11
与	yǔ	*conj.*	and	3

雨伞	yǔsǎn	*n.*	umbrella	13
语法	yǔfǎ	*n.*	grammar	12
语言	yǔyán	*n.*	language	5
预防	yùfáng	*v.*	to prevent	7
遇到	yùdào	*VC*	to run into	3
元	yuán	*m.*	*yuan*, unit of money	6
原谅	yuánliàng	*v.*	to forgive	13
约会	yuēhuì	*n./v.*	date; to have a date	14
月底	yuèdǐ	*n.*	end of a month	7
月经	yuèjīng	*n.*	menstruation	4
			Z	
杂志	zázhì	*n.*	magazine	3
暂时	zànshí	*adj.*	for the time being	8
脏	zāng	*adj.*	dirty	13
责备	zébèi	*v.*	to blame	13
责任	zérèn	*n.*	responsibility	5
增加	zēngjiā	*v.*	to increase	7
站	zhàn	*v.*	to stand	5
招聘	zhāopìn	*v.*	to recruit	14
照相	zhàoxiàng	*v.*	to take a photo	13
照相机	zhàoxiàngjī	*n.*	camera	13
者	zhě	*suf.*	person or thing	14
真性	zhēnxìng	*adj.*	real	10
真正	zhēnzhèng	*adj.*	true, real	10
正好	zhènghǎo	*adv.*	just enough	6
正确	zhèngquè	*adj.*	correct	10
正式	zhèngshì	*adj.*	formal	14
症状	zhèngzhuàng	*n.*	symptom	4
之	zhī	*part.*	of	2
之间	zhījiān	*n.*	between, among	8
支持	zhīchí	*v.*	to support	6
只	zhī	*m.*	*a measure word for certain animals*	9

值得	zhídé	*v.*	to be worth	2
职业	zhíyè	*n.*	profession, occupation	14
植物	zhíwù	*n.*	plant	9
只好	zhǐhǎo	*adv.*	have to	7
指	zhǐ	*v.*	to point, to indicate	8
指导	zhǐdǎo	*v.*	to guide	4
至少	zhìshǎo	*adv.*	at least	7
至于	zhìyú	*prep.*	as to, with regard to	14
治	zhì	*v.*	to treat	2
治疗	zhìliáo	*v.*	to treat	2
治疗费	zhìliáofèi	*n.*	of medical treatment cost	6
重点	zhòngdiǎn	*n.*	key point	11
周期	zhōuqī	*n.*	period, cycle period	4
周围	zhōuwéi	*n.*	around	2
逐渐	zhújiàn	*adv.*	gradually	2
主食	zhǔshí	*n.*	staple food	11
主演	zhǔyǎn	*n.*	leading actor, leading actress	12
助听器	zhùtīngqì	*n.*	hearing-aid	2
祝贺	zhùhè	*v.*	to congratulate	7
著名	zhùmíng	*adj.*	famous	12
抓	zhuā	*v.*	to scratch	9
专家	zhuānjiā	*n.*	expert	4
赚	zhuàn	*v.*	to earn/make (money)	6
赚钱	zhuànqián	*v.*	to make money	6
装饰	zhuāngshì	*v.*	to decorate	7
准确	zhǔnquè	*adj.*	accurate	5
准时	zhǔnshí	*adj.*	punctual, on time	3
姿势	zīshì	*n.*	posture	10
资源	zīyuán	*n.*	resource	8
仔细	zǐxì	*adj.*	careful	9
自动	zìdòng	*adj.*	automatic	1
自然	zìrán	*n.*	nature	8

走失	zǒushī	*v.*	to get lost	5
尊重	zūnzhòng	*v.*	to respect	10
作家	zuòjiā	*n.*	writer	12
作用	zuòyòng	*n.*	function	2
作者	zuòzhě	*n.*	author	12
座位	zuòwèi	*n.*	seat	7
做生意	zuò shēngyi	*VO*	to do business	4

专名 Proper nouns

		B	
北京大学	Běijīng Dàxué	Peking University	15
		C	
《草房子》	Cǎo Fángzi	*The Grass House*, a novel written by Cao Wenxuan	12
长城	Chángchéng	the Great Wall	
		H	
《海洋天堂》	Hǎiyáng Tiāntáng	*Ocean Heaven*, name of a film	12
		L	
李连杰	Lǐ Liánjié	Jet Li	12
		Q	
清华大学	Qīnghuá Dàxué	Tsinghua University	15
		S	
世界地球日	Shìjiè Dìqiúrì	World Earth Day (April 22)	8
世界睡眠日	Shìjiè Shuìmiánrì	World Sleep Day	3
世界睡眠医学学会	Shìjiè Shuìmián Yīxué Xuéhuì	World Association of Sleep Medicine	3
世界卫生组织	Shìjiè Wèishēng Zǔzhī	World Health Organization	3
首都国际机场	Shǒudū Guójì Jīchǎng	Beijing Capital International Airport	15
		T	
天安门	Tiān'ān Mén	Tian'anmen, the Gate of Heavenly Peace of the Imperial Palace of Beijing	15

W			
王府井	Wángfǔjǐng	Wangfujing, a commercial street in Beijing	15
Y			
亚洲	Yàzhōu	Asia	15
英文	Yīngwén	English (language)	12

全四册覆盖MCT大纲词汇表

第一册覆盖MCT大纲词汇				
家属	jiāshǔ	*n.*	family member	13
家庭	jiātíng	*n.*	family	9
解剖	jiěpōu	*v.*	to dissect	11

第二册覆盖MCT大纲词汇				
熬夜	áoyè	*v.*	to stay up	2
B 超	B chāo	*n.*	B-ultrasound	10
病历	bìnglì	*n.*	clinical case, medical records	10
查房	cháfáng	*v.*	to make the rounds of the wards	13
胆囊	dǎnnáng	*n.*	cholecyst	11
复查	fùchá	*v.*	to recheck, to reexamine	9
腹痛	fùtòng	*n./adj.*	stomachache, abdominal pain	9
腹泻	fùxiè	*v.*	to have a diarrhea	9
骨折	gǔzhé	*v.*	to fracture	3
挂号	guàhào	*v.*	to register	8
拐杖	guǎizhàng	*n.*	walking stick	3
核磁共振	hécígòngzhèn	*n.*	nuclear magnetic resonance	1
缓解	huǎnjiě	*v.*	to relieve	11
恢复	huīfù	*v.*	to recover	9
检查	jiǎnchá	*v.*	to test, to check	12
惊厥	jīngjué	*v.*	to have a convulsion	9
剧烈	jùliè	*adj.*	violent, strenuous, fierce	9
康复	kāngfù	*v.*	to recover	11

颗	kē	*m.*	*a measure word usually for sth. small and roundish*	12
口腔	kǒuqiāng	*n.*	oral cavity	6
模糊	móhu	*adj.*	indistinct	14
呕吐	ǒutù	*v.*	to vomit	9
切除	qiēchú	*v.*	to cut off	12
纱布	shābù	*n.*	gauze	15
神经	shénjīng	*n.*	neuro	4
石膏	shígāo	*n.*	plaster	3
视力	shìlì	*n.*	vision, eyesight	14
疼痛	téngtòng	*adj.*	painful	11
调整	tiáozhěng	*v.*	to adjust	8
听力	tīnglì	*n.*	listening	5
退休	tuìxiū	*v.*	to retire	4
胃镜	wèijìng	*n.*	gastroscope	10
息肉	xīròu	*n.*	polyp	12
消毒	xiāodú	*v.*	to disinfect, to sterilize	15
消化	xiāohuà	*v.*	to digest	9
消炎	xiāoyán	*v.*	to diminish inflammation	12
心电图	xīndiàntú	*n.*	electrocardiogram	1
心脏	xīnzàng	*n.*	heart	4
胸透	xiōngtòu	*n.*	chest X-ray	10
血压	xuèyā	*n.*	blood pressure	1
止血	zhǐ xiě	*VO*	to stop bleeding	15

第三册覆盖MCT大纲词汇				
办理	bànlǐ	*v.*	to handle	14
比例	bǐlì	*n.*	proportion	8
表现	biǎoxiàn	*n.*	performance	12
补充	bǔchōng	*v.*	to supplement	12
不良	bùliáng	*adj.*	unhealthy, harmful, poor	7
操作	cāozuò	*v.*	to operate	9
成熟	chéngshú	*adj.*	ripe, mature	14

刺激	cìjī	*v./n.*	to stimulate; stimulation	4
大便	dàbiàn	*n.*	stool, shit	12
蛋白质	dànbáizhì	*n.*	protein	12
导致	dǎozhì	*v.*	to cause, to lead to	11
定期	dìngqī	*adj.*	regular	6
发育	fāyù	*v.*	to grow, to develop	3
反应	fǎnyìng	*n.*	reaction	10
范围	fànwéi	*n.*	scope, range	11
分娩	fēnmiǎn	*v.*	to be confined	1
风险	fēngxiǎn	*n.*	risk, danger	2
辅助	fǔzhù	*v.*	to assist	13
腹泻	fùxiè	*v.*	to have a diarrhea	12
改善	gǎishàn	*v.*	to better	14
功能	gōngnéng	*n.*	function	3
过敏	guòmǐn	*v./adj.*	to be allergic to; allergic	4
含量	hánliàng	*n.*	content	7
呼吸	hūxī	*v.*	to breathe	11
化验	huàyàn	*v.*	to do laboratory test	7
怀孕	huáiyùn	*v.*	to get pregnant	13
患者	huànzhě	*n.*	patient	6
激素	jīsù	*n.*	hormone	15
疾病	jíbìng	*n.*	disease, illness	10
健全	jiànquán	*adj.*	sound, perfect	3
焦虑	jiāolǜ	*adj.*	anxious	14
戒	jiè	*v.*	to give up, to stop	6
精神	jīngshén	*n.*	spirit	5
就诊	jiùzhěn	*v.*	to see a doctor	10
空腹	kōngfù	*v.*	to be on an empty stomach	15
流产	liúchǎn	*v.*	to abort	13
门诊	ménzhěn	*v.*	to offer outpatient service	4
明显	míngxiǎn	*adj.*	obvious, clear	10

母乳	mǔrǔ	*n.*	breast milk	3
排除	páichú	*v.*	to exclude	15
胚胎	pēitāi	*n.*	embryo	13
剖宫产	pōugōngchǎn	*v.*	to have a cesarean section	1
强度	qiángdù	*n.*	intensity	13
清淡	qīngdàn	*adj.*	light, bland	15
情绪	qíngxù	*n.*	mood, feeling	10
缺乏	quēfá	*v.*	to be short of	12
缺铁性贫血	quētiěxìng pínxuè		iron deficient anemia	7
忍受	rěnshòu	*v.*	to bear, to suffer	1
失去	shīqù	*v.*	to lose	11
食物	shíwù	*n.*	food	7
适当	shìdàng	*adj.*	proper	12
蔬菜	shūcài	*n.*	vegetable	6
属于	shǔyú	*v.*	to belong to	10
死亡	sǐwáng	*v.*	to die	2
胎儿	tāi'ér	*n.*	fetus	1
胎位	tāiwèi	*n.*	position of the fetus	1
糖尿病	tángniàobìng	*n.*	diabetes mellitus	2
体重	tǐzhòng	*n.*	weight	13
危害	wēihài	*v.*	to harm	11
维生素	wéishēngsù	*n.*	vitamin	7
喂养	wèiyǎng	*v.*	to feed	3
吸收	xīshōu	*v.*	to absorb	7
狭窄	xiázhǎi	*adj.*	narrow	6
显示	xiǎnshì	*v.*	to show	2
消除	xiāochú	*v.*	to eliminate	5
心理	xīnlǐ	*n.*	psychology	10
形成	xíngchéng	*v.*	to form	12
血糖	xuètáng	*n.*	blood sugar	15
迅速	xùnsù	*adj.*	rapid	8

延期	yánqī	*v.*	to extend a time limit, to delay	14
痒	yǎng	*adj.*	itching	4
叶酸	yèsuān	*n.*	folic acid	7
液体	yètǐ	*n.*	liquid	3
饮食	yǐnshí	*n.*	diet	6
婴儿	yīng'ér	*n.*	infant	3
营养	yíngyǎng	*n.*	nutrition	3
预防	yùfáng	*v.*	to prevent	2
症状	zhèngzhuàng	*n.*	symptom	10
脂肪	zhīfáng	*n.*	fat	15
指标	zhǐbiāo	*n.*	index, target	15
指征	zhǐzhēng	*n.*	indication	1
专家	zhuānjiā	*n.*	expert	5
状态	zhuàngtài	*n.*	state	13

第四册覆盖MCT大纲词汇				
伴有	bànyǒu	*v.*	to be accompanied by	12
包括	bāokuò	*v.*	to include	8
保持	bǎochí	*v.*	to keep, to maintain	13
保险	bǎoxiǎn	*n.*	insurance	6
报告	bàogào	*n.*	report	11
避免	bìmiǎn	*v.*	to avoid	8
表现	biǎoxiàn	*n./v.*	performance; to demonstrate	10
并发症	bìngfāzhèng	*n.*	complication	15
病毒	bìngdú	*n.*	virus	8
病因	bìngyīn	*n.*	cause of disease	12
不足	bùzú	*adj.*	insufficient	7
部位	bùwèi	*n.*	(particularly the human body) position, location	13
场所	chǎngsuǒ	*n.*	place	1
程度	chéngdù	*n.*	degree, level	12
持续	chíxù	*v.*	to continue	3
充分	chōngfèn	*adj.*	full, sufficient	9

处理	chǔlǐ	*v.*	to deal with, to handle	9
传播	chuánbō	*v.*	to spread, to transmit	8
传染	chuánrǎn	*v.*	to infect	8
雌激素	cíjīsù	*n.*	estrogen	4
猝死	cùsǐ	*v.*	to die suddenly	1
措施	cuòshī	*n.*	measure	8
打喷嚏	dǎ pēntì	*VO*	to sneeze	8
蛋白质	dànbáizhì	*n.*	protein	4
发热	fārè	*v.*	to have a fever	8
发育	fāyù	*v.*	to grow	10
反而	fǎn'ér	*adv.*	instead, on the contrary	11
防止	fángzhǐ	*v.*	to prevent, to avoid	10
防治	fángzhì	*v.*	to prevent and cure	7
分泌	fēnmì	*v.*	to secrete	6
钙	gài	*n.*	calcium	6
感染	gǎnrǎn	*v.*	to infect	9
骨折	gǔzhé	*v.*	to fracture	7
骨质疏松症	gǔzhì shūsōng-zhèng	*n.*	osteoporosis	7
规律	guīlǜ	*n.*	law, regularity	4
患者	huànzhě	*n.*	patient, sick person	7
疾病	jíbìng	*n.*	disease	7
记忆力	jìyìlì	*n.*	faculty of memory	5
焦虑	jiāolǜ	*adj.*	worried	4
阶段	jiēduàn	*n.*	stage	14
接触	jiēchù	*v.*	to contact, to touch	8
接种	jiēzhòng	*v.*	to vaccinate	8
尽量	jǐnliàng	*adv.*	as far as possible	8
近视	jìnshì	*adj.*	nearsighted	10
精神	jīngshén	*n.*	spirit, mind	3
抗体	kàngtǐ	*n.*	antibody	9
抗原	kàngyuán	*n.*	antigen	9

空腹	kōngfù	*v.*	on an empty stomach	11
控制	kòngzhì	*v.*	to control	11
狂犬病	kuángquǎnbìng	*n.*	rabies	9
乐观	lèguān	*adj.*	optimistic	4
良好	liánghǎo	*adj.*	good	10
流感	liúgǎn	*n.*	influenza (flu)	8
难产	nánchǎn	*v.*	to have a difficult labor	12
内耳	nèi'ěr	*n.*	inner ear	2
年纪	niánjì	*n.*	age (*used to refer to the elderly*)	2
黏膜	niánmó	*n.*	mucous membrane	6
疲劳	píláo	*adj.*	tired	11
抢救	qiǎngjiù	*v.*	to rescue	1
青春期	qīngchūnqī	*n.*	puberty	4
全面	quánmiàn	*adj.*	overall	12
缺氧	quē yǎng	*VO*	to lack oxygen	12
确定	quèdìng	*v.*	to determine	13
弱	ruò	*adj.*	weak	8
伤害	shānghài	*v.*	to hurt	6
升高	shēnggāo	*VC*	to rise	11
失眠	shīmián	*v.*	to suffer from insomnia	3
食物	shíwù	*n.*	food	11
手续	shǒuxù	*n.*	procedure	1
睡眠	shuìmián	*n.*	sleep	3
死亡	sǐwáng	*v.*	to die	9
糖尿病	tángniàobìng	*n.*	diabetes	11
烫	tàng	*v./adj.*	to scald, to burn; very hot	13
特殊	tèshū	*adj.*	special	4
特征	tèzhēng	*n.*	characteristic, feature	11
痛苦	tòngkǔ	*adj.*	painful	13
涂抹	túmǒ	*v.*	to daub, to paint	13
脱离	tuōlí	*v.*	to separate oneself from	13

危害	wēihài	*n./v.*	harm; to harm	13
位置	wèizhi	*n.*	location	5
稳定	wěndìng	*adj.*	stable	4
物质	wùzhì	*n.*	substance	11
细菌	xìjūn	*n.*	bacterium	13
先兆流产	xiānzhào liúchǎn	*VP*	to have a threatened miscarriage	12
心悸	xīnjì	*v.*	to palpitate	1
行为	xíngwéi	*n.*	behavior	12
胸闷	xiōngmèn	*adj.*	chest tightness	1
酗酒	xùjiǔ	*v.*	to indulge in excessive drinking	7
眩晕	xuànyùn	*v.*	to get dizziness	1
血糖	xuètáng	*n.*	blood sugar	11
胰岛素	yídǎosù	*n.*	insulin	11
胰腺	yíxiàn	*n.*	pancreas	11
以及	yǐjí	*conj.*	and, as well as	14
异常	yìcháng	*adj.*	abnormal	12
疫苗	yìmiáo	*n.*	vaccine	8
因素	yīnsù	*n.*	factor	7
预防	yùfáng	*v.*	to prevent	7
预期	yùqī	*v.*	to expect	15
早产	zǎochǎn	*v.*	to have a premature labor	12
症状	zhèngzhuàng	*n.*	symptom	4
指导	zhǐdǎo	*v.*	to guide	4
治疗	zhìliáo	*v.*	to treat	2
智力	zhìlì	*n.*	intelligence	12
周期	zhōuqī	*n.*	period, cycle period	4
专家	zhuānjiā	*n.*	expert	4